D1408965

HARRY HARRISON!
HARRY HARRISON!

TOR BOOKS BY HARRY HARRISON

Galactic Dreams
The Jupiter Plague
Montezuma's Revenge
One Step from Earth
Planet of No Return
Planet of the Damned
The QE2 Is Missing
Queen Victoria's Revenge
A Rebel in Time
Skyfall
Stainless Steel Visions
The Stainless Steel Rat Goes to Hell
The Stainless Steel Rat Joins the Circus
Stonehenge
A Transatlantic Tunnel, Hurrah!
50 in 50
Harry Harrison! Harry Harrison!

THE HAMMER AND THE CROSS TRILOGY

The Hammer and the Cross
One King's Way
King and Emperor

HARRY HARRISON

HARRY HARRISON! HARRY HARRISON!

It Seemed Like a Good Idea at the Time

WEST HARTFORD · · PUBLIC LIBRARY 1320

TOR®

A TOM DOHERTY ASSOCIATES BOOK

NEW YORK

HARRY HARRISON! HARRY HARRISON!

Copyright © 2014 by The Estate of Harry Harrison

All rights reserved.

Designed by Greg Collins

A Tor Book
Published by Tom Doherty Associates, LLC
175 Fifth Avenue
New York, NY 10010

www.tor-forge.com

Tor® is a registered trademark of Tom Doherty Associates, LLC.

Library of Congress Cataloging-in-Publication Data

Harrison, Harry, 1925–2012.
  Harry Harrison! Harry Harrison! / Harry Harrison.
    p. cm.
  ISBN 978-0-7653-3308-7 (hardcover)
  ISBN 978-1-4299-6728-0 (e-book)
  1. Harrison, Harry, 1925–2012.   2. Authors, American—20th century—
Biography.   3. Science fiction—Authorship.   I. Title.
  PS3558.A667Z46 2014
  813'.54—dc23
  [B]

                                                        2014033723

Tor books may be purchased for educational, business, or promotional use. For
information on bulk purchases, please contact Macmillan Corporate and Premium
Sales Department at 1-800-221-7945, extension 5442, or write
specialmarkets@macmillan.com.

First Edition: November 2014

Printed in the United States of America

0 9 8 7 6 5 4 3 2 1

B
HARRISON
HARRY
H

ACKNOWLEDGMENTS

A word from Moira Harrison

My father never missed a deadline in his working life. He took great pride in his work ethic and he went to work every day as a writer. He always said, "Writers write, they don't just talk about it," and that is what he did. Even when he was seriously ill and very frail, he kept writing. When he could not use the computer anymore, he wrote by hand. When he could not write by hand, he dictated. We labored together to get his memoirs finished. It was a very tough task, and when it was finished, he did not want to celebrate with a glass of wine, as he would normally do. He knew that the book and his life were ending together, and four days after he asked me to type "The End," he passed away peacefully. He loved his life in science fiction and he loved all his fans. I hope you will enjoy this memoir, as you have enjoyed all his other works.

These are the words he asked me to write on his behalf:

Firstly, I would like to thank my daughter, Moira, for all her help in getting this book finished. I would also like to thank my children, Todd and Moira, as well as my late wife, Joan, for all the love and support they have shown me over the years—they had to put up with a lot! My son-in-law, Mark, deserves a special mention for all the support and practical help he has given me and my daughter over the last few years through some very challenging times. Finally, I would like to thank all my fans throughout the world who have bought and read my books and told me what they meant to them. Thank you.

The 1920s and 1930s

1925   Harry Max Harrison is born March 12 in Stamford, Connecticut, USA, the only child of Ria and Henry Leo Harrison.

1927   The family moves to Brooklyn, New York, USA.

1930   The family moves to Queens, New York, USA.

1938   Harry Harrison becomes a charter member of the Queens Chapter of the Science Fiction League.

The 1940s

1941   The May–June 1941 issue of the fanzine *Sun Spots* publishes a piece of artwork called "Robot" by a sixteen-year-old Harry Harrison.

1943   Graduates from Forest Hills High School. Attends the Eastern Aircraft Instrument School in New Jersey and becomes a certified aircraft instrument mechanic. Drafted into the U.S. Army Air Corps, he is sent to Keesler Field, Mississippi, for basic training, then to Lowry Field in Denver, Colorado, where he is trained as a power-operated turret and computing gunsight specialist.

1944   Sent to the Air Corps base in Laredo, Texas, where he maintains gunsight computers and acts as armorer, gunnery instructor, and truck driver.

1945   Transferred to the gunnery school in Panama City, Florida. When the school is closed, Harrison is promoted to sergeant and transferred to military police duties.

1946   Discharged from the army in February, Harrison works briefly as a hydraulic press operator. Then at the start of the fall term he begins an art course at Hunter College in New York City and becomes a student of noted American painter John Blomshield. Harrison leaves the class but continues to study privately under Blomshield for the next two years. At the same time, he attends the Cartoonists and Illustrators School.

1948   Teams up with Wally Wood while at the Cartoonists and Illustrators School, and they begin to produce comics and freelance commercial illustration work.

The 1950s

1950   HH chairs Hydracon on July 4 in New York: the first professional science fiction writers' convention.

HH illustrates the first two issues of *Worlds Beyond* magazine for Damon Knight, but illness prevents him from illustrating the third and drives him to the typewriter to write his first story.

1950 to 1952, Harrison is a freelance illustrator, operating his own art agency with two employees.

1951   "Rock Diver," Harry Harrison's first science fiction story, appears in the August edition of *Worlds Beyond*.

1952   Moves into editing, packaging, and publishing comics, often writing and/or illustrating much of the content of an issue.

      1952 to 1953, Harry Harrison is publisher of the magazine *On the Q.T.* and editor for Royal Publications, Inc.

1953   As the comics boom comes to an end, Harrison moves into writing for, and editing, pulp magazines. HH writes "true" adventures for men's magazines and "true confessions" for women's magazines.

      1953 to 1954, Harrison acts as editor of *Space Science Fiction, Science Fiction Adventures, Rocket Stories,* and *Fantasy Fiction*.

1954   Marries Joan Marian Merkler, June 4.

1955   Birth of son, Todd, May 21.

      September, Harrison delivers "Plotting Science Fiction," City College of New York, extension program.

      1955 to 1956, Harrison is art director of *Picture Week* magazine.

      HH begins writing *The Saint* comic strips and continues until the strip ends in 1960.

1956   Harrison becomes a full-time freelance writer. Moves to Mexico and begins work on his first novel, *Deathworld*.

1957   HH attends the 15th Worldcon held in London, England. Participates in a panel on "American Science Fiction."

The Harrisons move to England. Spends a short period writing *Jeff Hawke* comic scripts for Sydney Jordan in the autumn, as well as comics for Fleetway Publications.

First Stainless Steel Rat short story published.

1958   Moves to Italy.

Begins to write *Flash Gordon* scripts for the comic strip drawn by Dan Barry. Continues to write these scripts for the next ten years.

Returns to New York for the birth of his daughter.

1959   Birth of daughter, Moira, January 9.

Deathworld is completed and sold to John Campbell.

Moves to Denmark in the summer, where the Harrisons live for the next six years.

January, Harrison delivers "Science Fiction as a World Literature" to the Kopenhago Esperanto Klubo, Copenhagen, Denmark.

June, Harrison delivers "Science Fiction in Esperanto," Klubo Esperantista de Malmo, Malmo, Sweden.

Harrison begins work on *Bill, the Galactic Hero.*

The 1960s

1960   *Deathworld* published in *Astounding.*

       May, Harrison delivers "First on the Moon" to the Young Conservative Club of Hørsholm, Hørsholm, Denmark.

       September, Harrison delivers "American Science Fiction" to the Swedish Science Fiction Convention, Gothenburg, Sweden.

1961   *The Stainless Steel Rat* is published in book form.

       March, Harrison delivers "The Future of the Future" to the British Science Fiction Association annual meeting, Gloucester, England.

1962   *Planet of the Damned* and *War with the Robots,* Harrison's first short story collection, are published.

       April, Harrison delivers "American and British Science Fiction" to the British Science Fiction Association annual meeting, Harrogate, England.

1963   Harrison is the guest of honor at the British Science Fiction Association annual meeting, Birmingham, England, where he delivers the guest of honor address on "Sex and Censorship in Science Fiction."

1964   Founds *SF Horizons*—the first magazine of SF criticism—with Brian Aldiss.

       Vendetta for the Saint is published under the name of Leslie Charteris. *Deathworld 2* is published.

March, Harrison delivers "Criticism in Science Fiction" at the annual meeting of the Eastern Science Fiction Association, Newark, New Jersey, USA.

July, Harrison delivers "The Future of the Science Fiction Film" at the First International Convention on the Problems of Science Fiction, First International Festival of the Science Fiction Film, Trieste, Italy.

1965   *Bill, the Galactic Hero* is finally published, following difficulties in trying to get editors to accept its blend of SF and satire. *Two Tales and Eight Tomorrows* published.

HH moves to England.

April, Harrison delivers "Quasi-astronomical Sources in Science Fiction" to the Cambridge University Astronomical Society, Cambridge, England.

May, Harrison participates in the debate "The Existence of UFOs" at the Reigate Grammar School, Reigate, England.

September, Harrison attends the 23rd World Science Fiction Convention in London, England, where he participates in the panel "The New Criticism in Science Fiction."

November, Harrison delivers "Technology in Science Fiction" to the London University Science Fiction Association, London, England.

1965 to 1966, Harrison is editor of the English magazine *SF Impulse*.

1966   *Make Room! Make Room!* and *Plague from Space* are published.

February, Harrison delivers "The Future of the Biological Sciences" at Bromley Technical College, Bromley, England.

April, Harrison takes part in the panel "Editing Science Fiction" at the British Science Fiction Association annual meeting, Great Yarmouth, England.

July, Harrison attends the Third International Festival of the Science Fiction Film, Trieste, Italy, where he is elected judge of the festival prize films and takes part in the Astronomical Roundtable on the Possibilities of Extraterrestrial Life, where he discusses "Possible Forms of Alien Life."

1967   Moves to San Diego, California.

The Technicolor Time Machine is published.

November, Harrison delivers "Traveling with Science Fiction" at Kiwanis International, Long Beach, New York, USA.

1967 to 1968, Harrison is editor of *Amazing Stories* and *Fantastic Science Fiction*.

1968   Edits the first of nine volumes of the *Year's Best SF* with Brian Aldiss: the anthology is published annually until 1976.

Deathworld 3 published.

February, Harrison delivers "International Income Tax" to The American Society of Women Accountants, San Diego, California, USA.

March, Harrison attends the annual conference of the Science Fiction Writers of America in Berkeley, California, USA, where he is cochairman at the Nebula Awards Banquet and delivers "Needed Reforms in Authors' Contract Negotiations."

April, Harrison delivers "Writing and Selling Modern Science Fiction" at San Diego State College, San Diego, California, USA.

May, Harrison delivers "The Role of Science in Science Fiction," Mar Vista High School, Imperial Beach, California, USA.

June, Harrison delivers "Science Fiction, Spokesman for Science" at the First Unitarian Church, San Diego, California, USA.

July, Harrison is guest of honor at the Future Unlimited Convention, Los Angeles, California, USA, where he delivers the guest of honor address "The Year 2000."

August, Harrison delivers "The Craft of Science Fiction" at the Writers Summer Workshop, San Diego State College, San Diego, California, USA.

September, Harrison attends the 26th World Science Fiction Convention, Berkeley, California, USA, and takes part in the panel "Future Trends: The Writers to Watch."

1969   *Captive Universe* is published and chosen as the Book-of-the-Month Club selection for April. *Prime Number* is published.

The 1970s

1970   *In Our Hands the Stars, One Step from Earth,* and *The Stainless Steel Rat's Revenge* are published.

1972   *The Stainless Steel Rat Saves the World; A Transatlantic Tunnel, Hurrah!; Stonehenge;* and *Montezuma's Revenge* are all published.

1973   *Soylent Green* is released: the film wins Harry Harrison and the film's screenwriter the Nebula Award, presented by the Science Fiction Writers of America, for the Best Dramatic Presentation.

        Star Smashers of the Galaxy Rangers is published.

1974   HH returns to London.

        Queen Victoria's Revenge is published.

1975   Takes up residence in the Republic of Ireland.

1976   Organizes the first International Science Fiction Authors Conference, which is held in Dublin.

        Lifeship, Skyfall, and *The Best of Harry Harrison* are published.

1977   HH elected president of World SF.

Great Balls of Fire is published.

1978   *The Stainless Steel Rat Wants You* is published.

1979   *Planet Story* published.

The 1980s

1980   *Homeworld* and *The QEII Is Missing* are published.

1981   *Planet of No Return*, *Wheelworld*, and *Starworld* are published.

1982   *Invasion: Earth*, *The Jupiter Plague*, and *The Stainless Steel Rat for President* are published.

1983   *Rebel in Time* and *Stonehenge: Where Atlantis Died* are published.

1984   *West of Eden* is published.

1985   *A Stainless Steel Rat Is Born* and *You Can Be the Stainless Steel Rat*, an interactive game book, are published.

Harry Harrison becomes an honorary patron of the Universal Esperanto Association.

1986   *Winter in Eden* is published.

Harry Harrison is guest of honor at Windycon XIII in Chicago.

1987   *The Stainless Steel Rat Gets Drafted* is published.

HH attends the International SF Authors' Convention in Moscow.

1988   *Return to Eden* is published.

1989   *Bill, the Galactic Hero on the Planet of Robot Slaves* is published.

Harry Harrison by Leon Stover published in Twayne's United States Authors Series, the first full-length critical study of Harrison's works.

The 1990s

1990   HH is guest of honor at the 48th World Science Fiction Conference in The Hague. *Bill, the Galactic Hero on the Planet of Bottled Brains* is published.

1991   *Bill, the Galactic Hero on the Planet of Tasteless Pleasure; Bill, the Galactic Hero on the Planet of Ten Thousand Bars; Bill, the Galactic Hero: the Final Incoherent Adventure;* and *There Won't Be War* are all published.

1992   *The Turing Option* is published.

1993   *Stainless Steel Visions* and *The Hammer and the Cross* are published.

1994   *The Stainless Steel Rat Sings the Blues* and *Galactic Dreams* are published.

1995   *One King's Way* is published.

1996   *King and Emperor* and *The Stainless Steel Rat Goes to Hell* are published.

1997   Harry Harrison is guest of honor at the European Science Fiction convention in Dublin.

1998   March 5, *Stars and Stripes Forever* is published.

1999   Official Harry Harrison website launched at Octocon in Dun Laoghaire, Republic of Ireland.

        The Stainless Steel Rat Joins the Circus is published.

        December 16, "The Road to the Year 3000" is published in the journal *Nature*.

The 2000s

2000   March 11 to 12: HH is guest of honor at Mecon (the third Northern Ireland SF convention) in Belfast, Northern Ireland, where he celebrates his 75th birthday.

        April 6, *Stars and Stripes in Peril* is published.

        April 11, HH undergoes major heart surgery.

        HH is a guest at Chicon 2000 (the 58th Worldcon), Chicago, USA.

2001   October, HH is a guest at Octocon, Dun Laoghaire, Republic of Ireland.

2002   February 15 to 17 and 22 to 24, *Labours of Love*

presented by the Waimea Community Theatre at the Parker School Auditorium, Waimea, Hawaii, USA. Five one-act comedies on the theme of "men, women, and relationships" are performed, directed by J. Wayne Ryker II. Included is the play "For the Sake of Peace," adapted from HH's short story "The Day After the End of the World."

April 21, death of Joan Harrison.

April, *Harry Harrison: An Annotated Bibliography* by Paul Tomlinson is published.

June 6, *Stars and Stripes Triumphant* is published.

October, HH is a guest at Octocon, Maynooth, Republic of Ireland.

2004   July 9, HH is inducted into the Science Fiction and Fantasy Hall of Fame in Lawrence, Kansas, USA.

July 22, HH is awarded the Inkpot Award for Outstanding Achievement in Science Fiction and Fantasy by the Comic-Con International in San Diego, California, USA.

2005   March 12, Harry Harrison celebrates his 80th birthday.

November 19 to 20, HH is a guest at Comic Expo, held at the Hilton Metropole, Brighton, England.

HH attends convention in Kiev.

HH receives the Philosopher's Stone Award from the 2005 Kharkov convention for Service to Science Fiction.

2006   April, HH is guest of honor at the Eurocon held in Kiev and is made a European Grand Master by the Eurocon committee.

June 9 to 11, HH is guest of honor at the Atjaro Gateway Festival and Euroconference, Budapest, Hungary.

November 25, death of Leon E. Stover.

2007   April, HH attends ALT.Fiction in Derby, England.

September 21 to 23, HH attends Eurocon 2007 in Copenhagen, Denmark.

November 6 to 8, HH delivers a paper on "Speculating on the South: Reimagining the Historical South through Scholarship and Art," organized by the Institute of African American Research, Johnston Center for Undergraduate Excellence at the University of North Carolina at Chapel Hill, North Carolina, USA.

2008   May 17 to 18, HH is guest of honor at Roscon 2008, held in Moscow, Russia. HH is presented with the Golden Roscon Award for Lifetime Achievement in Science Fiction.

May 25, the spacecraft *Phoenix* lands on Mars; on board is a mini DVD created by the The Planetary Society, the contents of which being described as follows: "Personal greetings by space visionaries of our time to Mars settlers of the future are accompanied by eighty stories and articles by leading writers and scientists. A collection of Mars artwork, and classic radio shows narrated by Patrick Stewart, complete this unique tapestry of our knowledge and our dreams of Mars in the 20th century." The disc includes HH's *One Step from Earth* (1970).

2009   April 24 to 26, Harry Harrison attends the Nebula Award weekend in Los Angeles, California, USA, where he receives the Damon Knight Memorial Grand Master Award, presented by the Science Fiction Writers of America.

    The first world edition of *The Stainless Steel Rat Returns!*— the eleventh novel in the series—is published in Russia.

2010   *The Stainless Steel Rat Returns!* is published in the USA by Tor.

2012   August 15, Harry Max Harrison passes away in Brighton, England.

HARRY HARRISON!
HARRY HARRISON!

On the jacket of the German translation of one of my novels there appeared an expression that I had never stumbled on before. After the stern facts of *Geboren in Stamford, 1925* and *Er lebte en Mexiko, Italien, Dänemark,* it went on to refer to me as a *Weltenbummler.* Was I being called a "world bum"? Not nice. Professor T. A. Shippey, science fiction scholar, novelist, and linguist, set me right. "No, not a bum, Harrison—though others may think differently. It is an old and good German term, one not too different from our word 'apprentice.' Or better 'journeyman,' as in journeyman printer. A novice working at a skilled trade would go from workplace to workplace, learning new skills and crafts."

I think the Germans are right about me. *Weltenbummler* indeed. Everything new, different, interesting, educational becomes part of a writer's life. It is all grist for the creative mill. Many times the connection is obvious—I wrote *Captive Universe* after living in Mexico, seeing the life there in the isolated villages, discovering how these people understood their world. *In Our Hands the Stars* uses Denmark as a setting; the people, their attitude toward life, shape the structure of the novel.

Those are the obvious examples. But there are subtler threads in my writing; many times things that I am not aware of are there, that are pointed out by critics or friends. Or enemies? I do not wish to put down Peoria, home of that fine writer Philip José Farmer, but I do feel that there is more to the world than Peoria. I have lived for extended periods, for months and years, in a total of six countries. I have visited at least sixty more. I feel enriched by the experience. More important—I feel that my work has been enriched.

Circumstance, and residing outside my native country for some forty-four years, has certainly changed me. Changed the way I think, the way I write. I am an internationalist now, feeling that no single country is better than any other. Though there are certainly some that are worse. I speak Esperanto like a native, or as Damon Knight once said, "Harry speaks the worst English and the best Esperanto I have ever heard." I have traveled with this international language, learning other languages along the way, and have made friends right around the globe.

This is how it happened.

PART ONE

1

My generation of Americans were the first ones born in the New World. Without exception our parents were European—or at the most they were just one generation away from the immigrant ships. My genealogy is a perfect example.

My mother was born in 1882 in Riga, the capital of Latvia, which was then part of the Russian Empire. The family moved to St. Petersburg, where my grandfather worked as a watchmaker. They didn't exactly flee the anti-Jewish pogroms, but with a keen sense of survival they got out while they were still able. (I remember, as a child, that my mother still used the word "Cossack" as a pejorative.)

My grandfather emigrated first and went to work for the Waterbury Watch Company in Waterbury, Connecticut. Once he settled in and had earned some money he sent for his family, a few at a time.

My father, however, was a second-generation American; his father was born in Cork. Dad was born in the very Irish community in Oneida, New York, in the part of town named the Irish Ridge. This was where the immigrants from Ireland lived when they came to the United States to build the Erie Canal. However his mother was born in Ireland, in Cashel, Tipperary.

In the 1970s, while tracking down my own genealogy and searching for proof of my Irish ancestry in order to gain Irish citizenship, I found that I needed a copy of her birth certificate or other proof of birth. I knew that she was born in Dualla, a suburb of Cashel. After many years in Ireland I knew where to go for local information.

All of the medical records had been burned by the British, or so I was told. So I went to the oldest pub—where I bought a round of drinks for the oldest drinkers. It lubricated their memories.

"Moyles—yes, I remember the chap, that printer fellow who moved up to Dublin." Close. My family on my father's side were all printers. "Best to talk to Father Kinsella. He's here every third Sunday in the month." As the Irish population declined, the priests had to cover more than one parish. Another round of drinks and I had the vital information. On the correct Sunday I visited the good Father, with dire results. He was a tiny man with a white tonsure; his eyes flashed as he pointed to the tottering heaps of air letters. "Americans! It seems they all have grandmothers they're looking for. . . ." That was my cue; I jumped to my feet. "I see that you are a busy man, Father. I'm putting twenty quid in the poor box and I'll be on my way." Bank notes rustled greenly and the poor of Dualla were that better off.

"What did you say her name was?" the good Father asked. It took five minutes' time to find Margaret Moyles in the baptismal register, even less to make a copy of her entry. I was sincere with my thanks as I folded it into my wallet. For there, in faded blue ink, in neat Spenserian handwriting, the priest had entered *Margaret Moyles, 12 August 1832.* All for the price of a few pints. I took that down to the Irish passport office, to the "born abroad" authority, and that was the final piece of paper I needed to get—it wasn't a European passport in those days, it was a nice green passport with a golden shamrock: it looked like a real passport!

For the record: I was born in Stamford, Connecticut, but grew up in Queens, one of the five boroughs of New York City. My friends were the same as I, a step—or a half step—away from the Old World. Which was something we learned to look down upon as a weakness, not a strength. The Old World was part of the past. Forget that old stuff, we were all-American now (though this made for a linguistic pool that was only appreciated during World War

II, when there was never any shortage of translators in the army when they were needed).

My father, Henry Dempsey, started his printing career at the age of five when he began work as a printer's devil (the lad who opened the shop in the morning and turned on the heater for the diesel engine that powered the printing press). He went on to become a journeyman printer who worked all over the United States and Canada, as well as a quick look-in to Mexico. This history only came out bit by bit through the years.

––––––––––

The story of my name change, however, emerged sooner when I, Sgt. Harry Harrison, veteran of the U.S. Army Air Corps, applied for a passport. My mother showed some understandable discomfort when, most reluctantly, she produced my birth certificate.

The name on it was Henry Maxwell Dempsey. As you can imagine I was most interested in where "Harry Harrison" had come from. In tracking down the history of my name I discovered far more about my father's life as an itinerant printer than I had previously known. He explained. His family name was indeed Dempsey, but there were some hiccups along the way. It seems he had run into a bit of trouble in Mississippi. At the time he was a journeyman printer, going from job to job. Any town with a print shop and a newspaper welcomed him. Work was never a problem. To get between jobs he rode the rails, in empty boxcars, along with other bindle stiffs—the name for a skilled worker between jobs (as opposed to a regular hobo or bum). This was soon after the turn of the century, with employment very scarce. Riding the rails was an accepted form of transportation for men looking for work.

A lot of my father's early history I knew. What I didn't know— with very good reason!—was this missing episode in what certainly can be called a most interesting life.

It seems that the local police in rural Mississippi had rounded up all the itinerant workers from the boxcars of the train, including Henry Dempsey. If you had two dollars or more you were released as a legitimate worker between jobs. My father didn't have the two bucks so was sent to jail for a year for vagrancy. If this sounds a little exotic to you, think about the reaction of Sergeant Harrison with the strange birth certificate. Of course the whole thing was just a scam for the state of Mississippi to get guys to chop cotton for free. Nice. As my father explained, the end of this particular episode came rather abruptly, when a hurricane hit Mississippi one night. It had rolled up the corrugated iron roof on his barracks and blown it away. The prisoners followed the roof—and my father went with them, vowing never to return to the fine cotton-growing state of Mississippi ever again. And who could blame him?

Later on, after he was married and I was born—and certainly when I was still a baby—he changed his name to Leo Harrison. In those pre-computer days no questions were asked.

Later, during the war, he began to worry about the legality of all this—and was there the possibility that he was still an escaped prisoner? Like a loyal citizen he went to the FBI and told them all that had happened to him. Imprisonment, escape, name change, the works.

They smiled and patted him on the back and thanked him for coming in. And, oh yes, don't worry about Mississippi, their crooked vagrancy laws had been blown away in court many years previously.

I asked my friend Hubert Pritchard to come with me to the passport people, where he swore that he had known me before and after my father's name change, when we were both about three years old. No problem. I got a new passport. The story had had a happy ending. My father, the new Henry Harrison, went back to work. But this was all in the future. After years of working all over the country, my father had settled down. He was doing better and earning more money, working now as a highly skilled compositor and proofreader on newspapers—far away from the South. By the early 1920s he was teaching printing at Condé Nast in Stamford, Connecticut.

One of the printers he worked with there was called Marcus Nahan. They must have hit it off and become friends, because it was then that he met Marcus's wife Anna. She was a Kirjassoff, one of eight brothers and sisters (this family name was an Anglicized version of the Hebrew Kirjashafer, which in turn was a version of Kiryath-Saphir, a town in Israel). All three of her brothers had gone to Yale; all of them became track stars. Louis and Meyer both became engineers. Max went into the State Department and became U.S. consul in Yokohama, Japan—the first Jewish consul in waspland—and was killed in the earthquake there. Most of the sisters had gone to normal school and trained as teachers, except for Rose, who also went into government, ending up in the War Department with the simulated rank of colonel. One of the other sisters, my mother, Ria, also became a schoolteacher. Then, one day, her sister Anna invited her around to dinner.

That my parents met, and eventually married, is a matter of record. What they had in common has always baffled me. My mother was from a family of Jewish intellectuals; five out of her six grand-uncles were rabbis. My father's family was middle-class immigrant Irish. (Interestingly enough, almost all my Irish relatives worked in printing or publishing, both in Ireland and the States). Irish working class, Jewish intellectual—only in America.

But meet they did, marry they did, and had a single child. A few years later my father, as we have seen, changed his name and took that of his stepfather, Billy Harrison. (I never met Billy, since he had passed on before I was born. Ironically, he had died of silicosis after many years of sanding wood while working in a coffin factory.) I did meet my grandmother when she came to Queens to visit us. I remember a neat and compact white-haired Irish woman with a most attractive Tipperary brogue. She told me two things that I have always remembered. "Whiskey is the curse of the Irish" and "Ireland is a priest-ridden country." She had four sons and three died of drink. When I moved to Ireland I had some hint about the priests. After the child-molesting scandals broke, the whole world knew.

Back to history. When I was two years old we moved from Connecticut to New York City. Right into the opening days of the Great Depression, which soon had its teeth firmly clamped onto everyone's life. Those dark years are very hard to talk about to anyone who has not felt their unending embrace. To really understand them you had to have lived through them. Cold and inescapable, the Depression controlled every facet of our lives. This went on, unceasing, until the advent of war ended the gray existence that politics and business had sunk us into.

All during those grim years when I was growing up in Queens my father was employed at the *New York Daily News,* or almost employed, since he was a substitute, or a sub. Meaning he showed up at the newspaper at one A.M. for the late-night lobster shift every night, fit and ready for work. He then waited to see if someone called in sick who he could sub for, which was not very often. Then he would return home—often walking the seventeen miles from Manhattan to Queens to save a nickel.

Some weeks he would work only one shift; sometimes none. This meant that there was little money at any time; how my mother coped I shudder to think. But I was shielded from the rigors of grim necessity; there was always food on the table. However, I did wear darned socks and the same few clothes for a very long time, but then so did everyone else and no one bothered to notice. I was undoubtedly shaped by these harsh times and what did and did not happen to me, but it must not be forgotten that all of the other writers of my generation lived through the same impoverished Depression and managed to survive. It was mostly a dark and grim existence; fun it was not.

For one thing we moved home a lot, often more than once in a year, because even landlords were squeezed by the Depression. If you moved into a new apartment all you had to pay was the first month's rent, then you got a three-month concession. That is, no rent for the next three months. Not bad. Particularly when the iceman, with horse and cart, came at midnight before the third month was up and moved you to a new apartment with a new concession. The iceman received fifteen dollars for this moonlight flit.

This constant moving was easy on my father's pocket, but hard on my school records. Not to mention friendships, which simply didn't exist. Whether I was naturally a loner or not is hard to tell because I had no choice. I was skinny and short, first in line in a school photograph where we were all arranged by height. But weight and height did not affect children's cruelty toward the outsider. I was never in one school long enough to make any friends. Kids can be very cruel. I can clearly remember leaving one of our rented apartments and the children in the street singing—

> *We hate to see you go*
> *We hate to see you go*
> *We hope to hell you never come back*
> *We hate to see you go.*

The fact that I can clearly recall this some seventy-eight years later is some indication of how I felt at the time.

Forced by circumstance, I duly learned to live with the loneliness that had been wished upon me. It wasn't until I was ten years old that we finally settled down, and I went to one school for any extended length of time. This was Public School 117 in Queens. It was there at PS 117 that I made my first friends.

There were three of us and we were all loners, and as intellectual as you can be at that age. Hubert Pritchard's father was dead and his mother worked as a bookkeeper at the Jamaica Carpet Cleaning Company to support their small household. Henry Mann, rejected by his parents, was brought up in a string of foster homes.

He read the classic Greek and Roman authors in translation. Hubert was a keen amateur astronomer. I was devoted to science fiction. We were all outsiders and got along well together.

Did early incidents in my life cast their shadows before them into the future? Such as the one-act play that I wrote at the age of twelve for our grammar school class Christmas party. I remember very little of it save that it was about funny Nazis (perhaps an earlier working of the plot of *The Producers*?). In 1937, the Nazis were still considered butts of humor. But I do recall the song Hubert, Henry, and I sang to the melody of "Tipperary":

> *Good-bye to Unter den Linden,*
> *Farewell Brandenburg Tor,*
> *It's a long, long way to Berchtesgaden—*
> *But our Führer is there!*

For a nascent playwright this was a pretty poor start; scratch one career choice.

The poem I wrote at about the same time was equally grim. This was published in the PS 117 school newspaper and strangely enough was plagiarized a few years later by a fellow student. He actually had it accepted under his own name, James Moody, for the Jamaica High School paper. I recall the opening lines—which is more than enough, thank you:

> *I looked into the fire bright,*
> *And watched the flickering firelight . . .*
> *The shapes of fairies, dwarfs and gnomes,*
> *Cities, castles, country homes . . .*

My career as a poet stopped right there.

After school there was no avoiding the Depression; it was relentless and all-pervading. Pocket money was never mentioned because it did not exist—unless you earned it yourself. I spent most of my high school years working weekends on a newsstand. The widow who owned it knew my mother through the League of Women Voters. Her inheritance had been a wooden kiosk built under the steel stairs of the elevated part of the IRT subway on Jamaica Avenue. It supported her, two full-time workers, and me, working weekends.

Saturday was the busy night when there were two of us there. I sold the Saturday papers, magazines, and racing tip sheets, then unpacked the Sunday sections when they were delivered—all of the newspaper except the news section. When this main section was delivered about ten at night things became hectic, cutting the binding wires and folding in the completed papers, then selling them to the Saturday crowds that were out for dinner or a movie. Carefully counting the delivery first, since the truck drivers had a petty racket holding back a section or two. This continued until about midnight when, really exhausted, I took the Q44 bus home.

Sunday on the newsstand was a quiet day. I was responsible—from the age of fourteen on—for the cash and sales, and quite a variety it was. We sold *The Times,* the *Herald Tribune,* the *Amsterdam News* (a black newspaper—and just a few copies in this part of racially segregated New York). All these were in English. In addition there were two Yiddish papers, *Forverts,* and *Morgen Freiheit,* the Italian *Giornale,* the German *Deutsche Beobachter Herald,* and the Spanish *La Prensa.*

The newspapers were very cheap compared to today's prices. The tabloids were two cents daily, a nickel on Sundays, and *The Sunday Times* a big dime. However the two racing tip sheets for the horse players were all of one dollar, and I looked on the gamblers as rich, big-time players.

The newsstand job folded—for reasons long forgotten—and was replaced by my golf career. I worked as a caddy at the golf course farther out the island, but still in Queens. Reaching this resort required a bus trip to Flushing, then a transfer to get to the municipal golf course. It was not easy work. You carried the bag of clubs—no wheels!—for eighteen holes for a big buck; one dollar for a day's hard work. And I never remember getting a tip. The bus fare was a nickel each way and the temptation of a piece of apple pie—five cents in the caddy shack—irresistible after working the round, which meant eighty-five cents for a day's work.

Money was not easy to come by during the Depression—but a little did go a long way. Saturday was our day off and Hubert, Henry, and I headed for Manhattan, by subway of course. For a single payment of a nickel you had over a hundred miles of lines available. But we headed for Forty-second Street, the hub of entertainment in the city. We even managed to beat the subway fare by using the west end of the 168th entrance to the Independent. This entrance had no change booth but instead had a walled turnstile that was supposed to admit one passenger at a time. However there was no trouble squeezing two skinny kids in, one on the other's shoulders. Once—with immense effort—all three of us managed to squeeze through at a time; this was not repeated.

Forty-second Street between Broadway and Eighth Avenue had once been the heart of the legitimate theater district—with at least eight venues. The actors left with the arrival of the Depression and the theaters were converted to cinemas. It was ten cents for a double feature—with trailers. Three and a half hours at least; we stumbled out blinking like owls.

The Apollo was our favorite for it only showed foreign language, subtitled films. For budding intellectuals this was a wonderful look into these foreign minds. All of Jean Cocteau, Eisenstein, the best. Then up around the corner of Seventh Avenue was another theater—this one had only Russian films, and it was also very closely observed, we discovered much later. Only after the war was it revealed the FBI had an office there in the Times Building, overlooking the theater, where they photographed all the commie customers.

I had an early file with the FBI! It was a quarter well spent for our day out—a dime for the subway and another for the movie. The remaining nickel went for lunch. You could get a good hot dog for a nickel—or in a grease pit next door, a repulsive dog, and a free root beer. Thirst usually won.

There was, of course, far better food on Forty-second Street—if you could afford it. The best investment was a five-cent cup of coffee at the Waldorf Cafeteria. This admitted one to the busy social life there. In small groups at certain tables, like-minded individuals gathered together. I remember that the communists met on the balcony on the left side—of course!—with the Trotskyites a few tables away. On the right side of the balcony the deaf and dumb got together; dummies as we called them with youthful stupidity. Then, halfway between the two groups were the deaf and dumb communists.

New York was a big, big city and in this house were many mansions.

On the days when we had more than the basic two bits, there were the secondhand magazine shops around the corner on Eighth Avenue. Here, for a nickel apiece, were all of the pulps that cost as much as a quarter on the newsstand. *Astounding, Amazing, Thrilling Wonder Stories,* all the science fiction mags. As well as *Doc Savage, The Shadow, G-8 and His Battle Aces,* treasures beyond counting. But I had to count because one of the shops had a terrible and terribly attractive offer. Turn in three pulps—and get another one in return.

So I, in the fullness of time, must have read every SF magazine ever published. Read it and reread it. Then finally—and reluctantly—passed it back for the lure of just one more. . . .

In addition to the commercial joys of Midtown Manhattan there was, a bit further uptown—and free!—the Museum of Natural History, which contained the Hayden Planetarium. For an amateur astronomer there were delights galore here. There was a class where you learned to make your own reflective lens. The lens tool was fixed to a barrel, while a second glass blank was moved across it as you slowly worked around the barrel. With patience enough, grinding powder, and time, you ended up with a good lens that was still spherical. Then the careful slow lapping to turn it into a parabolic cross section, to be followed by silvering. If you did your work well you ended up with a parabolic lens and you had yourself a telescope, if you could afford the mounting tube and the eyepiece.

I had first started to read science fiction when my father had brought home one of the old large-size issues of *Amazing* in the 1930s when I was five years old. In the gray and empty Depression years the science fiction magazines rang out like a fire bell in the night. They had color, imagination, excitement, inspiration, everything that the real world had not.

At this same time, science fiction readership was taking on a new dimension. Through the readers' column of the magazines, readers found and contacted other fans. They met, enthused over SF, formed clubs—on a strictly geographic basis—and SF fandom was born. I, and other local readers, met together in Jimmie Taurasi's basement in Flushing and wrote a one-page constitution; the Queens Science Fiction League was born. In Manhattan the same thing was happening with the Futurians.

Far too much has been written about SF fandom and this literature is easily available. From a personal point of view it was just a pleasure to meet with other like-minded boys. (No girls! Ghu forbid!) Still in the future were fan feuds, conventions, fannish politics, fanzines, and all the rest of the apparatus of the true fan.

I sink into fanspeak. "Fen" is the plural of "fan." "Femfan," a female fan—but they came later, much later! "Ghu"—the god of fandom. "Gafiate"—get away from it all. Leave fandom. And more—a closed society indeed.

From a personal point of view I enjoyed SF and fandom. I went to the first ever world SF convention in Manhattan in 1939; couldn't afford the nickel entrance fee so had to sneak in. I read all of the magazines, *Astounding Science Fiction* in particular, and always felt myself a part of the greater whole of SF.

2

But there was thunder in the distance and my quiet world was about to be shaken to its roots and I must leave the early record at this point. I'm afraid that these brief entries must sum up my childhood years for the curious, all of the period right up until my sixteenth year and the traumatic event that was Pearl Harbor Day.

December 7, 1941. The day the Japanese bombed Pearl Harbor and America was at war. I don't believe that I even knew where Pearl Harbor was at that time. Nor was I filled with patriotic enthusiasm like my cousin Kenneth, who went out the next day and enlisted in the army. For the rest of us teenagers nothing basically changed. Yes there were shortages and rationing, gasoline was in great demand, but our already lean diet didn't change—and we had no car. So I—and my peer group—just went on serving time in school, numbly checking off the days until our eighteenth birthdays when the draft boards would reach out and seize us up. Other than volunteering there was nothing else that we could do.

However, we all found out quickly enough what the future would be like now that the United States had become a country engaged in a global conflict. America's industrial capacity grew and grew to meet the physical needs of a global war, almost incidentally ending the Depression. Now there was full employment—for those not seized by the draft boards. There was a shortage of printers and my father worked a full week now, so that our family fortunes were greatly improved. The military machine was expanding as well, and men were needed to man the mighty war machine that was being constructed.

I had been almost sixteen years old when the war began. As the months went by I, and all of the other male high school students of my age, became aware of the swift passage of time and its effect upon our future existence. The war was expanding and, if anything, was getting steadily worse for our side. The Allies appeared to be losing on all fronts. The fighting was bitter and deadly, with no guarantee that it would ever end in victory for our armed forces.

Time was running out for my peer group. If the war were still on—and it appeared that it certainly would be in a few short years' time—then we would soon be joining it. The draft age was eighteen and the culling was ruthless. Not only were pink-faced eighteen-year-olds being forcibly drafted into the army and navy—but were also being pushed into the theoretically volunteers-only Marine Corps. What could I, as an individual, do to get through this war alive? Was there anything that I could do to affect my destiny?

It must be understood that this was not a matter of patriotism or loyalty to one's country. I shared with my fellow teenagers a sense of fate inescapable. Whatever happened, no matter how we felt, no matter what we did, when we reached our eighteenth year we were going to be dragged into the military machine.

Up to this time, a middle-class or blue-collar child growing up in the '30s in America had few if any choices to make. The law required you to attend school for a good number of years, to be first fed into kindergarten and then pushed on into grade school, high school at fourteen, to graduate at eighteen. One maiden aunt of mine, Rose Kirjassoff, had even saved enough money to put me through college someday. My life was predictable and appeared to be about as orderly as life could possibly be. It was not to be questioned; just to be endured.

Then came the war. I would graduate high school in January of 1943. Two months later, on my birthday, the jaws of the draft board would open to consume and engulf me. What to do?

I remember being gloomily fatalistic about my future. I knew that if I did nothing I would be drafted into the army and would be shot. Or if not that, then I would go into the navy where I would drown. Or into the marines where I would be both shot and drowned at the same time. The prospects were not encouraging. What could I do that would separate me from the mass of other eighteen-year-old chunks of cannon fodder? I had no desire or intention of escaping the draft—it was unavoidable, and I really believed that the cause we were fighting was a just one. But how could I be fed into the meat grinder and come out alive? It was time for me to make a decision that could save my life. I am certain that my existence as an aware and separate entity began at this point.

The individual steps of my logic are a little vague some sixty-eight years later—but I remember the results quite clearly. I would go into the Army Air Corps, where the chance of survival was a good deal greater than in the other services. I had a boy's dream of being a pilot, impossible to achieve, since I wore glasses. Or even of being a glider pilot, since they were permitted to wear glasses (an opportunity happily missed, when the mortality rate of glider pilots is examined well after the fact). Simply, one had a better chance of living through the war in the U.S. Army Air Corps. At this time there were something like thirty-eight soldiers on the ground to every one in the air. I would enlist the law of averages on my side.

This was not any attempt to escape my military destiny. I was not a "draft-dodger," as they were so endearingly called at the time. I thought of this as a war that had to be fought and won. My mother's Russian-Jewish side of the family had helped relatives in Europe escape the coming Holocaust, among them that excellent photographer Philip Halsman. I have somewhere his portrait of me as a teenager, more a tribute to familial ties than to my physical assets at the time.

I knew very well what the war in Europe was about, since history was a subject that engrossed me: I did much extracurricular reading. So much so that someone wrote in my high school yearbook "To the guy who cheered up our history class," meaning that

I was the little shit who humiliated the young teacher by correcting her. American history, as taught then, and still I imagine now, was rather one-sided about the American Revolution. I had been reading Robert Graves's Sergeant Lamb books about American Loyalists, an unknown and probably taboo topic. So I cheered up my history class by pointing out that the revolution was not the inspirational one-sided affair that our textbooks told us about.

I knew my current history as well: I knew what was happening in Europe. I wanted an opportunity to get at the Germans—I just didn't want to die while doing my part.

It was three months to D-Day—Draft Day in this case. What to do? I had no money. Despite the end of the Depression my father never seemed to make a decent living; he had his personal problems. Since I was stone broke when I graduated high school I went to work in Macy's department store as a box boy at eighteen dollars a week. Only temporary, low-paying jobs like this were open to 1As, a status that meant instant drafting when the age eighteen was reached. I did my box-boy work during the days—then at night I went to the Eastern Aircraft Instrument School in Newark, New Jersey. Tuition paid courtesy of my labors at Macy's.

This school was fun. I liked machinery and I liked to work with my hands. By the time I was drafted I had a CAA-approved license as an aircraft instrument technician.

I turned eighteen and, the very same day, an official-looking letter arrived for me.

My childhood years were over.

My adult life was about to begin.

"Greetings." That is how the draft notice began. It informed me that a board comprised of my neighbors had decided my fate. I was to report to Grand Central Palace in Manhattan for a physical examination. This would determine if I were fit enough to join the military. Physical examination? We were all so naïve. I must have had visions of a friendly family doctor, complete with smile and stethoscope. But, oh, how different the reality was! The physical examination proved to be a more than sufficient glimpse at the harsh reality of the real world that existed out there, well beyond family, school, and all things familiar.

By hindsight, as an adult more than sixty years later, I still consider it a gruesome and horrifying experience, surrealistic and macabre.

I took the subway to Manhattan and joined the herd of teenagers there. Processing began. The first thing that they did was take all of our clothes away. Hundreds of boys of all sizes and shapes instantly lost their individuality and each became one more nude, shivering, goose-pimpled pink piece of flesh. Yes, all pink, because it must not be forgotten that America fought this war with a segregated military. The unreliable Negroes, they said, were not to be trusted with guns. So black-skinned Americans were called up by segregated draft boards and were herded into separate noncombatant maintenance and transport units. No weapons allowed.

There was some small comfort that, while stripped naked, we were still allowed to keep our shoes on. Each of us clutched a folder of still-blank records as we were herded to our destiny. Was this humiliation deliberate sadism? Probably not; just the military's total indifference to the individual as a thinking, separate human being. Into the elevators we went, giant cars holding thirty of us jammed tight. Up through the building to our first examination.

Well, not quite. Someone had pressed the wrong button. The doors slowly slid open before us to reveal to our horrified eyes an entire floor of female typists, all of them busily hammering away at their machines. I remember a slow rustle of movement as the petrified teenagers moved their folders in front of their shrinking genitals. The doors closed slowly, we moved on, the doors opened into the first level of hell.

Oh, Dante! How you would have relished Grand Central Palace in the cold winter of 1943! As you made your notes you might have paused for a moment in wry reflection. Here were circles of the inferno far beyond your wildest imaginings. Even the simplest medical procedure was inflated and traumatized into a surrealistic nightmare.

Consider hemorrhoids. Certainly no one could be drafted into the armed forces with hemorrhoids. Did we have visions of a pleasant proctologist, smiling and considerate? Don't mean to disturb you, young man. This won't take a second. . . .

Hah! The reality proved to be quite different. Shouted orders, first twenty men—step forward! Bend over, folders on the floor. Now reach back with both hands and grab your ass, wonderful. Now spread your cheeks—

I had a quick glimpse of a doctor all in white—your friendly family proctologist—masked and rubber-gloved and bent over in a crouch like Groucho Marx, running along behind us, flashlight extended. He must have had the keenest eyesight to spot piles in the half second of each glimpse.

Then on to the other levels of the inferno, the diabetes test. No enfeebled diabetics could be allowed into the armed forces. Pee into a numbered test tube; shuffle along in the shivering naked line, sample in one hand, folder in the other. Closer and closer to the scampering white-clad demon wearing great red rubber gloves. He needed them, for this was, to put it as delicately as possible, piss heaven. There was urine everywhere. His hospital whites were yellow with it and he stood on duckboards for the floor flowed with it. Working at speed he quickly decanted a sample into one of the racked test tubes that were each charged with reactive agents. The tubes were whisked away for a quick examination by another demon. Scribbled notes in files and on to the next level of hell.

It was a relief to sit down for a moment to prepare for the arduous psychological examination. Sexual orientation was most important in an all-male army. We were beckoned forward to be questioned by a gray-haired psychiatrist.

"Do you like boys or girls? You do like girls? Okay. Next!"

Next were the prophylactic injections to protect us against TB? Clap? Athlete's foot? We were not told; we just endured, slowly shuffling forward to our destiny like cattle in a slaughterhouse. Mechanized medicine. Step forward to be seized from both sides as a painful hypodermic injection was simultaneously thrust into the biceps of each arm. Some of the shots were quite excruciating. A push in the back so that the victim staggered forward a few feet for two more injections. Another push enabled the draftee to move out of shot range, to lean wearily on a waiting table. To be vaccinated while resting there.

But there was a disruption—the forward momentum stopped as one of the victims could not face the waiting needles. He was a teenage weight lifter with bulging muscles but no fondness for injections. One look at the waiting needles and his eyes rolled up and he fell to the floor unconscious. This did not interrupt the production line. Processing resumed as he was dragged forward to be injected and vaccinated. Then to be pulled to one side, his folder on his chest, to, hopefully, regain consciousness. Before we could witness his fate we were moved on.

Blood tests, sputum tests, and an eye examination that a totally blind man could have passed. Other, less traumatic examinations must have taken place, I am sure. Memory is blissfully blurred by time, but it seemed an eternity. Then, countless minutes—days?—later we were permitted to dress. We turned in our files and were ordered to go home. We would be informed of the results.

We staggered out into the chill afternoon. We were too young—and too poor—to drink to drown our sorrows. For me there was only the solace of the subway and the slow trip back to Queens.

My notice came a few days later. Probably printed out and mailed even before I left Grand Central Palace. I was physically fit (as was everyone else in my class at school) and I was in the army and due to report to Camp Upton on Long Island, to be sworn into the Army of the United States. Had I been assigned to the Air Corps or was I destined to be infantry cannon fodder? They didn't say. This was a mystery that would be revealed some time in the future. I was told—not for the first time—not to think but to simply follow orders. These were blurrily mimeographed and had a Long Island Railroad ticket stapled to them.

On the specified day I said tearful good-byes to my parents and left home for the last time as a child; this was indeed childhood's end.

Camp Upton was a monument of orderly disorder. Shouted at by sergeants, we passed numbly through a hectic first day of being issued clothing, shoes, towels, trousers, jackets, all the personal items we would need in the army. Heavily laden we were trotted off to the barracks where we were assigned bunks. We dumped our stuff and were herded off to a welcome meal in the chow hall. Hot dogs, my favorite food; maybe the army would turn out to be better than they said.

By then it was sack time, welcomed after a long and tiring day. The lights went off at nine but most of us had crashed by then.

To be hauled awake at five A.M. by a scratchy shellac recording of a tinny bugle playing reveille. Dress, eat, and then back to the barracks just in time to hear the order to fall out in formation. I turned to leave the barracks with the others.

This was when serendipity struck. A minor encounter that had a major effect on my life in the army. An older guy in the bunk next to me—he must have been at least twenty-five—looked on as I started to join the swarming crowd of recruits.

"Where you going, kid?" he asked, lying back comfortably on his bunk.

"Out. Orders. Go—"

"Just hold on a bit and think before you leap. This is a reception center. None of the permanent-party jokers who run this operation even know that you are here. The only thing you gotta do is once a day read the bulletin board—that's at eleven o'clock every day—to see if you are on a shipment. If you are not, then what you gotta do next is stay out of sight for twenty-four hours. Easy."

He climbed slowly to his feet. "Come with me. I been here a week and know the drill."

Instead of going out into the company street with all the other draftees he led the way to the rear of the barracks and through a door into the boiler room.

"The MPs never look in here until a lot later. My name is Blacky."

He was a treasure, Blacky was. He had been a cavalryman in the peacetime army, and had gotten discharged—just in time to be drafted again. But oh, how he knew the ropes. He was a world-class authority on what had been called goldbricking during the First World War, but was now referred to as fucking off. That is, avoiding work and not getting caught doing it. As we rested in the cool darkness he explained that our fellow draftees were now being assigned to work details. All we had to do was wait until they had all marched off, then we could emerge to spend a quiet day in the sun.

And it worked. During lunch I recognized newly minted soldiers from our barracks glumly working as KPs on the chow line. At eleven we checked for shipping orders; nothing. So back to dodging MPs for another twenty-four hours.

I was some weeks in the reception center resolutely dodging work—and the MPs who were sent out to round up the stragglers like myself. Camp Upton had lots of First World War underground ammunition bunkers, now empty. They made a good place to hide during the day—until the MPs got wise to this scam. They caught Blacky in a surprise raid. They shipped him out and I never saw him again—but I thank him fervently for his basic military education.

About this time I found the post library, far safer than the bunkers because the illiterate MPs never thought of looking there. In the weeks that followed, while waiting for my shipping orders, I happily worked my way through Wells and Verne and waited for events to unfold.

After a month of this literary life I was pleasantly surprised to discover that the Eastern Aircraft Instrument School had indeed saved my life. Every morning I emerged from the boiler room and, before my library assignment, I dutifully read the shipping orders posted on the bulletin board. There, at last, was my name. I was in the Army Air Corps and was being sent for basic training to Keesler Field, Biloxi, Mississippi.

That was the end of the good news. I was going to Mississippi in July. Remember, this was before air conditioners were invented. Even officers suffered the humid summer heat like the rest of us.

Two days later I dragged my barracks bag onto the troop train and the journey south began. After an endless, boring, and slow troop-train ride we reached our destination well after midnight and de-trained into the waiting fleet of trucks. Then, as soon as we arrived in Biloxi, the military made it very clear at once just where I stood. At two in the morning, temperature and humidity both in the nineties, I watched as my barracks bag, with all my worldly possessions, was kicked off the back of a six-by truck by a sergeant—and into the mud puddle below. Message received.

Hell began at five the next morning. Like at Camp Upton, reveille was announced by an ancient shellac record. Scratch, scratch, scratch—followed by the sour bugle call. Then the lights came on and the sergeant went down the rows of bunks—kicking each of them as he advanced—calling hoarsely, "Drop your cocks and grab your socks—you're in the army now!" Had there ever been any doubt? Pull on your fatigues, dress in a rush, pee, and wash, double-time to the chow hall, then a full day of unremitting labor in the ninety-degree heat. That often continued through the night as well. Skinny kids got skinnier as they sweated off the pounds— fat kids enjoyed an inadvertent slimming session. We didn't have time to think about it—just obey the screaming devils that tormented us.

Now, looking back through the telescope of time, it is obvious what they were trying to do—stress us to see if we broke. The majority of us were healthy eighteen-year-olds. Our drill sergeants—far older but far tougher—were subjected to the same stresses that we were. So logically we could not complain, but this basic training held a fierce and deadly truth.

The army was doing its best to strain us to the breaking point—and beyond. If we broke down, there would be a pat on the back and an honorary discharge. There was a fierce if terrible logic at work here. If we were going to break, they wanted it to happen in these first weeks, not later after we had received expensive training and the investment of plenty of military bucks.

It made horribly logical sense but the price paid was a disaster to the individual involved. I watched nice, happy kids get slowly worn away—then crack. Emotionally or physically; the military didn't care. The motto was shape up or ship out. Let me tell you—it was a very thin line between winning and losing. I remember coming right up to that line.

I had lost weight and had not yet started to put it back on as muscle. We were asleep in the barracks, dumbly and deeply, when the lights came on at midnight and we were shouted awake. A forced night march, twenty miles, field packs and rifles, let's go. We shuffled numbly out into the night.

It is hard to describe what we experienced. Tired to begin with, we dragged along the sandy track between the trees. The temperature was still in the high eighties, high humidity, silence, except for the sound of shuffling boots in the sandy track. The army expected us to fail. The column was followed by an ambulance—called the meat wagon—with lowered lights so as not to run us down. Orders were that if a guy dropped, the two nearest GIs were to pick him up and dump him into the back of the following vehicle. If and when he came to he was supposed to start marching again.

All of us were on the verge of exhaustion, staggering as we walked. Nor did it get any better as the night wore on. I remember stumbling as I walked, tormented by the sand under my shirt rubbing against the heat rash there, ground down by my pack. I was over the edge of exhaustion and ready to fall down. It was at that moment that I made a discovery about myself—I did not want to fall down. I did not want the bastards to win. This feeble spark of anger kept me going. Until the next five-minute break then through the rest of the march and back to the barracks to drop my pack and rifle and crash onto my bunk. Oblivion had never felt better.

Written out now, decades later, this may not sound like very much. But it was victory for that eighteen-year-old kid, something he would never forget. I had not let the bastards win. For many years I remembered this and from it drew strength when it was really needed. For a teenager with very little self-esteem I had finally felt some.

And it worked. I kept going. I managed to put on eight pounds—and all of it muscle. I finished the seven weeks of basic training, along with the survivors of my squad. We had lost a few guys along the way, for various reasons. The most tragic of these was Sol, who simply gave in. It was terrible to watch—particularly since he did not have to do it. He was well built and physically fit. It was purely mental, and the help he got from his bunkmate didn't seem to help. His name was Irving—he was also Jewish—and he took Sol under his wing.

I never found out if Irving was drafted or had volunteered. He didn't belong there. He was over thirty and a professor of hydraulics at Columbia but he did manage to make it through basic, doing his best all the time to help Sol. He sat and talked to him, encouraged him, did everything that he could, but Sol had given up. He used to complain about everything—and there was certainly enough to complain about. He dwelt on it, a reedy whine of complaint. He had stopped eating and then one day he wouldn't get out of his bunk. A couple of MPs came by and talked to him, then took him away. We never saw him again.

Irving kept track of him, bugging the detail sergeant. Then one day he told us that Sol had got a Section Eight and been shipped home—honorable discharge for psychiatric reasons. The bastards had simply ground him down, and in doing so had destroyed his life. It was a complete waste. If he had not been drafted he would undoubtedly have led a useful and productive life, but the military had found a little weakness and worried away at it until they had brought him down. On an ironic note: Irving got through basic and was assigned to the military scholastic program. They sent him back to Columbia to teach hydraulics.

Well—at least he was in far better physical shape than the other academics. When people want to know why I hate the military I don't know where to begin.

Meanwhile, even though I had finished basic, my shipping orders had not arrived. So I took basic a second time. I discovered that I was slated to go to a highly secret technical school, but the orders had not come in. No lazy bodies in the army! I breezed through basic this time—and a third time—until my shipping orders finally arrived. Before I could take basic training again—and let me tell you, was I in great physical shape!—the orders finally came. I was off to Denver, Colorado, to Lowry Field and a secret military school there.

It was almost Christmas by this time and I remember looking out of the train window at the snowy Rockies—absentmindedly scratching at the remnants of my heat rash.

3

I was on a troop train loaded with GIs, all heading for air force schools in Denver, Colorado. It was an endless, comfortless trip that went on interminably. Eventually we stumbled down to the freezing platform after five wearying days of two to a bed and a diet of stale white bread and leathery bologna. This had been loaded aboard in Mississippi in GI cans, galvanized metal cans used for food—or garbage, nice. It had to last for the five-day trip and was a little hard to choke down toward the end.

Now, bleary-eyed from lack of sleep, our guts concrete-solid from the revolting diet, my cadre stamped in circles to keep warm and, as fate would have it, we were the last ones to be trucked out to the technical school at Lowry Field.

My squad of budding technicians were all eager and willing to go to tech school. To study . . . what? We did not know, nor were we told. After all, there was a war on—a fact driven home by the dire warning stenciled in large white letters on the latrine mirrors: "If you talk—this man may die." Talk to whom, about what? We were never told.

Since we arrived on a weekend we actually had a chance to rest and eat some marginally better chow than we had at Keesler. Attached to our chow hall was a GI cooking school. So in addition to our normal food we were served some of their successes—few—and their failures—many. I shall never forget a large pan containing apple pie that was five inches thick at one end—and a half inch at the other.

Back in the barracks we found our orders posted. We were to

fall in on the Monday morning, when all the details of our future would be revealed, but what was first revealed was the usual military attempt at spirit breaking. Our first class was to be at six A.M., so of course reveille was sounded at three in the morning. Dress on the run with the sergeant's barked commands lashing you like a whip. Then we had to open all of the windows, stack the footlockers on the beds, and mop the floor. The fact that it was twenty degrees out and the water froze before it could wash anything clean was beside the point. Do it by the numbers and don't ask questions. Then out into the snow to freeze while a barely literate corporal worked his way through the roster of jawbreaking foreign names of our New York contingent. Then a mile's walk in the snow to the gratefully heated chow hall. Appetites sated, there was another mile to the school building for our class assignments. What technical secrets were to be revealed? Warmed and full of food we fought to stay awake long enough to find out.

"That is a Norden bombsight," the corporal said, pointing to the bundle being carried by two MPs who were passing through the hall where we were assembled. They carried the bombsight between them, holding the leather handles of the wash pail–sized, well-wrapped object. More impressive than the shrouded bombsight itself were the .45 caliber automatic pistols that they held ready in their free hands. This was a military secret all right!

Very impressed, we filed into a classroom and waited eagerly while our names were called out, ready and willing to learn the top-secret secrets of the Norden bombsight.

I was among those not called. Half the squad trooped eagerly away to delve into the mechanical mysteries of this secret device. The corporal turned his attention back to us.

"Okay. Next is Power-Operated Turret and Sperry Computing Gunsight School. Step out when I call your name. Harrison . . ." What on earth was a turret—or a Sperry gunsight?

I had a sinking feeling that I was soon to find out. We entered a classroom, found seats, and looked on with eager anticipation as our sergeant instructor locked the door and went to the front of the room. He pointed to a large square of blank cardboard with his index finger.

"This is the Sperry Mark 3 computing gunsight."

He turned the board over and there it was.

It was a lumpish black object with an angled piece of glass on its top that was framed by a metal cage. Nothing about it resembled any device I had ever seen before. I realized with a touch of panic that I had a lot to learn. The instructor flipped over the first card to reveal an even more interesting one. It could be seen now that the gunsight was mounted in the top of a tublike revolving turret, ominously close to two gigantic machine guns. There was a complex handgrip, and a folding seat for the gunner. Our instructor tapped the computing gunsight and informed us that it worked on the same principles as the bombsight—there were just no MPs with guns involved. With the aid of the computer the gunner aimed and fired the two .50 caliber guns that framed his head.

We were mystified. The instructor must have seen the blank looks on our faces; we hadn't the slightest idea of what he was talking about.

"Look—it's just like hunting birds with a shotgun—or shooting skeet."

He was talking a foreign language. What did a bunch of New York teenagers know about shooting a shotgun? Our instructor was remorseless.

"Just think about it. When you fire at the bird—or the clay pigeon—you've got to aim ahead of it because it's moving. You shoot at the spot where it's going to be, not where it is or was. Got it? That's called leading your target." He tapped the computing gunsight. "This does the thinking for you. The computer is a brain in a box. It solves the problem of where you have to aim, then tells you what to do. Now isn't that simple?" The answer was firmly *no*. He frowned at our gaping jaws and obvious stupidity. "I'll give you a for instance. It should be obvious, even to you bunch of adenoidal morons, that you have to allow for bullet drop. Grope through your feeble memories and try to remember your high school physics—and your basic training. Gravity pulls everything down at the same rate, right? So when you were firing on the range you were taught to aim your sights high on your target so the bullet would fall and hit the target. But what happens if you are firing from an airplane?"

He waited for an answer; none were forthcoming. His sigh was audible.

"I'll give you a clue. Another factor now enters the equation. The higher you go the thinner the air, the thinner the air the less resistance for the bullet. So as you fly higher it goes farther for every unit of drop. The computer allows for this with this rotating cam."

He held up a five-inch brass disc with a rising slope machined into it.

"As the plane gains altitude the altimeter controls the movement of the cam, which rotates. The higher it goes the thinner the air. The cam follower measures this drop in air pressure and feeds the changed reading into the computer. So the height of any point on the cam is analogous to the density of the atmosphere at that altitude. One is the analog of the other. That's why we have here a mechanical analog computer. There are other data inputs that you will learn about. All of them are used to compute the future position of the target. The optic head rotates and tilts so while it is still framing the enemy plane the guns are aiming at the point where it will be. It's just that simple. Do you understand?"

Hopefully, yes. Vaguely, but simply, *no*. Just what did the computer do to process the information? I had the fearful sensation that we were going to have to find out and that there was a long way to go.

In the weeks to come we would indeed learn not only the secrets of the operation of the computing gunsight, but all the faults and foibles these complex machines were heir to. And it was not only the gunsight that would be our responsibility. We discovered that we would be required to master all of the technology and secrets of the power turret itself.

And, if that wasn't enough, ours was to be an armament rating. Meaning that we would also learn the gunsmith's art of servicing the .50 caliber machine gun. Our Air Corps military specialty would then be a 678 power-operated turret and computing gunsight specialist. If we became proficient and worked diligently, after a year's experience in the field we could tack a 3 on the end of the number, making it 678-3, that is, a 678 skilled.

By the end of spring the survivors had finished the course and with the minimum of ceremony we were ready to be shipped out. I was now the proud owner of a triangular patch with a bomb on it—representing my new ranking as an armaments specialist. I sewed it onto my sleeve. Having qualified on a number of weapons during training I also wore a sharpshooter's medal on my pocket with pendant details: .50 caliber, Garand rifle, Reising submachine gun.

My orders were cut and I joined the next shipment to the air bases in Texas. I went first to a replacement depot—repple depple—in Kelly Field, San Antonio, to await my next assignment. It was boring just sitting around waiting for my shipment to come up. For the first time I actually volunteered. The detail sergeant wanted an assistant; that was me. We passed out all the jobs needed for our unit, sweeping up the company area, and such assignments. Also, completely by chance, I was wearing a faded blue class X jacket that I had grabbed from the pile (class X clothing meant almost-worn-out uniforms with some life left in them; grab what you want). It also had a faded blue patch where a sergeant's stripes had been.

Boy, was I popular!

Hi, Sarge.

Can I get you a beer, Sarge?

This privileged position only lasted a few weeks—but it was fun while it lasted.

My next assignment was a short trip south to Laredo Air Force Base in Laredo on the Mexican border. My home for the next two years.

I have written of the military mind elsewhere, particularly in my novel *Bill, the Galactic Hero.* I shall not cover that ground again here, other than to say that, like most other draftees, I managed to survive. Some years later, the war well over, I received my honorable discharge. But that was still in the distant future. The war was on and I was doing my bit. Of course I never saw an aircraft instrument again after being assigned to the aerial gunnery school in Laredo, Texas.

Laredo, Texas, was a specialist air base devoted to turning draftees into aerial gunners in eight weeks. There were thirty thousand GIs devoted to this task in one capacity or another, and I was one of them. I was assigned to the ground range where the students fired live ammunition for the first time. This was done from a Martin upper gun turret that mounted two .50 caliber machine guns. The turret was mounted on a steel frame bolted to the chassis of a six-by-six Chevy truck. There was a shortage of drivers so I was assigned to drive one of these monsters.

"I've been assigned here by mistake. I can't drive." He scowled at me grimly over his clipboard. "What sort of chicken shit is this? All patriotic American kids can drive." He reached out a great claw of a hand and reeled in a pudgy, gasping GI who was passing. "Grab one of those six-bys over there and Grubinsky here will bring your driving up to snuff." Muttering and rubbing his shoulder, Grubinsky found a truck with a key and hauled his lardy bottom up into the front seat. "Okay, kid, get in the driver's side. That's it, bang on. Now turn the key."

I learned to shift, to double-shift (much needed in those days before synchromesh) to brake and accelerate. The truck bucked, the gears ground noisily, the engine died. My instructor fell asleep. I practiced some more then punched him awake.

"You really got it now, kid." He yawned. "Road test. Head out toward the gunnery range road." He fell back asleep. I drove out into the desert. When I had enough of the cactus, I found a wide spot in the road and, with much heaving and bucking and killing the engine, I turned the truck around and headed back to the base. It was almost time for chow. I found the fleet base, parked, turned off the engine, and left my instructor peacefully sleeping. I went to chow.

The working day began before dawn when, in convoy, each truck was driven to the ground range some thirty miles from the air base. I came last, bucking and braking—terrified. I made it eventually and once there I was lined up with fourteen similar rigs and the working day began.

The guns were serviced by an armorer who cleaned and bore sighted them, and loaded the ammo. The student climbed into the turret where an instructor taught him how to fire the guns at a cloth target mounted on a remote-controlled jeep. I had no complaints when a driver was assigned to our truck. I had enough to do maintaining the turret and servicing and adjusting the Sperry Mark 4 computing gunsight that was mounted between the guns. We used cotton earplugs because when the firing whistle blew thirty guns firing twelve shots a second each made a soul-destroying sound. An easy job, until someone with an IQ a bit above vegetable life noticed that there was one warm body too many per truck. The driver could be sent to the field of combat and the armorer could drive the truck, as well as service the guns.

It didn't stop there. Now that the rot had started someone else noticed that since I had been to armament school I could service the .50s as well as work on the turrets and computers—and after a bit they decided that I could drive the truck as well. (The mere fact that I still couldn't drive did not bother the army. Next day in the dark, white-knuckled and absolutely terrified, I was once again driving out of the base in a convoy.)

The handwriting was on the wall. In about a month I knew just as much about instructing as did the instructor—he was overseas like a shot. I—and the other 678s stayed on at the range, each doing four jobs. We were so valuable that we were all frozen in category and grade for the duration. Meaning we couldn't change jobs, or get promoted or transferred from the airfield, until the war was over; wonderful.

So I serviced my computer, and my power turret, drove the truck, changed barrels and cleaned the .50 calibers and went slowly deaf, as we did ground-to-ground firing every day. This went on with monotonous repetition until the war was over and the airfield closed.

I have very few memories of this period—good or bad. It was very much like serving time in prison. You put up with it, one day at a time, and looked forward to the unbelievably happy day when your sentence would be complete, your time served. The army food was terrible, but a bit better on weekends when we went into town on pass. Laredo was an overcrowded dump, but we had passes that allowed us to cross the Rio Grande to Nuevo Laredo, Mexico. The food was good and cheap there, drink the same, and the *zona roja,* also called Boys' Town, beckoned to the GIs who wanted to try out their government-issued rubbers.

But wait—one memorable thing did happen. There was to be a lecture one evening at the post church about Esperanto. I remember that my father had some Esperanto books and I was intrigued so, for one of the very few times in my life, I went to church. The lecturer, a fellow GI, was an ardent Esperantist—and he told us why.

Esperanto is a simple second language that is quite easy to learn. It does not attempt to replace natural languages but instead supplements them. It was invented by the good Dr. Zamenhof in 1887 and has grown from strength to strength since then. I was intrigued. For seventy-five cents I bought a booklet titled *Learn Esperanto in 17 Easy Lessons.* I could and I did. I ordered books and read them with pleasure, then began to correspond in this new language. Not to Europe, of course, with the war on, but there were plenty of waiting correspondents in Central and South America, all of this without ever hearing a word of it spoken aloud since that first lecture. I remedied this in New York after the war, and became quite an ardent Esperantist. This linguistic hobby paid off tremendously when I first voyaged to foreign lands. You will hear more about Esperanto later.

In Europe, great fleets of American bombers were blasting the Third Reich. An impressive number were being shot down as well and we were certainly doing our part to man the new bombers. We worked a twelve-hour day and a seven-day week. (That's working seven days in a row with the eighth day off—then starting the whole thing over again.) Working, sleeping, and getting drunk in Mexico on that day off. We were so busy that we scarcely noticed that the war, even in Laredo, Texas, was about over. A fact we really began to appreciate when they closed the whole thing down. Bang. That was it. No more gunners needed, at least not in Laredo.

We had a few blessed weeks of just lying on our bunks and drifting down for chow now and then. The army couldn't have that. They must have heard a rumor that the gunnery school in Panama City, Florida, was open, so they shipped some of us down there, but when we reached Tyndall Field their gunnery courses had been canceled as well. I wondered what the future held. I believed, with good reason, that when I got my discharge no one would really want to employ a power-operated turret and computing gun-sight technician, skilled. Nor, as it happened, did anyone in the Air Corps, where I was still serving my time. After the years of servitude I had slowly crawled up in the ranks to buck sergeant. Back at Panama City the assignment officer frowned over my records, turning the pages and muttering to himself.

"Don't need any 678s, Sergeant," he said. "It looks like you're going to be assigned to the stockade. They're short of MPs." I didn't like the sound of it and told him so. The officer made my position very clear. "KP or MP, Sergeant. That's your choice." The choice was easy. "I've always wanted to carry a gun for my country, sir."

It had been an easy choice; I loathed kitchen police and had pulled it almost every month that I had been in the army. Whatever happened in the military police would be better than the kitchen. It turned out to be the happiest part of army career. You must realize that at this time most MPs were from the Deep South. They sneered with contempt at anyone from north of the Mason-Dixon Line. Chortling with glee they saw me and reeled me in. A Yankee—from New York! They gave me the worst assignment they could possibly think of, but one that was just perfect for me. I was going to the black stockade. Remember that this was a completely segregated army. Even the jails were segregated. But what these ridge-running cretins didn't realize was that I had finally joined my peer group.

With very few exceptions the black prisoners were from the North. The South was a new and hated part of the USA for them. They loathed segregation, and most had mouthed off at a white officer. They were garrison prisoners—terms of up to a year in jail could be given as company punishment—and this didn't warrant a court-martial. So all that the prisoners wanted was to serve their time, get out with a clean army discharge—and all of the benefits that went with that.

So I spent these happy days riding shotgun on a garbage truck, guarding the prisoners while they picked up and dumped the refuse. After we had dumped the boxes and crates from behind the kitchens, we headed for the officer's club. They were a drunken bunch and the bottles piled high. In the rush the barmen always left a bit behind in the bottle. Now each bottle was carefully drained into a clean bottle, using a funnel. No attempt was made to differentiate. Bourbon, Scotch, rye—drop by drop they went into the bottle until, by the end of the day, we had an almost full bottle of loathsome liquid. Hidden by the mountains of rubbish we drank our spoils.

We had a first sergeant in our ranks who had told his CO—commanding officer—to go fuck himself. He got a year in the stockade for this needed advice. Now he produced a filthy, small glass with scratched markings on it. He held up the bottle to the light, squinted, muttered a bit—then poured out the first portion. Since I had the gun I drank first. Choked, coughed, and gasped, to the amusement of the troops. Then we set up bottle targets and took turns trying to hit them with the shotgun—the prisoners seemed to have stolen an endless amount of cartridges. As further punishment I had to accompany them to meals and eat at the black mess hall. This turned out to be paradise!

You must realize that it was an unbreakable military rule that any qualified cooks who were drafted into the army instantly became riflemen. Ridge-running morons from the Deep South were trained as cooks. But, since the white officers assumed all blacks were equal and without skills, mistakes were often made. This mistake was really a doozy. The head cook in the black mess hall had been salad chef at the Waldorf Astoria in New York.

How we ate! There was never anything wrong with the basic food ingredients sent to the army. It was just the incompetent cooks who loused everything up. Since I was the guard I made one of my charges hold my shotgun while I ate first. It was true bliss.

This state of affairs went on until my number came up, literally. Every GI had to have a certain number of points, determined by some arcane military formula, before he could be discharged. As I remember you got one point for every month in the army, two points a month if you were serving overseas. A medal or a Purple Heart earned extra points—not a bad way of getting the boys back home, while favoring the combat veteran. At a point a month and no extras I had to wait while a lot of other guys said good-bye to the military.

My life at the time was quite boring in content and can be summed up quite easily. It was the same as every other draftee of my generation. We grew up, starting as teenagers and ending as army adults perfectly adjusted to the military life. We learned to curse constantly, to chase girls when we got a pass to town—and to avoid work whenever possible. I could now fieldstrip a .50 caliber in the dark, could drive a truck—double-shifting the clutch, now a lost art—had heard untold live rounds fired on the ground gunnery range, where I ended up—and have been deaf ever since.

In 1946, I received my discharge and returned to the civilian life as an adult totally adjusted to military life—and totally unprepared for my future as a civilian.

I was not alone in being disoriented. Whatever kind of growing up or maturing we teenage draftees had done had been on strictly military terms. We were proficient at dodging work details and we had also been well trained in cursing profanely, drinking heavily, and lusting vigorously after the opposite sex. I quickly discovered that the civilian world did not need oversexed gunnery instructors; nor were any of my other military skills exactly in great demand.

It must be remembered that in the '30s and '40s, high school students led pretty sheltered lives. While we were in school we were treated as children—not as adults. As children we were drafted into the military. A lot of us did not survive the treatment, as we have seen. The vast majority of us who survived this initial bout of sadism went on, in our various ways, to win the war. Although we all hated the military, we were completely adjusted to military life. We were all zealously happy to finally leave its stern embrace—not realizing that we would be facing a future as adults in a society that we knew nothing about.

Honorary discharge in hand, Sergeant Harrison went home, to a cloying maternal embrace. Much as I loved my mother I could not accept her belief that I was still six years old. For all of her intelligence and wit she was still a Jewish mother. (Freudians will love this.) In her eyes, I never grew up and would always need her love and loving control. The fact that my father never did lose his love of freedom and fleetness of foot, and would disappear for months at a time, would only increase her acceptance of my need for supervision in all ways. This was a silent war with no winners. (Goyish readers can find a detailed delineation of this relationship in Roth's *Portnoy's Complaint*.) Simply—there are no winners. Accept and spend your life being run by motherly love. Reject it and spend a life of guilt. Or not; I rejected it and moved out of the family apartment into a cold-water fifth-floor one of my own. Warmth, food, comforts all left behind for happy solitude and large and aggressive roaches.

Why leave home? The uninformed goy may ask. It's not the apocryphal Jewish Mother of the jokes: Mother gives two neckties for Christmas (read Hanukkah), he wears one; she asks what's wrong with the other one. I'm not talking instant guilt—I'm talking year-long, decade-long guilt. For example, no one had any money, but when I had a furlough, two weeks to go home and visit, I was pleasantly surprised when my mother sent train fare. Then, long after the war, the fateful words, "I didn't want to tell you, but . . ." The money was earned by her painful, awful, arthritic hands working for the post office during the holidays. "I sometimes would cry with pain, but for my *sonileh* . . ." (Small son—Yiddish diminutive.) Write the copy yourself. Guilt is the gift that goes on giving. I moved out.

One way or another, I suppose all the ex-GIs managed to survive the change. Having done their best to kill us, the government relented and now eased the way for us to live. The first, and best, contribution to our benefit was the readjustment allowance. Ex-GIs could draw twenty dollars a week for a year. We called it the 52-20 club and drank most of it away. I muttered and complained about life—and tried not to remain sober.

This went on for almost six months before I had enough. I had better shape up and do something constructive: the answer was not at the bottom of a bottle. I went to work and found a job in a factory, stamping out pliers on a hydraulic press. I lasted three days and quit before my brain petrified. The idea of going back to school suddenly became more attractive. The GI Bill was waiting out there, willing to pay for my education and give me a small amount of pocket money to boot. I was not sure what I wanted to do, what I would become. I always liked to draw—but enjoyed writing as well. A decision had to be made. I would just have to go back to school and try to sort myself out somewhere along the way.

4

For almost all my life I had had two equal ambitions. I wanted to be an artist—then again I wanted to be a writer just as strongly. Both had equal appeal. In the end I decided to be an artist.

Was this a wrong decision? The past cannot be altered so the question really has no answer. Am I happy at having had an artistic career? Yes and no. Yes, I did enjoy myself, and there is a great pleasure in executing a competent work of art. And yes, an artistic career surely added a visual context to my writing. But there is also a niggling *no* answer in that, for a long time, I felt that I had lost all those years drawing when I should have been writing. But the clock of time cannot be turned back.

The year was 1946 and the Second World War was over. A generous government passed a law that enabled veterans to go back to school. All tuition paid by the government, books and supplies provided for too, and a living allowance paid out as well. Something like thirty-seven dollars a month that permitted you to starve in style. (I remember one art student who did manage to stay alive on it. He ate only cheap day-old bread that had been returned to the bakery by restaurants, and peanut butter. After some months of this diet his complexion became very peanutbutteryish. Then he dropped out of school and we never did find out what happened to him.)

Endless numbers of art schools were opening up to get the government dollar. I tried taking classes at some of them and they were pretty bad. However I did take some courses at Hunter College; one of them was a painting class with John Blomshield. He was a wonderful portraitist, the last mannerist he called himself, and a fascinating man. He had been in Paris between the wars, with the other American expatriates, and was a font of fine stories. I dropped out of Hunter but continued taking private classes with John for a number of years.

Then I found Burne Hogarth, an excellent artist and teacher— and at that time still drawing the Sunday *Tarzan* comic strip. He was a true professional and taught the meat and bones of drawing that attracted student after student. His single classroom eventually grew into an entire school, the Cartoonists and Illustrators. But it was a joy to be there in the beginning. All the students were ex-GIs, many destined for highly successful careers.

Some of Burney's first students were Roy Krenkel, Ross Andru, Mike Esposito, John Severin, Al Williamson, Ernest Bache, and Wallace Wood. We learned to draw, and the best of us were soon moonlighting artwork in class to eke out our government grant.

Ernie Bache was an accomplished artist even before he came to class. He and I teamed up for some time until he left school and we drifted apart. This was after I worked with Wally Wood; always Woody to his friends.

Woody was developing into a great artist, but at the time was still unproven and insecure. He could pencil but not ink. I had two things going for me: I could ink—and I was a salesman for our joint efforts. We drew up what we thought were some great samples and I took them around to the various comic book publishers. Most of them turned us away. By hindsight it is obvious that our work was still just not that good.

But we did find a home with Victor Fox.

His was really a crap publishing operation—because publishing was not his real business. He was a printer with great thundering web presses roaring away somewhere in the South. And he was a hard-nosed businessman. He knew that presses lying idle did not earn money. Therefore he opened a New York office to supply comic books. These piled up in the printing works. Then, as often happens, when other publishers did not deliver work on time, or he lost an account, he would dig out his own comics to keep the presses humming.

And boy, were his comics bad. The New York office was manned by one incompetent who was named Ganz. He had greed—but no artistic sense whatsoever. He bought the crappiest art because he paid the crappiest prices. DC was paying ninety dollars a page at this time for artists of the quality of Dan Barry. Marvel was around forty-five dollars, and other publishers a bit less.

But not Fox. The price there was twenty-five dollars a page, but even that wasn't paid. Ganz made it painfully clear that he only assigned artwork to artists who kicked back five bucks a page.

This was real hardship, because twenty dollars was not much to get for a ten-panel page, even one that had been hacked out at great speed, with plenty of blacks to fill the empty places. The worst part was that Ganz had to be slipped the money in cash before he accepted the artwork and vouchered it. Then came the many-week wait for the check.

But it *was* work and Wally and I did it. The stories were long. There were thirty-two pages in a comic in those days, and two pages of text as required by federal law. Most comic books broke up the stories, five and six pages, some one-page fillers. Not Fox. There were three ten-page stories—and that was that.

They were easy enough to draw. Most of them were really cruddy romances that had been written by total incompetents. And Ganz was so lazy he barely looked at the pages. So Woody and I would do a really spectacular opening page for each story with a large and fiercely illustrated splash panel. Plus two well-drawn and elaborate following panels; good stuff.

The next nine pages were usually pretty desperate art, close-ups that filled the panel, plenty of silhouettes, balloons coming from a parked car, that sort of thing.

Every time we turned a story in, our hearts were in our mouths. Ganz would look at the first page and grunt. A porcine emission that may have meant he thought it well done—or perhaps he was enjoying the deep cleavage on the girl with adenoids. Then he would fan the illustration board pages out and count them–ten— he would push them back into a neat stack and fill out the voucher— without looking at any of the last nine pages.

I don't believe he ever even glanced at anything other than the first page.

And, wow, didn't we really knock out nine pages of tripe!

For one thing, the dimwitted little girls who wrote this pathetic romantic nonsense all had logorrhea. We had to cut the copy, usually in half, or there would have been no room for the art. (Once, when we were working all night and the art was due in the morning, we lettered in all the script in the last pages. There was so little room for the art that I remember one panel with only space enough for a talking eyeball.) We paid no attention to their dim artistic instructions and drew whatever we felt like. After all—no one was ever going to look at the stuff until some hapless girl dropped a dime for the finished product.

We weren't allowed to sign the art so we used artifice instead. I remember one page where the girl opens the door for her boyfriend in the first panel. For the next eight panels they walk through room after room—an eight-room house, obviously. She is talking over her shoulder with deathless prose like, YES, JOHN, YES! I WILL ALWAYS BE YOURS! Then in the last panel they arrive in the kitchen and she takes down a package of cereal and holds it up so it fills the panel. It is labeled in large caps HARRISON WOOD.

But this was no way to make a living. Thank goodness our art was improving with time and we began to crack into better markets. One of them, small but very promising, was EC Comics.

EC was short for Educational Comics. The original publisher, old man Gaines, brought out *Stories from the Bible* and such titles and made a tidy living. But he snuffed it and his son, Bill—who had a reputation as a playboy—took over the firm, and he was not interested in Bible stories, no indeed.

When we started working for Bill we first did rangeland romances. Dreary kissing cowboy stuff, but we did manage to liven it up. Bill had a great reputation as a practical joker and was a connoisseur of the same. We gave him something to laugh about.

The first page of a comic story is called the splash page. About 80 percent of it is a large splash panel, with one or two panels below it. Romance stories opened with a turgid, long paragraph of prose at the top, leading into the boldly lettered title. Such as:

> *Although she slaved for her widowed mother, her*
> *heart was awash with romance and . . . [another*
> *four or five lines of this nonsense, ending in] . . .*
> *then her entire life, her entire being, changed when*
> *she met the man who*
> WOULD BE THE LOVER OF HER LIFETIME!!

This title being lettered big and bold. The art was a turgid drawing of the couple smooching.

So what Woody and I did for one story was letter in this nonsense, following the script exactly. Then we pasted some illo board over the title with rubber cement so it could be easily pulled off and discarded. The copy now read . . .

> *she met the man who*
> HAD NO BALLS AT ALL!!

And all around the title were baseballs, basketballs, tennis balls—you get the picture. Bill laughed like a drain, showed it around the office, then peeled off the fake title and sent the story to the engraver. Good fun.

Until one time we almost lost it.

It was a loathsome rangeland romance that we hated. Since we knew nothing about the anatomy of the horse we had to root around to find artwork of horses that we could copy. This was called a swipe, because that is what we did. And we were slowly building up a swipe file that we could use.

Somewhere we found a really great drawing of a black stallion rearing up, front feet high in the air. We filled the splash panel with it, with the cowgirl in the saddle throwing a lasso to seize her smirking lover. The entire underside of the horse was black.

Then came the fun. We cut out a piece of illustration board the shape of the horse, and rubber cemented it in place. And drew on the horse a very large and very human set of testicles with erect penis. If this wasn't bad enough, we adorned it with a spider in a spider web and many crabs. (The kind with claws; a visual pun.) It was gorgeous.

Bill was very impressed. He showed it to an admiring Al Feldstein, then left it on his desk to show to his head salesman, who was coming that afternoon.

The rest was almost history. The messenger from the engraver came when Bill was out and our story was sent off with the other art. No one at the engraver or the printers ever looks at the comic pages. It is just so much salami to be processed. Our well-hung, crab-ridden horse was well on the way to being comic history. If it hadn't been for the schmuck of a colorist.

In the comic book publishing process the black plate is the key to all the other colors. Silverprints are made, comic-book size, and these are sent to a colorist. For two bucks a page he indicates where each color will go and in what intensity for the engravers to fill in. In order to do this he has to look at the artwork.

Bill almost had a heart attack when the colorist asked him wasn't there something funny about the splash panel. What a great opportunity for collectors was missed!

Woody and I had personal differences and the partnership was dissolved. I became a fast and talented inker and found myself drawing less and less. It was then that I started a partnership with Warren Broderick, a talented artist. He came from South Jamaica, very close to where I grew up in Jamaica. It was a nice, middle-class family. His father was a railroad porter; one of the few jobs open to intelligent blacks at the time. Walter was a shy guy and didn't like to face art directors. So we had a good relationship. I went out and sold the stuff. He penciled the stories and I inked them. We worked together until I found myself doing more packaging and writing. As the work slackened we drifted apart, since I was doing very little art.

What little I did, I would hire a penciler or a breakdown artist to rough in the panels. I would tighten the pencils of the faces and hands, and render the rest directly into ink with a number seven Winsor & Newton camel hair brush. Clean and fast.

My variegated skills would be very useful on the next project that came up—or exploded up, so outrageous was the idea. MGM had invested a lot of money in what they hoped would be a blockbuster. They had worked a deal with DC, who would publish the comic of Samson and Delilah to tie in with the release of the film. Then a comic book packager named Barney was struck with this tremendous and obvious idea.

You can't copyright the Bible—right? It was there for all to see. Meaning that anyone can bring out a Samson and Delilah comic on the day the film was released. With this surefire deal to hand, Barney made the rounds of all the dicey publishers who would surely love the idea. But he struck out! There were no takers. These guys who would normally run their grandmas through the presses if it made money had suddenly got religion or something, wary of the Bible tie-in. This lasted quite a while until one publisher realized he was turning down a win-win deal. Negotiations were begun, contracts hammered out until Barney had the deal. Then he began counting on his fingers and broke into a cold sweat. There were exactly twenty-four hours left before the finished comic had to be turned in. Barney got on the phone and thus began Operation Deadline. Sometime during the night I had a call and was swept up in the plea for aid and the offer of lots of greenbacks if we made the deadline.

It was a strictly by-the-numbers project, in the hope that the final product might have some consistency. Fat chance! The breakdown men practically grabbed the script from the two writers. They passed it in to the pencilers, who tightened the figures. Background men roughed in their bit and it then went to the inkers.

Around two in the morning fatigue began to strike. Cardboard cartons of coffee were distributed and a contest organized. The six inkers, including me, were going to have a contest and see who inked the fastest. This woke the troops up and the betting began. Freshly finished pencils were distributed, facedown. Lap boards were adjusted, pens cleaned, brushes pointed. Unknown to us someone had found an authentic starter's pistol, which made an incredible bang when the starter shouted GO! Bending low under the cloud of smoke, shivering in reaction to the explosion, we began to ink.

Watching inkers ink is like watching paint dry. I can say with some pride that I won, having finished my page in seventeen minutes. As far as I know my record still stands.

For the record, we finished by deadline. Our super-hack comic appeared on time and we thumbed our nose at the licensed one.

Being ambitious I also began to do packaging for smaller publishers. For a fixed price I would deliver a camera-ready comic book. Lou was a perfect example of the small comic publisher. He had managed to collar a contract with Kable, the biggest distributors of comics. And then he hired me. The money was miserable so the comic was just as bad. I wrote the stories myself so that money was saved. If the fee was slightly better than usual, I got a good artist to draw the cover. If not, not, and I drew it myself.

After the cover, there were still thirty-two pages to fill. If it was a romance comic, I used the two non-art pages as a letter column and let the readers tell their troubles to Aunt Harriet. I stopped the column when real women wrote in with their real problems. Pregnancy advice from a twenty-four-year-old ex-GI—I just could not do it. After that I settled for a quick thousand words of fiction to fill the spot.

The art was terrible but Lou couldn't tell the difference. He passed on the romances but only exercised his editorial prerogatives on the horror comics. He was a necrophiliac of a specific kind. He loved bones. When I brought in the cover art I also brought along some illo board and rubber cement. Then I drew skulls and crossed bones, shards of skeletons, and more bones until the cover looked like some kind of comic ossuary. When I left Lou's office most of them dislodged and a trail of comic bones fluttered to the hall behind me.

As I began to package more and more titles I found myself drawing less and keeping busy enough editing. What little art I drew was for the science fiction pulp magazines, since SF was still my first love.

I was saved from comics by a congressional investigation. Horror comics were getting pretty repulsive. When a Dr. Wertheim put them on television, during his investigation into the horror comics industry, they looked even worse. The moment that comics died was when Bill Gaines was cross-examined. Wertheim was a renegade Freudian who was a little exotic himself but his impact on the industry was dramatic. Bill volunteered—and we all wished that he hadn't.

After some meaningless bumf, Wertheim whipped out a pretty horrible cover. It was a close-up shot of two hands. One was holding a decapitated head by the hair. The eyes were rolled up and just the front of the neck was showing. The ax held in his other hand was dripping blood. Wertheim asks: "Now, isn't this horrible?" A laid-back Bill says, "No, not bad, in fact quite mild in this competitive world. We toned it down—it could have been a lot worse."

"Worse!" Wertheim shouts, bits of spittle on his lips. "How could it be worse?"

"Well, you know, we could have shown an end shot of the chopped neck. With all the tubes and blood and all the bones and things. . . ."

He killed it. Bundles of comics were returned unopened and the comic book industry almost collapsed. The big, quality firms like DC and Marvel stayed in business, while the fly-by-night operations went to the wall. Before the investigation there had been over six hundred different comic titles on the newsstands. After the investigation this number dropped to a little over two hundred. Unemployed comic artists wandered the cold streets of New York, and I was one of them, but not for long.

A new professional career was opening up for me. Since I had not been drawing very much, but had been editing comics and writing scripts for them, it was very easy for me to take a step sideways and go into editing pulp magazines. This was when science fiction saved me.

5

When I was in the army I had continued to read the science fiction magazines. I still read them after getting my discharge. When I was beginning to be an illustrator, fitted in between my comic book stints, I did book jackets for Gnome Press, a small SF publisher, as well as illustrations for *Galaxy, Marvel Stories,* and various other SF magazines. I became a part of the professional New York scene in SF publishing—albeit as Harry the artist, not yet the editor and writer.

And New York was the place to be in science fiction after the war. All of the SF magazines were published there; eventually paperback and hardback SF would be published as well, and New York had always been a hive of fanac—or fan activity. I had been there at the beginning; as I have said, I was one of the founders of the Queens Science Fiction League, along with the same superfan Sam Moskowitz who also helped found the Newark club. In Manhattan there were a group of fans—many of whom would eventually become pros—called the Futurians. They were the nucleus of the Hydra Club.

There were nine founding members of the club—the nine heads of Hydra—and this organization became the center of science fiction activity in New York. Most of the meetings took place at the apartment of Fletcher Pratt on Fifty-seventh Street in Manhattan. Fletcher was a longtime and well-established professional writer, so, along with his wife Inga, a top-notch fashion artist, he opened their rather luxurious doors to the science fiction riffraff. Some, like Fred Pohl, Don Wollheim, and Damon Knight, were already employed as editors. Others, such as Fred Brown, Mack Reynolds, Lester del Rey, and Cyril Kornbluth, were established freelancers. Martin Greenberg, a glazier by trade, was also publisher of Gnome Press. The rest of us were trying to break into publishing with various degrees of success.

I was still grinding out comics when I did a book jacket for Gnome Press. On the strength of this Marty took me around to a Hydra meeting. It was like coming home. This was SF fandom come of age; I took to it as a fish to water.

It really was a good time to be alive; the birth of a new world. When book publishers began to consider SF they came to the Hydra Club. Basil Davenport, of the Book-of-the-Month Club, became so involved that he began to host Hydra meetings in his Gramercy Park apartment. All was going fine there until I initiated a mini-tragedy. I slipped into Basil's bathroom for a pee, locking the door behind me. I lifted the seat, which polite chaps are wont to do, and it fell to the floor. Bladder pressure rising, I grabbed it up, turned about, and saw a waiting hook on the back of the door—I hung it from the hook and did what I had to do. Then I left, thinking nothing about it.

Not for long. The hum of voices bullshitting about SF was cut through by the elegant Southern drawl that was Basil at his best.

"You will kindly lock thu doors—and join me in thu hunt for thu low scalawag who has stolen mah TOILET SEAT!"

Panic among the troops. Much rushing about and looking under Basil's bed with no result. Of course everyone who searched the toilet threw the door against the wall, thus concealing the pinched article of sanitary hygiene.

It all ended not with a whimper but a yell. I had sneaked in between searchers and put it back—to be miraculously discovered. The meeting at Basil's broke early that night. We put the toilet tragedy behind us and the Hydra Club carried on.

When Doubleday was considering hardback SF, one of their executives, Walter Bradbury, became a regular Hydra attendee. In true fan tradition, the Hydra Club was social as well as commercial. I remember that we had a chess tournament going and Fletcher Pratt was champion. I was at the zenith of my not-so-great chess powers at the time, doing illustrations for the *Chess Review* and rubbing shoulders with chess greats like Sammy Reshevsky and Arnold Denker. Some of their genius must have rubbed off because I finally managed to beat Fletcher. However, Frederick Brown thrashed me royally after making sure I was drunk first; gamesmanship at its very best. Life was filled with richness.

There was talk of turning the Hydra Club into something more businesslike, an official SF writers' organization. I remember at the organizing meeting that Alfie Bester kept asking if it would be an official trade union like the Screen Writers Guild. There was some leaning this way, but Judy Merril led the artistic opposition. This would be no proletarian trade union—but a true meeting of intellectual minds. George O. Smith was elected president. George was a full-time radio engineer, a part-time SF writer, and an almost-across-the-borderline alcoholic. He never held a meeting of our new organization. In the absence of an official organization, the Hydra Club stumbled along with its monthly meetings. We all chipped in quarters to buy the beer, and that was the extent of our official organization at the time.

But we did publish an occasional journal, which I partially edited, then produced and pasted up. A few years later, the Hydra Club even managed to run a convention at the Henry Hudson Hotel, which I chaired. There were many whiffs of fandom still about the Hydra Club; I remember Will Sykora, still leader of the Queens Science Fiction League, passing out pamphlets denouncing me at the convention. I forget what I was supposed to have done, but it was claimed that I had been bought off with a lifetime comic book contract. Despite the fact I was through with comics. As always in fandom, uneasy lies the crown. Later there was a putsch engineered by Fred Pohl—I remember Doc Lowndes was brought in to pad out the vote—when I went from being president of the Hydra Club to nonmember in one evening.

There were a lot of visiting firemen at the Hydra Club. Tony Boucher was editing *Fantasy & Science Fiction* from the West Coast—and was mobbed when he made one of his rare visits east. Other visitors included Olaf Stapledon, dean of SF writers, who had a more restrained audience.

Then there was Garry Davis, World Citizen Number One, who became a close friend and companion. Judy Merril or someone in the Hydra Club knew him and brought him around to a party. People threw parties in those days and you'd bring your own beer. Garry and I had both been in the Air Corps and we just hit it off very well. He was becoming quite famous at the time, becoming the first "world citizen." We shared an office for a while. I helped him to design the World Passport, which was in English and Esperanto. My wife, Joan, designed and sewed the World Flag, which she made out of one of her old dresses.

Garry's father, Meyer Davis, was Jewish and his mother was Boston upper class—silver hair and real rubies, you know, and a good Boston accent like Kennedy. I met her once or twice and she was strictly upper-upper. She went to Europe, and came back from Greece by train. Trains were still in use in those days; through Yugoslavia and Czechoslovakia. Garry had given her a World Passport, with her photograph in there, and she had an American passport, but she thought she'd try out the new one. When the train came to the Yugoslavian border she passed them the world citizen passport. She was a very upper-class woman in a first-class carriage, and she gave them the World Passport, and they stamped it. And once it was stamped, all the other borders she crossed, they stamped it too! Even France—she got it stamped at each one. A small success perhaps, but an interesting one.

Garry was always brushing up against authority, but it often proved that they were in the wrong and he was right.

He was a very good actor and was in London, acting in *Stalag 17,* and was in Britain on a visa to perform. Once the show was over, he was out of a job, and his visa expired while he was in London. The English said, "Go back to the land of your birth." And he said, "I don't have an American passport anymore." He'd torn it up and carried his World Passport instead. What the Brits did was to grab him and put handcuffs on him. Then they took him down to the *Queen Mary* and put him in the brig and locked him in.

They threw him out of Britain because he was in the country illegally now that his visa had expired. With the addition of this little sea trip in the brig of the superliner.

They unchained him in New York and gave him an envelope, and in it on nice white stationery was a letter saying, "I, Garry Davis, born in the United States, wish to return to the land of my birth—signed Garry Davis." To get his signature they had taken a letter he'd written in prison, on gray prison stationery, and had cut out the signature and pasted it on the white stationery. That may look pretty illegal to us simple peasants, but it must have made the American authorities happy, because they let him back into the United States.

He came to our office and we fixed up a publicity release, wrote to all the newspapers, television, and radio, then marched on the UN. We arranged an interview, and made photocopies of the letter—we had a couple of hundred copies—and Garry had the original letter there, and he held it up for all the press to see. The next day the newspapers and television featured—nothing, not a word about this heinous, illegal, international collusion. The syndicated papers said only that "Garry Davis Raises World Flag at United Nations."

Come on, buddies, where's the real story? There was illegal agreement in high places, but I suppose people don't want to rock the boat. Deep sigh.

I was still working in science fiction. At that time I was illustrating most of the stories in *Worlds Beyond,* an SF magazine edited by Damon Knight. A bout of tonsillitis put me to bed; my hand shook too much to draw. But I could still type, and I wrote a story called "I Walk Through Rocks" and gave it to Damon. Who bought it, wisely changing the title to "Rock Diver," and gave me a hundred dollars for it. Since he was only paying me five dollars each for the small illustrations that I was doing for the magazine, this was quite an improvement. My then agent, Fredrik Pohl, put the story into an anthology he was editing and I had another hundred bucks. I did not realize it at the time, but my career as an artist was drawing to a close.

Driven out of comics, I was more than happy to edit some SF magazines for a very cheap and crooked publisher. I edited *Science Fiction Adventures, Rocket Stories,* and even one issue of *Sea Stories.* When my budget was too small to pay for enough stories for an issue I wrote them myself. I illustrated the magazine—and even wrote the letters in the letter column. Including a letter column in the *first* issue of a new magazine—which shows more brass than intelligence.

Harlan Ellison came to see me when I was editing these magazines. Bob Silverberg gave him my address. We had no receptionist; this was just a basic publisher based in a warehouse floor. There were no offices there, no partitions, just people drawing, writing, laying out, and pasting up, the works.

Harlan walks right into this publishing madhouse and says, "Mr. Harrison, I'm Harlan Ellison, and I'm doing a fanzine. . . ."

He was in the office, so I gave him a sales pitch about the magazines and I talked to him about how when a story ends in a magazine, you have up to half a page blank sometimes. John Campbell used to put a picture of a spaceship there. Or you put an ad for the next issue.

In addition to editing I wrote anything that would earn a few bucks. This was a very natural progression. As a commercial artist I drew for money. "Listen, Harry," the editor would say. "I need an illo of a girl with big boobs being eaten by a monster by Thursday." On that day I would turn in a 48-D-cup screamer being tentacled to death. Money!

I saw very little difference in writing for any market that would pay me. And, oh my, they were a disparate lot! I wrote true confessions, men's adventures, Westerns, most anything. I even did the occasional picture shoot, one of which I remember all too clearly.

Alex Kylie was a former marine raider and a very good photographer who I had worked with before. He talked a lot about the war and how all the guys in his outfit were real war dogs, trained to kill. They landed first on the invasion beaches and wiped out anyone in their way. Most of them did not live through the war—for the obvious reason. The few survivors got their discharges like the rest of us. However, unlike the rest of us, their total indifference to matters of life and death made them quite different from the rest of the ex-GIs. So I should have been more wary and asked a few questions when Alex asked for help with a picture shoot.

We had worked together before, on mini-articles for this same agency. They bought picture sets, pics with some copy about them, which they sold to the numerous picture magazines then crowding the newsstands. The mags then expanded the set into a very short, illustrated article. I wrote the copy to go with the pics so the purchaser could amplify the whole package into an article.

On a typical picture shoot Alex would take the pics and I would write up some imaginary copy for the article. For example—*meet Felicity, the fearless female, who bares her beautiful body for the lecherous eyes of The Beast. . . .* You get the idea. Many times I would use his second Leica. He would set the openings and exposures so all I had to do was shoot and advance the film. With my art background I could frame a picture well enough that some of my shots were selected from the contact prints for use by the agency. The partnership worked well.

This one picture shoot, Alex had somehow managed to meet this retired Texan who was in New York, doing some work with a charity. It seems that he had a domesticated lion who wandered around with him. Somehow Alex talked him into doing the shoot for us. We would do the obvious—along with a girl, we had Beauty and the Beast. For this we had hired a model named Jet for the job—with our own money, which we paid to her agent, who kept a paternal eye on her.

We had rented a room in hot-bed hotel and we were all to meet there at two in the afternoon. We could only afford an hour of Jet's time and we needed to make the most of it.

However, when I met the lion I had instant doubts about the wisdom of the entire matter. Her owner was an ancient leathery Texan complete with traditional five-gallon hat and deep drawl. The lion, on a short leash, was a half-grown female—who did not look happy.

We met in the hotel lobby and introductions were made. We were not introduced to the lioness, who sprawled beside Tex's chair. We asked at the desk; Jet and her agent were already in the room. We headed for the elevator. Remember—the year was 1954 and the hotel was an old and crummy one, built in the days before electronic circuitry and push buttons. It had an ancient, decrepit, hand-operated elevator. The operator was black and frightened out of his mind when we entered with the lion. He was shivering, staring straight ahead as he worked the handle and the gate. The whole thing began to look like the setup for a racist, silent one-reeler film. "Five," Alex said as we shuffled in, then turned back to Tex. The lion loped in and settled down with a thud, sprawling across the tiny elevator. The shivering operator closed the folding inner gate. I suddenly felt as terrified as the operator—as the lion's tail flopped out through the folding brass grill. I couldn't believe that Alex and Tex were still nattering away happily to each other, not looking at the lion. The operator, paralyzed with fear, was staring straight ahead, seeing nothing. I suddenly realized that when the elevator moved it would catch the lion's tail between the elevator and the sill—and cut off the end of the beast's tail. What would it be like in this tiny elevator if that happened . . . ?

I had no time to think—I just reacted. I reached down and grabbed the end of the lion's tail and, as gently as I could, pulled it out of the gate just as the elevator shook and started up.

The tail was soft and warm in my hand. I held it loosely, not daring to drop it. The lioness looked up at me with cold, hate-filled eyes, then growled deep in her throat. "Nice lion . . ." I said. I dare not let go. We rattled slowly upward while I waited for the teeth, claws from that beast of the jungle. . . . Time stretched, endlessly. Then we reached the fifth floor and the operator opened the inner and outer doors. I dropped the tail, the lion got to her feet, we got out. I was last of all, walking ever so slowly, staying as far away as I could from the queen of the jungle.

Jet and her agent were waiting in the room, crowding it even more. No one noticed that I was shaking, soaked with sweat, clutching the wall, staying as far from the lion as the tiny room would permit. I could not believe what had just happened. I numbly went ahead with the shoot.

The theme for "Beauty and the Beast" required them to be in bed together—at least that was required by the kind of magazine that would be buying our picture set. Alex pulled the covers back and, with a lot of gentle pushing and Tex tugging on the leash, the lion was finally prodded into lying on the bed. She wasn't happy—if the constant twitching of the end of her tail meant anything. I stayed against the far wall. Jet stripped and slowly, with understandable trepidation, got into the bed. She was beautiful—radiantly so, with perfect, round breasts and dark nipples. She was also very stupid, which helped when doing this kind of thing. We turned the lights up and Alex started shooting, while I adjusted the baby spots we had brought up to the room earlier. The lion rumbled deep in her throat. Jet stretched and turned. The cameras clicked. Jet arched her back and the lion rolled over and dropped her paw onto Jet's magnificent, deep cleavage.

There was silence. Then Jet spoke in a worried nasal monotone. "This lion has its hand on my breast." Alex clicked off some shots.

"That's all right," he reassured her. "It's a female lion." Jet thought about that for a while and relaxed. "That's all right then," she said.

With our model reassured, and the lion still being amiable, we finished the shoot. I paid Jet's agent, then went to the lobby. I took the stairs, as did Tex and the lion. We all said our good-byes.

I was in luck. There was a little bar just off the lobby. Alex joined me and I pushed a whisky over to him. "That went okay," he said, then drank. "Sure had a great bust." I nodded agreement, drinking deep. "And no trouble from the lion." "No trouble," I agreed, still feeling the round, smooth weight of that tail. "No trouble at all." I don't think that I'm a coward—but I thought a lot about destiny then, and never worked with Alex again.

In addition to doing these picture sets I found myself writing more and more confessions. I was very good with true confessions, mainly since they paid a nickel a word—while the pulps were a penny, two cents at most. The confession magazines also liked their stories long. Ten thousand words translated into five hundred dollars. When you consider that my pulp editor's job earned seventy-five dollars a week, the lure of the freelance life became mighty attractive. My old friend Hubert Pritchard was then in medical school, and furnished me with many a true story that turned into plot. I specialized in medical true confessions.

Then there were the men's magazines, dozens of them, with stories of men's adventures that were about as true as my true female confessions. I was doing okay; between editing and writing commercial fiction, otherwise known as junk, I was staying alive. Happily to meet, fall in love—and marry. Joan Merkler was a petite and gorgeous professional dancer, as well as being a talented and experienced dress designer. I must take a moment to tell you about Joan. Simply—she was the best thing that ever happened to me. I wasn't certain about love or marriage in my life—she was. With infinite patience she gave me all her freedom and affection until the happy day when I realized this, finally appreciated it. Marriage was fun. We worked hard all day: she was a dress designer at that time while I was editing and freelancing. How we partied then, many times all night! Be assured that the art scene in New York in the late '40s and early '50s was very, very nice. We didn't have much money—but we did manage to have a very good time. Such a good time, I must add, that Joan stuck by me through a good bit of thin and, eventually as my fortunes improved, through a lot more thick.

Losing Joan was the most terrible catastrophe that ever occurred to me. With tears and the heaviest of hearts I must report that she died in April 2002 of lung cancer. She was just seventy-two. I will always miss her radiant presence. We were together for fifty years. We could have used fifty years more.

But this is now the 1950s and that terrible day is fifty years in the future. Let us settle for now with the golden past.

Someone once bemoaned the end of the pulp magazines, because with their demise there was no place left to be bad in. Meaning that there were no markets remaining that paid tiny sums for indifferent writing. Nonsense!

By hindsight, it was quite fortuitous that I started my career by being a graphic artist. There is no illusion in commercial art; you work for hire. When I first started drawing comics I illustrated far too many romance comics—because these were the only kind of scripts going for a newcomer at the time. I was very happy to go on to adventure, war—and science fiction—even if I had to write the scripts myself. To earn a buck I would take on any kind of assignment. I illustrated magazines, designed book jackets, did scratchboard jewelry ad designs, whatever the editor wanted I would draw; that's the name of the game.

When I launched my writing career I was as liberal with topics as I had been with art. I was a writing gun for hire. I sold first to the comic books, a market I knew well since I had been drawing the things for years. Then I met a writer who sold articles to the men's magazines and he tutored me in their needs. This is the craft of writing: knowing the market and writing just what the market wants. It's a win-win situation. You have discovered what certain editors and readers want. You have satisfied that need and earned a few bucks in the process. There is certainly no shame involved. To put it simply: writers write.

But how is this done? First you must face the truth that writing is a conscious craft. Yes, the good old subconscious works and inspiration helps. But as a wise man said, "Writing is 1 percent inspiration—and 99 percent perspiration." It is very hard work.

So how to begin a genre career? First, analyze the stories and articles and find out what makes them tick. Try not to be snide or superior. There is an art to writing—but there is also the craft. No one can teach you the art. Good teachers can help guide you. But in the end we are all alone—and must learn for ourselves.

The craft is easier. You can get tips from books on writing, from analysis—and best of all from practitioners in the field. I'll be ever grateful to Jackson Burke, who explained the simple formula for men's adventures to me. We met a bit later in Mexico. I was there for the cheap living that enabled me to write. He was there for the same reason—plus the fact that Acapulco gold was a dollar a kilo. When not stoned, he lived on men's adventures. There is always a formula in the category markets. Articles in men's magazines usually ran about two thousand words. They were written in a very specific manner. "A very simple formula," Burke explained. "You open with a cliffhanger. Maybe literally one, such as a climber reached the top of a terrible climb." *Below me was a thousand-foot drop. To the left and right sheer ice without a handhold. I was stretching upward to the limits of my strength, clutching the small projecting knob of rock. And I could feel it crumbling. . . .*

This is called the establisher. As soon as the hero is in extremis there is the flashback:

How did I get into this terrible position?

Now the build, which explains what happened, how through a series of circumstances the protagonist finally reaches the cliff where he is hanging on by one fingernail. Then the justifier gives him an unexpected chance at salvation, he wins by guts and ingenuity, and he is off the cliff. All in twenty-five hundred words. Type "THE END," send it round the editors. Top markets like *Argosy* paid up to five hundred dollars for one of these. Salvage markets—the dregs who bought most anything—paid seventy-five dollars, more than enough to live very well for a couple of weeks in Mexico.

That's the formula, the craft. The readers expected it and the editors bought it. The art, in any kind of writing, is in the authorial skill that must disguise the fact that you, the author, already know what is going to happen, but must never reveal that knowledge to the reader. The art is also the skill in writing, the talent that keeps the reader turning the pages.

I have written and sold such diverse items as men's adventures, Westerns, a small biography of Lena Horne, and detective stories, each with its specific needs. That's the secret of genre writing: study your market.

Then there are the true confessions. They are always written in the first person to maintain the illusion that there is actual truth behind each revelation, each confession. When of course there is not. It is best to think of these fictions as moral lessons. No matter how tortuous the plotting and complex the situation, in the end justice must triumph. Good and right must prevail and a moral lesson must be taught. And the reader must get involved with the protagonist's troubles. The more realistic they are, the more response there will be. When I did get it right I had up to fifty letters from satisfied readers.

Do not sneer. Category fiction exists because people enjoy reading it and pay good cash for the privilege. A bit of advice for those of you who want to write. You are not Graham Greene. Not yet. Begin by finding some corner of the literary marketplace for which you have some sympathy. Analyze the whys and hows of this particular branch of fiction—then try your hand at writing it. If you have any drop of residual talent you should be able to sell what you

write—because for every salable writer there are ninety-nine others who will never make the grade.

I was earning a living but I was getting a little tired of turning
out commercial prose. My constant love was always science fiction. I wrote pulp fiction to stay alive. The same reason that after
the war I had worked on a hydraulic press in a pliers factory—or
packed boxes for Macy's. To stay alive and eat. But my heart and
soul were in SF. There was not much money in it—but I labored
hard at my short stories and felt the thrill of accomplishment when
they sold. It was a creative field and, for the first time, I could exercise my writing skills to produce something of worthwhile value.
And I had a novel working away in the back of my mind, a real
novel, a science fiction novel, something to be proud of.

But how on earth was I to get the time to sit down and write a
work of fiction thousands of words long? There was no way I could
squeeze it in between commercial assignments while surrounded
by the busy life in New York with the phone ringing and friends
dropping by at all hours. It would be impossible, but I had to do it.
But how?

Joan and I were both getting fed up with the New York scene
for plenty of reasons. And there was one idea that we had considered. Move to Mexico.

6

Life is a process of change. When our son, Todd, was born in 1955, Joan had to quit her dress designing job. A loving, lovely, feminine and maternal person, she felt that family should come before work at that time. Life was still fun, but not completely without its problems. New York City was hot, dirty, damp, and miserable that summer of 1955. The tar in the streets was so soft that your shoes stuck to it. Without our air conditioner, life would have been intolerable. I was grinding away at a men's adventure titled "I Went Down with My Ship," theoretically written by Captain Matson Wilner, when Joan returned from a visit to the pediatrician with the baby.

"Everything okay?" I asked.

"The baby? Todd couldn't be better."

"Then why are you scowling?"

"The doctor said that with this heat wave and all the pollution, tramps, and dog crap and broken glass in the park, it would be best not to take him out of the house. He thinks that we should keep him indoors with the air-conditioning."

"That's no way to live!"

"Tell me about it."

This was not the first time that we had this conversation; we were going over familiar ground. Things were beginning to pile up; one little bother after another. The Spanish have a word for this: *molestias*. Small things that trouble or annoy you. Each one not important by itself—but put enough of them together and they begin to grind you down. This grinding was well started when Joan returned from her visit to the pediatrician.

The one-bedroom apartment—with a tiny study—had been more than large enough when we were both going out to work every day. Now I was freelancing at home, Joan was home all day as well—and the baby was omnipresent in his crib. And it was a bitch of a summer, torrid and humid as only New York, and the Everglades, can be. We rarely seemed to get out anymore; what with the fuss about the babysitter and all the rest. And the grandparents dropped by far too often. They couldn't be blamed for wanting to see their grandson—but it was just one more *molestia*.

"We could move out of town to the suburbs, where things are cleaner, maybe cooler," I said brightly. "Get out of Manhattan."

"Where—Queens? Near your parents?"

I shuddered. "Or to Long Beach—near yours?"

Only silence followed that. I pulled the first page of "I Went Down with My Ship" from the typewriter and scowled at it. I was writing a lot of men's adventures at the time, fake-true fiction disguised as fact. I could see an endless procession of these potboilers stretching out into the future. What I wanted to do was write more science fiction, someday even start on the great SF novel that was still simmering away in the back of my head. I needed time, space, privacy, no phone calls. I wasn't going to get that in New York—even in the suburbs.

"Let's go to Mexico," I said.

"Is it possible?"

This was not as impulsive as it sounds. We had talked about this before, but always in an abstract way. I had been stationed on the border for most of the war, in Laredo, Texas. I had spent all my passes in Mexico and thought it was the best place I had ever been. It was a warm country, an interesting country—and incredibly cheap. And, best of all, it was hooked to the States by roads. We could drive there.

"We would need some money in the bank before we leave," I said. "That's for starters. Bruce is publishing those little magazines now and he offered me a job. Art director or copy editor, I can take my pick."

This was Bruce Elliott, a writer and an old friend—and now the publisher of a number of small magazines. "I think I'll grab the art job and keep my gray cells pristine for freelance writing evenings and weekends."

Joan looked around at her home. It was important to her, I knew. "We'll have to sell the air conditioner," she said. Ever practical, she had made up her mind. Our lives and our marriage were more important than four walls. I have always had the opinion that when it comes down to basics—and survival—women are far more realistic than men.

I nodded agreement. "And I'll sell the folding bicycle. I'll be happy to see it go." It was war surplus, built for paratroopers. To save weight there were no fenders on it and I got a streak of mud up my back when I rode it to work in the rain.

It all seemed simple enough. We had been over the details many times in the past. I would work hard and get some money ahead. Whatever of our goods that we couldn't take with us, we would store in the cellar of Joan's parents' house. Our Ford Anglia wasn't the biggest car in the world—but it was certainly the sturdiest. And leaving New York would not be forever; this would be a trial run to see if I could hack it at full time and get into some serious freelance writing. We would stay just long enough for me to get out of the writing-to-stay-alive mill and get tucked into the fiction that really counted.

We took a worst-case scenario. What if it didn't work and the money ran out? The answer was simple. Joan's father was well enough off, with his own garment embroidery factory. There was no way that he would allow his daughter and grandson to fester in the depths of Mexico. The money to bail us out would be sent as soon as he got our cable. We would then have enough to drive back to New York. When we were back we would find another apartment, buy another air conditioner—and I would get another editorial job. And eventually we would pay the money back. It would work out and, basically, we would be right back where we had started. But at least we would have tried.

The more that we thought about it the better it sounded. We were filled with enthusiasm, feeling that at this time anything was better than New York. We thought the logic behind this move was impeccable—our friends thought that we were raving mad. What our parents thought about this resolution—which included taking their year-old grandson south to the jungles and deserts—does not bear repeating.

The plan to get out was a simple one. I would take the job with Bruce, working days—and keep on freelancing to get some money ahead. In those penurious postwar days writers actually helped each other. When I was editing I bought as much as I could from friends; they did the same when they were employed. Bruce Elliott had written many articles for me, before becoming managing director of a group of pocket-sized magazines. I had already called him about a job when exploring all possibilities. The choice between art director and copy editor was an easy one to make. Art. That way I could save the writing bits of my brain for freelance work. I took the job.

As the new art director of *Picture Week* I had to lay out the articles, design the interior, size the photographs, paste up the copy after it had been set, then screen the pics when they came back from the engraver. I had to do this for sixty-four pages every week. Child's play for someone who had helped to hack out endless pages of comic art.

I was filled with such enthusiasm, the future began to look brighter. Language was going to be a problem—we couldn't live in Mexico without at least trying to speak Spanish. I had studied it in high school and hated it. Except for the preterite of *ir,* all of it had long vanished. Joan had studied French so had a Latin language background. We turned to an Esperanto friend, Jim Donalson. He had come from his home in Delaware to New York to teach high school Spanish, and appeared to be starving to death. Tall and thin, he had the world's best appetite. We traded Spanish lessons for meals and both sides were satisfied. Although Joan was worried that she wasn't making big enough meals, since he finished everything served to him and still looked hungry—even after seconds and dessert. He ate at least three times what I did so I did not share her concern. Nevertheless she planned to fill him at least one time. To this end she prepared one of our staple—and most filling—meals. Hot dogs stuffed with cheese and wrapped with bacon. A single one of these cholesterol nightmares was a meal; two stretched the stomach's capacity. I think Jim ate twelve before raising the white flag.

1955 had faded into 1956 as I worked to get the money ahead for our trip. Although I didn't know it at the time, art directing would be the last paid job I would ever have. Early in the year, when we had saved up the incredible sum of $250, we packed up, reluctantly sold our air conditioner—for a New Yorker the final act—and loaded the car. I put on a roof rack for the baby's crib and part of our luggage, then covered the backseat with a thickly padded board so he could roll around in comfort. We said our last good-byes to horrified parents and gloomy friends and headed south.

That was over fifty years ago, and the world then was a very different place indeed. America had fewer people and fewer roads. No divided highways or freeways—it was two-lane blacktop all the way. The motels we stayed at were more like the Bates Motel than the giant Holiday Inns and Ramadas we know today. They were mostly little decaying wooden buildings where you always borrowed the room key before checking in, then inspected the place before dropping three bucks for the night. Joan could always sniff out the mold. I checked the plumbing and threw back the covers; wrinkled sheets and the odd pubic hair indicated that the linen had not been changed and thank you, no, not this time. All the cottages had a kitchen of sorts, which made it easier to feed the baby and saved a lot on restaurant bills.

South first to Washington, D.C., to spend two days with my aunt Rose, sleeping in her Murphy bed. (Are they gone now too?) She was almost as good as our parents at laying on the guilt and reminding us how we were imperiling our infant, putting our lives and his in danger, and generally making a mess of things. Time to leave. A storm front was coming south from Canada and we wanted to stay ahead of it. We waved bye-bye and crossed into Virginia. Then down through Tennessee to Alabama where, when we stopped at a traffic light, we heard a local girl look at our car and say, "My, my . . . what a cute little Jag-uar!"

You must realize that the undersquare, underpowered, undersize Ford Anglia 100E is probably the ugliest car in the world, after the Citroën 2CV. But she was right about something: at least it was as English as a Jaguar. We were really getting pretty far away from civilization and the sophistications of New York.

I had taken some magazine assignments with me so we could top up our funds when we finally reached our destination. While doing some research, I had stumbled over the interesting fact that at the battle of San Jacinto, when the Texicans whupped the Mexicans, they had gone into battle shouting "Remember Goliad—and the Alamo!" This wasn't the way I had learned it when I was stationed in San Antonio. So we stopped at Goliad, Texas, for a day and I rooted through the library and the local dusty museum. (For those who care—the story is true. Santa Ana's men had massacred a great number of locals at Goliad, getting all the Texans very annoyed. The Alamo was small stuff compared to this—they just had some big names there and better publicity in later years.)

Then we reached Laredo and the Mexican border. The American officials didn't even look up when we left the country and drove across the international bridge. Bored and uniformly paunchy Mexican police waved us to the office there. We filled out the tourist forms that allowed us and the car into the country for a stay of six months. If the visa was renewed every six months one could live in Mexico forever, as a lot of Americans did.

We weren't thinking about that at the time. Just being in a foreign country was excitement enough. We drove out into the desert and headed across it to Monterrey, Joan and Todd's first visit to Mexico. They took it all in their stride. The food was great, lodging clean and cheap, with gasoline at two pesos a gallon—about sixteen cents.

We drove on with no certain plan in mind. Monterrey was no place to tarry—big, dirty, and industrialized—nor was Ciudad Victoria any better. In those days the main road from the border to Mexico City ran through tropical and ramshackle Tamazunchale, and then wound up into the mountains. The wide river shrank to a tiny silver trickle below as we climbed the cliffs above a mile-high drop. Burst tire fragments, brake marks on the pavement, and holes in the trees beside the road indicated that some cars and trucks had indeed made that drop. There were no guardrails. Joan held the baby in absolute silence while I clutched tight to the steering wheel with very damp palms. The Mexicans have an endearing custom of leaving little crosses and name markers by the road where their loved ones have met their deaths in accidents. We passed a great number of these impromptu shrines. We relaxed only when the highway left the mountains and the road stretched out onto the central plateau. Then we were through Pachuca and were in the outskirts of Mexico City and still had seen no place that tempted us to stop.

This was well before the endless Mexico City smog, but the slums and shantytowns of the outskirts of Mexico District Federal, or D.F., or just plain "Mexico" to the Mexicans, were very offputting. We had had enough of big cities for a while so we kept driving south. Driving higher and higher, up almost to the pass of Cortez, which ran between the two volcanoes Iztaccíhuatl and Popocatépetl. Popo, as the locals called it, was snow-covered in winter and still active; smoke rising from its white cone. We drove quickly through the damp, cold city of Amecameca and down the slopes beyond, through forests of great pine trees, before finally emerging on the fertile plain below. It was late afternoon when we passed through the market town of Cuautla and crossed the bridge over a small river just south of town and braked to a stop when the pavement ended.

"Am I wrong—or is the road ahead made of dirt and mud and filled with ruts and rocks?" Joan said. I could only nod dumb agreement. "We can't go any further."

"I remember seeing a sort of motel back there," I said. "Let's spend the night and figure out what we do next in the morning." This was Cuautla, Morelos. We did not know it at the time, but it was to be our home for the next year.

It was a horrible night, the worst we had spent since leaving New York. It certainly did not augur well for our Mexican future. The so-called motel was nothing more than a connected row of rooms built of concrete blocks. There was no front door to these cells, just canvas curtains, which were no barrier to either the street noise, nor the mosquitoes that appeared in ravenous swarms as soon as the sun went down.

Dawn found us wide awake, exhausted, swollen with bites, the none-too-clean walls now splattered with bloody patches where satiated mosquitoes had been squashed. "I don't like this place," Joan said, straightening the blanket on Todd. He was sound asleep and unbitten; well protected by his dutiful parents during the long night. "If by 'place' you mean this dump—correct. But we still don't know anything about the town. Certainly the climate seems right. Why don't we see if there is a better hotel to stay for another night? Take a day off, get some rest—and some sleep. We have been a long time on the road. Let's put off any major decisions until tomorrow."

Joan reluctantly agreed. I did not want to admit that to me, hammered by fatigue, things were looking very black indeed. We had been in Mexico for over a week and still did not know what we wanted to do. And low as the prices were, every day meant a little trickle out of our cash hoard. Had the entire thing been a big mistake? Was this reality speaking—or just depression and weariness? A day off might very well be a good thing. Surely this was a way of avoiding any decision for the moment, a way of not admitting defeat, that we might have to turn back. We were too tired to argue or disagree.

After breakfast in a nearby cafe, with many cups of good black Mexican coffee, we drove back down the main street, until we saw a sign with an arrow pointing east. HOTEL VASCO, it read. We bumped through unpaved and rocky streets with a growing feeling of depression. What were we doing here so far from civilization? If we had not been so tired we might have turned back to the main road and headed north toward home. Instead we persevered and eventually we found the hotel. All that could be seen from the road was a high wall, overgrown with flowering vines. Filled with suspicion and foreboding we drove in through the open gate to the patio beyond.

For a wonderful surprise. Here was a wealth of flowers, blossoming trees, neatly trimmed grass, everything modern and clean. This was a vast improvement over the fleapit where we had spent the night. The hotel was Spanish colonial in design although recently built, and designed with style and taste. There was a cool lobby, an English-speaking receptionist to go with all these lovely gardens, and immaculate rooms. We checked in, unpacked, and showered. And discovered what must have been the only, tiny fault in this otherwise paradisiacal retreat.

Apparently, when the hotel was being built, a slight mistake had been made in laying out the water pipes. The plumbers had reversed the hot and cold water systems. Since the pipes were buried in the concrete floors, nothing drastic could be done about correcting the error. It could be lived with; we found that the Mexicans were very fatalistic about things that could not be changed. And apparently the error could be modified quite easily. All the faucet handles on the sinks and showers were removed and reversed. Foreigners might confuse C with COLD, when it really meant CALIENTE. But that, and F for FRIO, would be quickly sorted out.

Only one small problem remained—and it was a rather frightening one when first discovered. While sitting comfortably on the commode, after answering a call of nature, one would happily grab the handle and flush the toilet.

And move away rather quickly when steam rose up from the bowl. Many interesting things happen in life; we found that this was one of the more disconcerting.

But if the Vasco had any other faults, they were not easily observed. I had a beer in the tiny bar while Joan unpacked our bags and gave Todd his bottle. Milk in Mexico can be very suspect and we tried to avoid it. Instead we had brought numerous cans of powdered milk with us from the States. This, mixed with boiled water—or sterile water bought in the drug store—formed a basic part of his diet. Once he had been fed we tried out the hotel restaurant. After a fine lunch of guacamole salad, tacos de frijol, and enchiladas we felt better able to face the world. After a nap during the siesta we went out to explore, and soon discovered that Cuautla was a lovely little town. Our spirits began to rise.

This compact city was set in the middle of the fertile plain that stretched southward from the base of the volcanoes. Natural springs abounded and cool water ran along the streets in open aqueducts. Corn grew in the fields that began just at the outskirts of town. Here was sugarcane as well, pineapples, and all manner of vegetables, including some that we had never seen before. Cuautla was the market town for the entire area—the market itself a joy to explore, sheer paradise. There must have been four acres of stalls, shops, butchers, flower stands, hot chili vendors, vegetable shops, bakers, hardware stores, ramadas, outdoor kitchens with tables and stools—and wandering mariachi bands filling the market with music. It put to shame every other market we had seen in Mexico. You could buy everything there—from a set of furniture down to a handful of fresh limes. These from the Indian women who sat on their heels saying *veinte, veinte* while holding out a handful of limes to the people who passed by. (They were saying "twenty," meaning twenty centavos. With the peso worth eight cents, the four or five freshly picked limes cost under a cent and a half.)

Sometime during that first day we met Jim Touhy. He heard us talking English and introduced himself. In these simple, bygone days this sort of thing did happen. It wasn't an approach or a con— just friendliness and curiosity. Only Spanish was spoken here and the sound of English was a novelty. Jim was one of the only four Americans who lived in Cuautla. There were absolutely no American tourists to be found in this purely Mexican market town at the end of a dead-end road. With the exception of Adam, who had retired from a car dealership, the Americans were all war veterans who had ended up in Mexico. They had their tiny pensions, which would have enabled them to starve to death back in the States, but which went a long way here. On these minute sums they could live very well indeed. This was particularly true of Herman, who had a pension from the First World War. And also true of Willy, who was existing quite comfortably on a pension from the Spanish-American War. It could not have been more than fifteen dollars a month—but it sufficed.

Jim was renting a small apartment in Don Carlos Tornel's hacienda. He took us to see it and it was wonderful. If we could find something like this, why then Cuautla would be a good place to settle down in. We stayed on at the Vasco and every day toured the streets of Cuautla looking at apartments and houses. It took us almost a week to locate anything inhabitable.

It happened by accident. We discovered a hidden motel completely by chance after we had strayed from the center of town. There were very few paved roads in Cuautla. Only the highway that cut through the center of town was paved, this and the few residential streets that ran off it. Within one block, like on the highway itself, all paving vanished and the streets turned to rocks and ruts. The Anglia, with its big wheels and eight-inch clearance under the differential, the lowest part of the car, took all these in its stride. That is how we found the Camerones Motel.

It had been recently built, had verdant gardens, banana trees, and grassy areas, all of this hidden behind the high walls. There were ten house-sized units, and the rent was incredibly cheap. We did not question circumstance but paid for a week in advance and moved in. It turned out that we were the only occupants of the motel. It took us a long time to put together the story, and it turned out to be a fascinating and very Mexican one.

It seemed that the motel builder and owner was a very rich doctor. Very rich because he ran the best abortion clinic in Mexico City, solely for the Yanquis. But his services were not expensive in American terms. The clients would be met at the Mexico City airport and would be escorted to one of the first-class hotels in the city. He had a modern clinic and was a skilled surgeon. Everyone was quite happy with the arrangement and the dollars rolled in. But like all good capitalists he was always on the lookout for investments.

He had seen an opportunity to increase his wealth with a shrewd move when it was made known to him that the highway that ended in Cuautla was going to be improved. It was to be paved and extended on to Oaxaca. To widen the road they would have to bypass the town center and use this now unpaved and very rugged road. Here was an opportunity. The land was cheap, the opportunity golden, and the motel was built.

We learned later that Mexico is a land of harsh realities and wild fantasy. The new road proved to be more wishful thinking than truth. The highway was indeed paved and extended to Oaxaca. But it was not moved; that part of the plan was abandoned—if it had ever existed.

So here, many blocks from the highway, sealed off by unpaved streets and unseen by cars on the distant highway, the motel stood in solitary, empty splendor. On national holidays there would be a

few other Mexican customers, who came to Cuautla for the sulfu-
rous stink and supposed healing powers of the thermal baths there:
Agua Hedionda.

All of this may have been a setback for the good doctor, but it
was surely a boon for us, since we had the entire establishment to
ourselves about 99 percent of the time: manager, gardeners, guard
dog, night watchman, and day manager, the lot.

Besides being rich, the good doctor was also quite eccentric. He
had designed the construction of the units himself and they were a
marvel of modern utility. Upstairs in each there was a large bedroom with a tiny screened balcony. Next to it was an immense
bathroom complete with shower, toilet, sink, and bidet, since hygiene in the tropics was most important. Downstairs was a kitchen,
as well as an architectural novelty that I had never seen before—or
since, with good reason, for the doctor had invented what every
weary traveler needs in a motel: a combination garage and living
room.

That is exactly what it was. The front of the structure was filled
by a large garage door, the only entrance. Open it and you had a
place for the car. Drive out and close the door, put in some furniture,
and it became a living room. The concept took the breath away. We
looked at the oil stains on the concrete floor, the bare room and
walls, and decided that we preferred the living room configuration.
There was a nice selection of furniture that could be moved in; the
Anglia lived outside under the banana trees.

We settled in happily. I appropriated the balcony, which was
just wide enough for a tiny table and chair. Since Cuautla has the
most ideal climate in the world I could work outside all year long.
I caught up with my men's adventure assignments and thought
about the novel. Thinking was easy, for time moved at a very tran-
quil pace here. The sky was always blue and cloudless, the gardens
in front of the building bursting with the most colorful of tropical
foliage—and always empty of visitors. Just beyond the screened
balcony were the green fronds of a banana tree. The only movement

that I was aware of, if it can be called movement, was the slow growth of this banana tree. I discovered that I could live—and hopefully create—with this kind of wild excitement.

In the year that I lived in Mexico, and I wrote on this balcony, the green trunk of the banana tree reached slowly up toward me, putting out immense flat green leaves as it grew. When it had reached its desired height, just before my balcony, it ceased growing leaves and produced an immense purple, fruiting flower instead. Gravity tugged at this purple spheroid until it hung down toward the grounds. One by one its petals fell off—and from each petal's truncated stem a single banana grew. It must also be admitted that there was darkness behind this beauty. The flower slowly dripped acidic juice down onto our car, parked below. I had to move the car, but not before this corrosive sap ate a hole through the Anglia's many layers of paint.

As the weeks passed the bananas slowly changed from green to yellow. Then a pair of jewel-feathered hummingbirds came and inspected the bananas just before they ripened. Satisfied, they made a nest in their upstretched bowl. Soon after this the female laid a clutch of infinitesimal eggs. In the course of time, as I typed out my stories, I watched life unfold before me. The green bananas slowly turned yellow. The eggs broke open and hatched into three very tiny fledglings. Their parents dutifully fed them and they grew quickly. In the end they all hummed mightily, then flew away. The bananas were now ripe. One day the gardener came and the tree was chopped down, the fruit carried off to market. A new tree would grow from the stump and the entire cycle would be repeated. New York was becoming just a bad memory.

I had the time and opportunity to enjoy my work. Joan had settled in quite happily in what was, to us, most spacious accommodation. She had a full-time maid to help her, not really a luxury at $3.75 a month. Since the only time we talked English was in the house, our Spanish was coming along quite well. Survival is the mother of linguistic skill. If we wanted to eat bread we had better learn how to pronounce *pan*. Not to mention *carne, leche, cerveza,* and all the rest. Early morning was the time to shop, when the Indians from nearby villages brought in the fresh produce. The bread was freshly baked—as were the tortillas. Mexican food was wonderful.

We also had a satisfactory amount of a social life, seeing and being visited by the handful of resident Americans. And there was all of the surrounding countryside to explore on weekends. We were well off, comfortable, and happy. I had found safe haven for my family. For the first time in my life I had the time and peace, financial security and lack of pressure, to start on my first novel. I was thirty-one years old and I felt that I had better get cracking.

My ambition at this time was to bring some life, color, and action back into science fiction. This may sound ludicrous today in our age of atomic guns and exploding skulls, all of the pornography-of-war SF as well as all of the empty violence of crap TV SF and unspeakable SF films. But in the 1950s, science fiction existed for the most part in the magazines. I had them sent from the States and I read them all. I had the feeling then that the better stories were getting cerebral and slow. *Fantasy & Science Fiction* published too much fantasy for my liking—though Tony Boucher had brought on a stable of impressive new writers. Horace Gold at *Galaxy* had done the same. Even *Astounding* was featuring molasses-like plots and tedious think-pieces. My years of churning out men's adventures had taught me that, with some effort, action and thought could be combined. I would apply what I had learned and write an SF novel in the classic tradition. A serious theme carried forward by an action-filled plot.

What I wanted to do was to deal with the myth of the superman. Not the comic book one; I had had enough of comics. I wanted to deal with the German so-called supermen, who had fought and lost the recent war. My ambition was to pit cerebral man against purely physical man, to see which one came out ahead. So in my novel I designed a race of real, living, realistic physical supermen—and superwomen—then turned around and asked the important question. If there actually were this physical superrace—what would they really be like? I typed a cover page for *Deathworld,* put in a fresh sheet of paper, and started on chapter one.

The work was going well and Cuautla was fun for all three of us. Todd had the house and the garden to crawl in and explore. It was all very secure since a high wall ran all around the grounds. It was topped with broken bottles and separated us from the road and the world outside. Our watchdog was an immense and ferocious mixed-breed bitch, with great white fangs and pendant dugs, who guarded the gate. She had been taught to hate Indians and would savage any that tried to come in. But she would also drool with pleasure when she saw us; Todd was her special favorite. Her name was Villiana, villainess, and that she certainly was.

Life was comfortable and incredibly inexpensive. Which meant that one sale of an article, two or three days' work, would pay for a month's living. Our rent was about thirty-five dollars a month, including electricity and gas for cooking. The Coca-Cola truck brought ice and bottled water—and fine Mexican Carta Blanca beer at five cents a bottle. The delivery men—who were Indian of course—carried clubs to beat Villiana away with, so they could drive in and unload without being savaged.

The class structure soon became quite clear to us. Indians, Aztecs, were on the very bottom, although they must have comprised 95 percent of the population here in the state of Morelos. Then there were the mixed breeds, next step up in the pecking order. On top were those individuals with white, or near-white skin, the descendants of the Spaniards who had conquered the country. After five hundred years they were still right at the top of this society. We soon discovered that it was our skin color that determined our place in the society around us. We were getting our first education, very much firsthand, about life in a very different society from the one that we had grown up in.

Since there were no tourists or strangers in this part of Mexico

at this time, everyone seemed to accept us as linguistically handi-
capped Mexicans, not foreigners. Gringos and other strangers were
what you saw in films, never in the flesh. The only outsiders who
came to Cuautla were also Mexican. So, necessarily, we were as
well.

It was an unusual experience to be accepted as part of a totally
new and different culture. Fascinating and educational, though
fraught with small and large stumbling blocks, which we had to
discover as we went along.

Speaking Spanish came easily; most of the locals spoke the Aztec language Nahuatl first, then learned Spanish as a second language, as did we. However there were little traps everywhere. The
Spanish word for eggs is *huevos*. That's what the dictionary said,
even our Mexican dictionary. Then why the strange looks and gig-
gles when Joan bought them in the grocery? Some comprehension
came when she heard another woman ordering *blanquillo,* literally
"little whites." It took quite a while for us to discover that *huevos*
was slang for testicles.

Cultural traps. We soon found out that Mexico was a land where
no hay reglas fijas was the rule, not the exception. It was true in
every walk of life. There were no fixed rules. Meaning that the
mordida, the little bite, a bribe, was what represented the real culture. The more you could bribe, the more you could do. The poor
man could do nothing; the rich man anything. He could get away
with murder. Actually he really could. In a discussion one evening
the subject of *pistoleros* came up.

"These are gunmen you can hire quite cheaply," Don Carlos
said. "But most of them die young—my gardener, Pedro, is one of
the very few I know who have reached advanced age. Listen to him
and you will understand why. Pedro." The gardener looked up from
the border he was trimming. "Tell us of your life." Pedro had gray
hair and the dark skin of the local Indians and was of indetermi-
nate age. He held his hat respectfully across his chest and spoke

quietly and without any emotion, since these matters were about things long past.

"When I was a young man there was fire in my blood. I was very hotheaded and I drank in the *cantinas*. We all drank, and perhaps we were all hotheaded. There were arguments and sometimes we were carried away, becoming impetuous, insulting even. Of course when another man insulted you in public it meant that he was insulting your manhood, your honor. It could not stop there. I saw this happen many times, and always with the same result. The men would draw their pistols and fire at each other. One would be faster, or a better shot, or more lucky, and the other man would die. I also noticed that after someone had killed a few men he would begin to think very well of himself, put on airs and look for fights. If you were very good, why then you were accepted as a *pistolero* and others walked quietly in your presence. I saw this and envied these men. But I also saw how dangerous this work could be.

"When I grew older, and bought my first gun, I had my first difference of opinion in a bar. Since I wanted very much to live I had determined that I would wave my left hand in the air as I drew my gun with my right. I was pleased to see the other man's eyes move automatically toward my left hand as I shot him.

"After this my reputation grew and I was a well-known *pistolero*. I have killed many men, how many I am not sure. It was a good life and I had much respect."

He hesitated and looked down and I noticed, for the first time, that he was holding his straw sombrero in his right hand. Now he withdrew his unseen left hand and held it up.

"But this life was very hard on my left hand."

His story might have been true, or a very pleasant and entertaining lie. Perhaps as a gardener he had caught his left hand in a lawn mower. In any case, he only had stumps for fingers, as though they had all been shot away.

Don Carlos dismissed him and nodded in agreement. "That is the sort of man you must deal with. If you have an enemy you want killed they will be happy to do it for sixty pesos [about five dollars]. Which sounds a bargain at first. Until some time later when the *pistolero* gets drunk and comes around for more money. If you are foolish enough to pay him he will keep coming back. So in the end you must hire another one to kill him and on it goes. Very expensive in the long run. Far better to go to the *alcalde,* the mayor here in Cuautla. I'll introduce you to him, a fine man. You simply pay him twelve hundred pesos [one hundred dollars] and he will give you an official death certificate for the man you want to dispose of. Dated the next day—with cause of death listed as an accident. Then you can shoot the man down anywhere yourself, and it doesn't matter who sees you. Simple and clean."

Simple and clean. At this time Mexico led the world in deaths by violence. And Morelos, the state Cuautla was in—also Zapata's home state—led all the other states in deaths by violence. But it was really quite safe as long as you knew the rules. As you can well imagine, we learned the rules very quickly.

- Never go out at night without a gun.
- Lock your gate at sunset and see that the top of your garden walls have broken bottles stuck into them. If anyone ignored all this and broke in you were expected to shoot him and no questions would be asked. The penalty for murder was five years in jail. But killing an intruder was seen as a normal and respectful act and would certainly not be prosecuted.
- Stay away from low bars at night. Probably a good bit of advice for any country in the world.

Our maid was still not too much of an excessive expenditure, even though we had raised her salary and it now came to $3.87 a month. Plus she had her perks of all our empty tin cans, which she sold in the *mercado* for a few centavos each. And she was happy to cook some of the local dishes for us: Joan was learning an entirely new cuisine, since true Mexican cooking has no resemblance to the Tex-Mex restaurants in the north. *Taquitos, guacamole,* home-made *frijoles refritos,* and many other dishes. We ate very well indeed. We did not dare try the highly attractive food in the market stalls, since amoebiasis and other gut infections were endemic in this part of the world. But there was one very good and clean restaurant in town, the Green Lantern, Lanterna Verde, which we went to as often as we could. They had a special fish dish called *pescado Veracruzana* that we have never found in a Mexican cookbook. Joan re-created it by taste and it became a staple in our diet. Not only in our home, for the recipe passed on to those of many friends who have dined on it at our table.

We were learning the language and settling in. Learning the culture as well, and enjoying every moment of it. Well, some bits, like the outdoor butchers, were really not that enjoyable. There was a row of butcher stalls in the *mercado*; none of them had refrigeration. The cattle that would be that day's meat supplies were driven to the nearby abattoir before dawn and slaughtered in a singularly brutal manner. By the time we went shopping, the thatched butcher's stalls would be displaying their selected pieces of carcass. Joan fought her way through the linguistic barrier, as well as the fact that not only all the cuts of meat had strange names, but they were also butchered in a totally different manner from in the States. Through trial and error—and we chewed some very tough errors—she found a cut of meat that could be carved into small but tasty steaks.

But you can't really cook and eat meat that was walking around just twelve hours before. We had an icebox that wasn't too efficient. Meat would go off long before it aged. So Joan followed the local practice of slicing the meat thinly and putting it into the icebox between slices of fresh papaya. This fruit contains papain, a natural enzyme that is processed and sold as meat tenderizer. By dinner-time the meat would be aged enough to be cooked quickly in the pan: in, over, and out.

We also learned that you only ate vegetables raw that you could peel or cook. Night soil was used as fertilizer by the local farmers, thereby assuring that all the parasites and bugs were kept in constant recycle. Joan would impale tomatoes on a fork and peel the skin off over the gas burner on the stove. Then peel the cucumbers and onions, boil the potatoes. Lettuce was very much out of our diet. Mexico was still a bit of an adventure—but a good one. We were settling in.

7

It was the rainy season in Cuautla, which meant that it rained twice a day: at four in the morning and four in the afternoon. Not precisely to the second, but if you were out walking in the afternoon and four o'clock was approaching—you looked around for a doorway. The rain began suddenly, a drenching tropical downpour that usually lasted about five minutes. People stood patiently under shelter until the rain stopped, then left and walked carefully around the puddles that were steaming and vanishing in the warm sun.

You knew that winter was there by looking up at Popo (Popocatépetl)—not at the calendar. There would be snow on the volcano's summit, which looked even more dramatic when trails of smoke would rise up from the crater there. Our first Christmas in Mexico was almost upon us now and there were plenty of *navidad* activities. All of the northern Christmas props looked very much out of place here in the sun, where the occasional ratty cardboard Santa, or shining shreds of tinsel, were placed in the store windows. But these were alien imports borrowed from the cold country to the north. The Mexican celebration centered around the *piñata*. These were gaily decorated pottery bulls or pigs—cheap pottery because they were slated for destruction. They would be filled with small gifts and hung from a rope that had been passed through a hook in the ceiling. At the Christmas celebration children would be blindfolded, then would take turns trying to break the *piñata* with a stick. This would be made more difficult by an old uncle who would pull on the rope and lift the thing up out of the way of the wild swings. We decided that we had to get a *piñata* for ourselves; not to break, but just for a decoration.

The *piñata* stall in the market was right next to the *chumile* lady. We had watched her at work with horrified appreciation of her trade. *Chumiles* were flat green insects about the size of a fingernail that looked very much like wood lice. They were gathered alive in the forest, then displayed in the market in an enamel washbasin. They would climb about on top of each other until a customer appeared. Then the *chumile* lady would fashion a cone out of paper, and with her bare hand would scoop the cone full of the bugs. (We discovered later that they would be mashed in a *liquidador,* a local carved-lava version of mortar and pestle, to make the essential part of a very popular sauce—that we never had the courage to taste.) When the cone was full and sealed, the saleswoman would brush back into the basin the insects that had escaped becoming sauce by crawling up her bare arm. She would brush them off just as far as the elbow, though. Any higher than that she popped into her mouth, a tasty treat. . . .

We bought our *piñata,* took it home, and unwrapped it proudly. Our maid was there, babysitting a small relative as well as Todd, and greatly admired it. As I held it up, a *chumille* bug crawled out of its interior. The maid squealed with pleasure, picked it off—and popped it into the baby's mouth. Wasn't it the Romans who said *de gustibus non disputandum est*?

I was happy in Cuautla since the work was going well. Joan was happy because life was going well. We had been living in Mexico almost a year now and had settled in nicely. I was selling short stories, and the occasional men's adventure, so we had more than enough money to live on. And I was about a quarter of the way through the first draft of the novel. I tried not to work more than six days a week so we could take Sunday off.

Upon rereading this I realize that a bit of explanation is in order since most people don't work on Sunday. Writers are a case apart; their writing schedules are exotic and individualistic. Every author is different. Jim Ballard always worked a five-day week when his children were small, so he could have the weekends with them. Bob Silverberg, in the years when he was producing voluminous amounts of copy, only worked a four-day week. On Friday he would rest— and deliver the week's stories to editors and pick up assignments for the next week. Another writer friend was always late for deadline, suffered dreadfully over his tardiness, then would eventually write the promised story in a twenty-four- or thirty-six-hour sitting. As for myself, I very quickly discovered, after my second or third novel, that if I broke off work, even for a day, I had trouble getting back into the book. So my routine became very simple. I would work every day, sometimes for a month or two, until the first draft was finished. This was hard on the family, I know. But as Joan said, writers eat people. Meaning simply that writing comes first, always, and friends and family must learn to put up with it. If they don't, then, sadly, they become ex-friends and in many cases ex-family.

But in Mexico I was still a beginner at the freelance writer's life, and still working out what I wanted to do and how to go about it. So I settled for a five- or six-day week and took Sunday off with the family. We explored the surrounding countryside in our little car and found the perfect picnic spot above us on the slopes of Popo. Gigantic pine trees covered the hillside, their needles so thick on the ground that nothing else could grow there. Under the trees there was just a ground covering of pine needles and no undergrowth at all. It was cool and silent in the pine forest, with the branches forming a giant green cathedral above our heads, the pine needles a soft carpet on the ground below.

We were enjoying our picnic one Sunday when we heard a sound like distant falling rain, a growing rustle between the trees. But the sky was blue, as always, so it could not be rain. Then, between the tree trunks, a herd of goats appeared. The goatherd, a man in his sixties at least, though possibly older, stopped to greet us in a civil and most formal way. We discussed the crops and the weather until I offered him a drink of tequila. He squatted on his heels and accepted with pleasure, downing a large water glass of the potent spirit. After a few minutes he closed his eyes and fell sound asleep, head lowered, perfectly in balance. The goats milled about until, about ten minutes later, he awoke again. Stood and said his goodbyes and led his charges off among the thick trunks of the pines. We were a long way from Manhattan.

After the picnic we always stopped on the way home at the Wienervald. This was an Austrian restaurant on the road to Amecameca owned, of course, by a refugee Viennese, complete with *lederhosen* and sturdy paunch. He butchered his own pigs and made his own sausage that he first smoked in the giant fireplace then hung from the rafters to season.

They were hard as leather—and the most delicious that we have ever tasted, and we much favored them. We drove back through Cuautla many years later and found the Wienervald closed and silent. We have found that it is the truth, all too often, that you cannot go home again.

In these pretelevision days we tended to read a lot in the evenings. The lights were good, the chairs comfortable—but something disturbed me very much about our garage-living room. This was the large unbroken wall. It was painted a pale, sick pink, a good 160 square feet of it. We could have hung pictures on it, though I didn't think much of the idea of driving nails into plaster in rented premises. Joan enjoyed the bareness just about as much as I did. "All that plaster. If we can't hang pictures on it we should get Michelangelo to do a Sistine Chapel mural on it."

The seed was planted. Why shouldn't we have a mural? I looked at that great expanse of pink plaster, and my artistic ambitions, long dormant, stirred in my bosom again. In the market they sold little bundles of charcoal twigs that were used to start the cooking fires with. I bought some and tried them on the wall. They were as good as, or better than, the charcoal I had used as an art student when drawing the antique.

"It won't hurt the wall—and it can always be washed off," I said. I made a quick sketch of a cactus on the plaster, blurred it, and wiped it off with a cloth. "What will you draw?" Joan asked. "Something local, historical, and very Mexican." We had recently visited the Paso del Cortez high up on the flanks of Popo. The route that stout Cortez had taken after he had landed at Vera Cruz. He and his handful of soldiers had crossed through the mountains on this path, on his way to the invasion of the valley of Mexico. A very suitable topic for this area: I went to work with enthusiasm. If the mural was more comic book than classical art, why then my years of laboring in the comic factories were certainly to blame. But Mexican art is colorful and realistic in part, sometimes even garish and bigger than life to Northern eyes. Why not?

Why not indeed! With manic dedication I drew in the mountains and jungles, jaguars and Indians lurking in the background. While Cortez, helmeted and armored, his sword waving, led his followers on to victory. Over the mountains and through the pass that would one day be named after him. I just had his figure roughed in, a sketched outline, when we had a visit by Carlos Mendoza. At that time he was a well-known and popular Mexican actor, who was in Cuautla shooting a film. We invited him in for a drink and his eyes blazed with Latin pleasure when he saw the mural. He tore off his shirt and insisted on the spot that he pose for the figure of Cortez. He did, and I drew him in, adding the sword and helmet later. He was a very pleasant man and while the film was being shot would stop by often to admire my creation. I enjoyed doing it.

I little knew how well I had wrought until Jorgé, the hotel's manager, joined us for a drink one evening and saw my mural. Not only did he not mind my defacing the wall, but appeared to take great pride in what I thought was a garish piece of artwork. I went back to work on the novel and was surprised when, some days later, he knocked on our door. He had brought the chief of police with him. What crime had I committed? But, no, he just wanted my permission to show the chief my mural. I let them in and turned on the lights. The policeman pursed his lips and nodded approvingly at my garage-long piece of art. Shook my hand and thanked me before he left. For the rest of our stay in Cuautla, Jorgé brought many friends, and local notables, including the mayor, to see my mural. Artistic fame at last!

Though we visited Cuautla many years later we forgot to see if the Motel Camerones still existed, to find out if the mural was still there. I like to think that it is.

Meanwhile I was working quite hard, grinding out stories and the occasional men's adventures, to keep us eating, and getting in more work on the novel. The months slipped by. I went to the post office every day to pick up our mail and of course to send out my completed articles, a complicated process. Since the international postage on a manuscript being sent to New York was more than the weekly salary of a postal worker, one did not simply drop a stamped envelope into the mailbox. It would understandably have instantly vanished. So I stood in line and took the envelope to the window, where I had it weighed. Then I stood and watched as the clerk fixed the stamps in place—and carefully canceled every one. Then I paid. It was not humiliating at all but a very practical ceremony.

One day on the way back from the post office, I passed a stranger who appeared to be having trouble with his car. He had stopped in front of the local automobile mechanic's establishment and was explaining his troubles. The only problem, I realized as I passed close by, was that he was describing his mechanical difficulties in French. A traveler in need, far from home. I had to help, but at that time my French was nonexistent. But perhaps he spoke English? It was worth a try. He was a tall man with a sparkling smile that lit up when I talked to him. "Of course! Your help would be greatly appreciated."

The problem was a minor one; my Spanish, by this time, and knowledge of car mechanics, were well up to sorting it out. While the repairs were being made, we talked, and I found out that we had very much in common. He was a Dane, named Preben Zahle. An artist of some renown in his home country, as well as being art director of *Tidens Kvinder, Today's Women,* an important magazine in Denmark. He was visiting Mexico with his wife on an American art scholarship. I took them back to our living room–garage for drinks while the repairs were being done and we hit it off at once. Joan instantly invited them to dinner, and the next day they rented the apartment next door. They only stayed a week, but we had a good deal of fun together. When the Zahles returned to Denmark we corresponded for a bit. Preben talked to the other editors on the magazine and convinced them that Joan and I should write some travel and cooking articles for them. We did, and it was very nice, and Danish kroner turned into Mexican pesos just as easily as dollars did.

We did not realize it at the time, but this chance meeting was going to have a most profound effect on our lives.

Mexico was very good for us and I don't know how long we would have stayed there if Todd had not taken ill. And it wasn't your usual childhood illness. Dr. Ugalde diagnosed it without a blood test, just by putting his hand on the baby's forehead to take his temperature, then feeling his swollen spleen. *"Paludismo,"* he said with authority: malaria. It was endemic in Mexico in the '50s and he had seen far too many cases of it. At this time malaria was very easy to cure with the drug Plaquenil. This was well before the mutated and deadly varieties came into existence, the ones that plague us today. Todd was medicated and completely cured, he still is, but his parents were understandingly very frightened at the time. Had our parents indeed been right? Were we exposing their grandson to scores of deadly diseases? Right or wrong, we had had a good scare, followed by intense feelings of guilt. The bright sheen was off Mexico and our *Wanderjahre* was just about up. We made plans for our return and got the letters off. Needless to say our parents were overjoyed. We were of two minds—but the decision had been made. It was time to pack up, to say good-bye to our Mexican friends, and point the sturdy Anglia north, back to the land of our birth.

When we said our good-byes we realized how many good friends, both Mexican and the few resident Americans, we had made here. And it was hard to say good-bye to Mexico as well. We drove north with very mixed emotions. This country had been very good to us. Every meal we stopped for was one more to remember. We were not going to get food like this in New York City.

Nor would we see many disastrous accidents there like the one we passed a few miles outside of San Luis Potosi. A one-vehicle accident on a straight stretch of road, the truck was an old one, the tires completely bald. There must have been a blowout; the truck swerved into the ditch and overturned. The driver had already been taken to the hospital—but what of his cargo? There had been a full load of live pigs in the stake body of the truck and a goodly number had been killed when it overturned. The survivors wandered among the corpses of their brethren, while the farmers from the nearby village took advantage of this gift from heaven. Since it was a hot day and no refrigeration was available the outcome was obvious. The pigs were butchered in the road, the pork carried away. The highway patrolmen looked on benevolently; they weren't their pigs. I took some photographs for the record and we drove on.

Our trip back to the States coincided with the rainy season. Some of the storms were quite severe and floods covered the desert—and the highway. The Anglia stood so high on its large wheels that we had no difficulty driving on the flooded roads. We could not tell the road from desert, but helpful highway crews had marked the shoulder with lengths of wood stuck into the ground. Stay inside them and you were okay. One tanker truck had not done this and had skidded off the road and lay on its side in the flooded waters. I took photographs of this as well.

The border approached. We knew that we would miss Cuautla but we were excited about going back to the States. Outside of one brief trip to the border to renew our tourist visas, we had not seen that country for over a year. What would it be like? Unfriendly, for openers. We crossed the border and were a few miles into Texas when we were greeted by sirens and flashing lights and were pulled over by a Texas Ranger. "You know that you're driving with illegal plates," he drawled warmly as he wrote out the ticket. "They're not illegal—just New York plates," I protested. "Illegal there too," he said as he handed me the ticket. "Last year's plates. You have twenty-four hours to get Texas plates. County seat is just down the road."

We had left the land of no fixed rules and had returned to the rule of law. (In Cuautla the chief of police drove a car with expired California plates. Who would question him?) And this was sure a good racket for the state of Texas. How many returning tourists did they grab every year? Eight dollars for registration and new license plates was a lot of money in those days. Only when I had bolted on the plates did I realize that this was a blessing in disguise—and a very cheap one at that.

"Do you know what has happened?" I cried aloud. "We have been washed whiter than white and can take our place in New York society again." Joan frowned in puzzlement—then burst out laughing. "Of course—the tickets!" I can now admit, and hope that the statute of limitations has indeed run out, that in 1955 I was a scofflaw. New York City takes a very dim view of people who amass a pile of unpaid parking tickets, and I had amassed quite a few. Not on purpose, of course. When Joan was pregnant and expecting, I had parked the car outside our apartment house at night. Parking was allowed until eight A.M.—when it became a non-parking zone, with tickets and fines ready and waiting for the guilty lawbreaker. Only too often I had rushed down to move the car and found a ticket on the windshield. Once it was there at five minutes past eight; the traffic wardens started work a lot earlier than I did.

I don't know how many tickets I had, but it was a good handful. I paid the really old ones when I could, since in those precomputer days they investigated by dates. The oldest tickets were tracked down first. This feeble ploy had worked well enough and the fateful knock on the door had never come. Nevertheless, it was with a feeling of great relief when we left New York for Mexico. Chortling with glee we had torn them up and thrown them out of the window when we had reached the New Jersey Turnpike. And now we were driving a Texas-registered car and our record was clean. There was another fringe benefit as well. In the brief time that we had been away, America had apparently changed. No longer were the filling station attendants the usual surly and silent lot. Now they greeted us warmly and called, "You'all come again, hear?" as we drove happily away. Realization dawned slowly. When we had driven south we had been Yankees, and our license plates identified us as New York Yankees at that, the worst kind there is. We had been changed by our Texas license into honorary Southerners. Now, as we drove through the South, we were real live Texans in a funny car. The War Between the States was still fresh in Southern memory in 1957.

We returned to New York and a great wave of black depression washed over us. Everything was different—or was it we who had changed? After Mexico, Long Beach was terrible. We had to get out—but where to? Not Mexico again; although Todd's malaria had been a simple one and was now completely cured, we were still frightened. No more tropics with an infant; once had been more than enough.

Life with in-laws was getting pretty terrible as well. We were staying with Joan's parents and the inevitable frictions began eating away. It was pretty obvious that they thought that our lifestyle sucked. It all came to a head one day when I was hammering away at the typewriter, finishing off yet one more men's adventure to keep us in funds. Joan and Todd were out so I had some quiet and peace of mind. Despite our Mexican year I was still an inexperienced freelancer—and not the world's best researcher to boot. I would gather all my scraps of notes together and mumble over them while I sorted them into some kind of order. When they were clear in my head—along with the fictional-fact outline—I would slip paper into the mill and begin to type like crazy. I could usually get the first draft done in a day. Once it was completed, I could then rewrite and polish. But at this point in time if I were interrupted, while getting the copy from head to paper, I would lose the whole thing. Everything would come crashing down from my brain and that would be that. A day's work shot. Start again in the morning and hope for the best. I was in full two-fingered flow when the door opened.

The door never opens while I am at the typewriter. Joan knew that—the children imbibed that knowledge with the first air they breathed. Still the door opened, my fingers froze, my jaw gaped wide. My mother-in-law looked in and said: "Harry, since you are not doing anything, would you go to the store for me?"

What a storehouse of content, meaning, and attitude in that single sentence. How neatly it summed up the nonwriter's attitude toward the writer's craft. This sentence was so perfect—of its kind—that I have passed it on to many other writers. Years later it was quoted back to me; now part of the Apocrypha of our trade.

It was the end. We had to leave. And science fiction would save us. SF fans had been holding conventions on and off since the 1930s. In 1939 the first so-called World Convention, or Worldcon, took place in New York City. Apparently the science fiction world, up until 1957, had consisted of the United States, with the generous addition of Canada the last few years. But in this landmark year the Worldcon was going to live up to its name. It was going to be held in London, England. Outside of North America for the first time.

An old friend, Dave Kyle, longtime fan and one-time publisher of Gnome Press, was organizing a fan flight. At this time the only way to cross the Atlantic by plane, with any kind of reasonable fare, was by charter. Sign up enough fans and a fan flight would be possible. Dave managed to do just that. I sent him our names and payment, something like two hundred dollars round trip for two, and the baby went for free. With great enthusiasm we began to pack. Proving once again to our parents that we were certifiable.

The Anglia went into storage. My typewriter, a Corona office standard, was bolted into a war surplus army footlocker, padded about with blankets, pillows, clothes, and books, and shipped to England by sea. We said good-bye once again to parents and friends and headed for Idlewild Airport.

This might be a good place to stop and ask the question—what was running through our minds at this time? Probably the same thoughts that had got us out of New York the first time around. Nothing had changed in the year that we had been away. To stay there meant returning to the same situation that we had worked so hard to leave. But we had done it, we had fought our way out of the city and to Mexico where we had lived and prospered. Lived quite well, thank you very much. If it had been done once it could be done again.

We had no idea of what we would find in England. But at least they spoke English there. And the fan flight did contain a round-trip ticket if it was all too awful. So what had we to lose? Well, a good deal, as our parents so kindly pointed out. Rational—to us—arguments did not prevail. They believed this was madness heaped on madness. In the end, all we could do was simply shrug our shoulders, take on the burden of guilt, and turn away yet again. Buoyed up by what we thought was still-reasonable logic and adequate explanation.

That it seemed like a good idea at the time.

8

With great excitement we headed for Idlewild Airport (JFK now) and Forest Hills, one of the suburbs in Queens, where I had grown up and had attended Forest Hills High School. This side trip was necessitated by the fact that the tiny, by today's standards, Super Continental, the four-engine, triple-tailed wonder we were flying on, could just about manage to cross the Atlantic with a full load of maybe twenty-five passengers, with minimal luggage. But it couldn't lift the weight of the food to feed them. So before takeoff we were bused to a restaurant in Forest Hills, where we dined there among the mock-Tudor buildings, then back to the airport. There was a heat wave, close to one hundred degrees, and we sighed with relief when the plane's doors closed and we buzzed down the runway and heaved ourselves into the sky.

We headed for Gander, Newfoundland. Not only couldn't our tiny craft carry enough food for the passengers—it couldn't manage to carry enough fuel to get across the Atlantic nonstop from New York. We landed, sweat still damp on our clothes, and stumbled through the freezing air to the terminal. After refueling we were loaded back aboard and our transoceanic voyage began. No food, of course, just candy and soft drinks—but this was an adventure.

Todd slept, but I don't think anyone else on the plane did. We all knew each other, all science fiction fans, carrying the plane high on wings of excitement. Some of the fen joined a quiz to see who was the most knowledgeable about the true history of science fiction. The finalists were Sam Moskowitz and Ozzie Train. They hammered at each other mercilessly.

"Who painted the cover of the January 1935 issue of *Amazing Stories*?"

"Frank R. Paul. Now—who wrote the cover story in the first issue of *Air Wonder Stories*?"

We were young and the world was young in those days. Eventually we slept a bit and awoke to the good news that because of a strong tailwind we had overflown Shannon Airport in Ireland and were going directly into London North Airport. First we dropped down from the blue sky into the blindingly thick clouds. After this our plane passed through a layer of clear air—then ever downward into more clouds. As we dropped lower and the sky grew ever darker, our spirits darkened as well. We knew that England had a rainy reputation—but this was ridiculous. I counted seven ever-darker cloud layers until a leaden and damp landscape finally swam into view below us. We came in low over a road and, horrified, I saw a gloved and goggled motorcyclist who was dressed all in leather, complete with a sheepskin jacket. New York City and the Labor Day heat wave were far behind us. But not Forest Hills, it seemed, for the suburban homes we passed over appeared to be mock-Tudor as well. Or real Tudor? We would soon find out.

Customs made us welcome in a very suspicious way. The reception of foreign visitors seemed to be dependent upon the way they were dressed. This was our first thrilling encounter with the British social system. Young Robert Silverberg, nattily attired in suit, shirt, and tie, along with his fashionably dressed wife, Barbara, was greeted warmly and they each received a three-month visa in their passports.

Our little family group was not so lucky. Was I that scruffy? Or was it the presence of an infant that drew instant suspicion? Perhaps they thought we were American peasants trying to immigrate. They were quite thorough—actually inspecting the contents of my wallet to see if I had enough money to support my indigent dependents. Passports were expensive in those days so we were all on one passport, joined in a single family photo. I have it before me now. I am dark-haired but already balding. Joan is tanned and gorgeous; Todd goggle-eyed and startled. Next to the photo is a rubber-stamped visa that reads:

PERMITTED TO LAND ON CONDITION THAT
THE HOLDER DOES NOT REMAIN IN THE
UNITED KINGDOM LONGER THAN. . . . .
. . . .

On the dotted line ONE MONTH has been written in. To drive the gracious reception home the further message appeared below:

AND DOES NOT ENTER ANY EMPLOYMENT
PAID OR UNPAID

We were exhausted by this time and looked forward to some rest. But not before food! We had had nothing to eat on the plane so we perked up greatly when we were all ushered into an elegant dining hall, courtesy of the airline. This was it! No American greasy spoon here. We had left the colonies and were now in the bosom of culinary civilization. Tables covered in white linen, silver cutlery stretching out not only on both sides of our plates but above them as well. And the waiters . . . They could have been ambassadors, or symphony conductors, in their black tailcoats.

And the food—what civilized old-world joys lay ahead for us! Trundled in on little wagons, hidden under rounded silver domes, served by skilled and cheerful servitors. Our plates were filled and we tucked in. It was unbelievably terrible. Cafeteria steam-table food at its absolute worst. Chunks of stringy, greasy, cold chicken. Poisonously green peas with the texture of bullets. Globs of over-cooked and watery cabbage. Three kinds of potatoes; all indigest-ible. We ate in silence. Telling ourselves that the meal must contain sustenance and calories because all the Brits we had seen so far were alive. Well, almost all, if you excluded the zombie-faced customs officers.

Full, if not fed, we forgot our travails in the warm welcome of British fandom. They were there in great numbers, as cheerful and as excited as we were, turned out before dawn to bid us welcome. Ted Carnell, editor of *New Worlds,* with whom I had corresponded, led the pack. They had provided a transport of delight—a red, double-decker London omnibus. Fatigue forgotten, we reveled in the joys of conversation with our peers. Fanac—fan activity—at its finest. We trundled majestically through the green fields, to a London familiar to us all from countless films and novels. To Queensway and the Kings Court Hotel, site of the convention and our home for this magical weekend.

It was an interesting hotel. It had apparently been made by knocking holes in the walls to connect a number of ancient and adjoining buildings. The corridors rose up and down as one passed from building to building. Our room had a double bed, a window, a sink, and a curious metal construction in one corner. This proved to be a shower of sorts. Old-world charm—and we were charmed. After some of the fleapits we had stayed in in Mexico this was indeed a form of luxury.

Not to all. Next day a tearful Dave Kyle wanted to know if we were leaving too? Why on earth should we? Apparently most of the other Americans found the accommodation too primitive. Obviously none of them had ever been to Mexico. Eventually the rebellion was put down and they stayed. Probably because a few scouts had looked at the other accommodation in the neighborhood.

We all retired early, Joan and Todd instantly asleep. I was too excited to sleep so I dressed quietly and went down to the bar off the lobby. A real English pub—I had a real Scotch whisky and some real English ice. (Two melting slivers served out of a fake pineapple ice tub, along with the advice from a florid customer that ice would freeze my tum.)

None of the American fen seemed to be present, and I didn't recognize any of our hosts. Yes, there was one. Wasn't that the chairman of the con himself, a budding author named John Brunner? I introduced myself—why not?—we were all one big family united in fandom.

Two countries separated by a common language and culture. Apparently I was being pretty gauche on British terms, pushing in like this and introducing myself. With a great effort John extended his hand and, with even greater effort, on the third try, turned to me and said *howdjado*. Let the joy commence.

All conventions blur in the memory and this one is no exception. I do remember, at the so-called banquet, the convention president, John Wyndham, proposed the loyal toast to Her Majesty the Queen. Just like in a historical novel, spoiled only by those few fen of republican leaning who did not stand up and join in, yet another social discovery.

I had my first pint in my first pub and that was good. Passing through the hotel dining room while on my way to bed, sometime after midnight, I was astonished to see that not only had the breakfast tables been laid—but every bowl had been filled with cornflakes. What efficiency.

Brian Aldiss and I first met at the Worldcon in 1957. Neither of us has any memory of it, but I know we did meet. I only really got to know him when we later corresponded and met up at various English Eastercons.

The rain stopped, the sun came out briefly, the rain started again. Since we were in London we took the opportunity to see a bit of it. Only when we had left the security of the hotel did we begin to appreciate what the war had done to Britain.

Wasn't it General Westmoreland who wanted to bomb Vietnam back to the Stone Age? As we walked through the smoggy, sooty streets it looked as though Hitler's mob had bombed London at least back to the Middle Ages. Almost every row of buildings had gaps in them, blackened openings like missing teeth. Great wooden beams and heavy bolts held up the remaining buildings on each side. The center of London, around St. Paul's Cathedral, was nothing but a series of bomb sites. Almost twelve years had passed since VE Day and an impoverished Britain still bore the scars of war. I realized how lucky we had been in the mainland United States to have avoided the destructive forces of modern warfare. If anything the war had dragged the States out of the Depression and had built a booming production economy. Not so in Britain. The few cars on the streets were prewar antiques. Rationing was still on, as we quickly discovered. We had to sign on with National Health since orange juice and vitamins for the baby were by prescription only.

But the convention was almost over and we had no idea of what we would do next. Once again our money was running out and we had to make plans. One of them was to try and sell the return flight part of our tickets. Unhappily, there were no takers.

We had made lots of new British friends, and we sought their advice. Joan had been talking to Myrtle, a femfan she had grown friendly with, who lived in a nearby suburb called Bromley, Kent. It sounded nice, a quick commuter train trip to London, and Myrtle assured us it would be a lot cheaper than central London, and it was. We found a residential hotel named Smith's not five minutes' walk from Bromley North station. We could have two rooms, bath down the hall, with three meals a day for the three of us for twelve guineas a week. (No guinea existed, we were to find out. A guinea is, or was, one pound and one shilling, written £1-1-0. All hotel rooms at this time were priced in guineas, as well as books and expensive clothing.) The pound then was worth $2.80, so our all-in room and board came to about thirty-five dollars a week. Not too bad, we thought. This was before we tasted the food.

Now I hate to carp on what might seem only a cultural difference, but this was a true and strong reaction. It should be noted that I am not fond either of my native American meat-and-potatoes-and-three-vegetable meal either. I loathed the army chow and I didn't really appreciate food until I went to Mexico, or later Italy,

France, and Denmark. During my years in England I have had wonderful British meals. It is just that the average postwar British meal was—let us face it—pretty dismal. Things have improved of late but in 1957, with rationing still on, there was not much variety. We were beginning to realize what a battering the country had taken during the war and afterward.

Smith's Hotel represented the absolute worst in British cooking, possibly because the chef, the owner's son, had learned to cook in the British Army, or perhaps because the rates were so cheap. In any case I found it so terrible that I couldn't eat it at all. Before we left, a few months later, I had lost twenty pounds. Joan, who likes potatoes, managed to put on a few pounds. I have a photograph, taken for a police residence permit at the time, where we look like Hungarian war refugees; me hollow-faced and gaunt, Joan plump-faced under a headscarf.

We weren't the only ones put off by the food. A young naval officer stationed nearby and living temporarily at the hotel would bug his eyes each night at the food going by and order canned spaghetti instead. The ancient retirees, who were the main residents, ate the food with, if not pleasure, a degree of indifference. Perhaps they really liked oxtail soup, made from powdered concentrate, seven times a week.

Still, we had reached safe harbor of sorts. We had gone onto the panel of a local doctor in order to get the needed prescriptions for orange juice and vitamins for Todd. The footlocker from New York had finally arrived so I unbolted the typewriter and set it up. I was forbidden to do any work, paid or unpaid, by the stamp in my passport. Maybe writing fiction wouldn't count, particularly if they didn't know about it. Fed up with hack writing, I was now doing short SF stories, but they took some time to sell and the money to hand was almost gone. Could I write anything locally that would top up our funds while we waited for transatlantic checks? I suppose I would be breaking the letter of the law—but feeding my family, if that's what it could be called—came first.

Through Ted Carnell, editor of *New Worlds,* I met a number of artists. Brian Lewis was a fine artist who had painted many covers for Ted, and we soon became friends. This was when I first realized that SF was truly international—in many ways an extended global family. I was beginning to feel that coming to Europe had really been a good idea, but could I earn a living here?

I looked in the comics scene, always a good fallback. At the convention I had met Sydney Jordan, who was then drawing a newspaper comic strip called *Jeff Hawke.* We had talked a bit and he liked the idea of some transatlantic SF input. So I wrote some scripts for him. Through Syd I met more of the London comics people, in particular Andy Vincent, editor of a comic book line for Fleetway who was a nice guy who became a good friend. We began a working relationship that would last for years. Also working for Fleetway at that time was a lean and clean-shaven Mike Moorcock. He was a subeditor then, his successful writing career yet to come. I opened a bank account at Lloyds Bank in Bromley and they deposited my sterling checks with pleasure. Interestingly enough, I still have the same account some fifty-plus years later.

While all this was going on I was doing my best to help a friend of a friend: Hans Stefan Santesson, an editor I had worked with in New York, who was very active in a number of charities. One of these was for Indian seaman; subcontinent, not American. Before we left for England he had asked me to talk to Massoud Chowdry, who was having problems with American immigration. Massoud wanted to immigrate to the States to join his family there, but was having immense trouble with the bureaucrats. I did what I could to give him a hand. I even made an appointment to meet with the consulate officer who had been sitting on his application for some years.

I knew her type; my heart fell when I met her. She was an ancient virginal time-server in a dead-end civil service job, letter of the law and no exceptions. And the letter this time was that poor Massoud was trapped in a catch-22 situation. He had been with an

Indian regiment during the war and had been captured by the Japanese after the fall of Singapore. He had spent some months in a prison camp and had not liked it at all. One day he escaped into the jungle and decided to walk back to India. Yes, they are on the same Asian land mass, but over fifteen hundred miles apart. It took him a year, going from one village to the next, working to earn his keep. It was a heroic adventure that he never discussed very much. Then why couldn't he join his family in the United States? Because, while London had a record of his entering the army, there was nothing on record of his leaving it. He could be anything; a deserter perhaps. His records had been destroyed by the Japanese in Singapore. What could be done? I groped for a way out. A piece of paper, that was it. A letter of some kind, the document so sacred to the bureaucratic mind.

"You know his records were destroyed by the Japanese?" I said with enthusiasm.

"That is what he says." Sniff of suspicion.

"What if I got the British Army, someone in charge of documents, to give you an official statement that his records were destroyed, along with those of everyone else in his company? And that the entire company was captured by the Japanese. Would that suffice?"

She turned the idea over and over for long moments. I smiled ingratiatingly and made charming comments about the importance of her job and how nice it was to see this matter in her competent hands. Flattery—or fact—won the day. The idea was approved. I wrote the letter for Massoud and, within a few days, the important paper came back from the British authorities. He and his English wife, Barbara, would soon be on their way across the Atlantic.

Meanwhile the money was running out. My New York agent was not answering letters and we were in hock to Smith's Hotel for almost four weeks' room and board. I worried about money and couldn't write—and we couldn't get out of the place until I wrote something and got some money. I was trapped in a catch-22 of my own. It was last-resort time. I took a deep breath and typed out an outline for a confession story. I bypassed my noncommunicative agent and sent the outline directly to *True Confessions*. They had liked my work in the past and had bought everything that I wrote. And they paid five cents a word—as opposed to the SF magazines' one to three cents—and equally important they would take stories up to ten thousand words, and could we use five hundred dollars!

I wrote good confessions—but I loathed them. I had to get very feminine and weepy for a week at least, since you can't write category material and fake it. I had to believe sincerely in what I was writing, feel it throbbing to the very core of my being. I hated it but I did it. I had always managed to come up with ideas that would grab the readers' attention. At this time there were lots of young adults in America who had been victims of the poliomyelitis epidemic, some of them so paralyzed that they spent all of their time in a chamberlike apparatus called the iron lung. It did their breathing for them. Those luckier could manage outside the iron lung for longer periods, usually just spending the nights in the machine. I had talked to doctors and made notes before leaving New York, but had never written the piece. I did now, and it was called "My Iron Lung Baby." Sensational? Yes, but true as well. I got a good deal of fan mail, all approving. And the five hundred dollars bought us out of Smith's little suburban hell.

But where should we go? I mentioned my problem to Massoud and he said that there was a bed-sitter vacant in the rooming house where he lived and it was very cheap. We grabbed it and thus began some of the most fascinating months of our lives. Massoud and his wife Barbara had moved out of their room, into the frigid attic of the building, so we could have the room. This was a true kindness that we never knew about until some years later. We arrived in the building as friends, not strangers, and were soon good friends with everyone else living there as well. They were all Pakistanis, most of them cooks in the new curry restaurants that were springing up all over London. They were all warmhearted and social, and living there was more like Mexico than the frigid north. We loved it.

The best part was that we hadn't eaten curries since Hans Santesson had introduced them to us in Harlem, some years previously. Like Mexican food it was very tasty, spicy, interesting. We were converted. Joan was practically a professional cook before we left, having learned to cook curries side by side with chefs in the communal kitchen. Todd didn't take to the food too well, but he was a dab hand at helping to mash dal.

Money was still in short supply since nothing had come in since the *True Confessions* check. London publishing had shut down over Christmas and we were slowly freezing to death. Central heating was unknown in Britain at this time. I remember that I did an article for a New York magazine on English public houses. In this I scotched the rumor that the English served warm beer. They did not. Their beer was served at room temperature. However, English room temperature was about the same as American refrigerator temperature.

In our furnished room we had a gas fire with attendant coin meter. Insert sixpence, turn the knob, and light the fire, which extinguished itself with a popping sound in what seemed like an incredibly short period. Only a lucky accident kept us alive. For some reason we had a lot of American pennies with us—and they proved to be the same size as an English sixpenny piece. We fed them one by one into the meter and stayed warm. But they ticked away there like a time bomb; we had to find a way to get out of town before the man came to empty the coins and discovered our crime.

Our communal Pakistani Christmas dinner, while not traditional or Western, was simply incredible. The season of joy was upon us, but apparently doomed to be a dry season. Joan didn't drink, nor did the Moslem Pakistanis, which left only me and Barbara to represent seasonal Anglo-Saxon alcohol swilling. We chipped in one and three each for a grand total of two and six. Two shillings sixpence; thirty-four cents American. Just enough to buy a pint bottle of VP sherry. A particularly loathsome drink made of powdered Cyprus grapes, sweet and vaguely alcoholic. We toasted and wished a merry Christmas to all.

We had to leave. The dreadful winter, and the threat that our crime would soon be exposed when the meter box was emptied, drove us on. This was before the Clean Air Act in Britain and a time of killer fogs. The coal soot in the air would combine with the water drops in the fog to make an impenetrable wall. You could not see more than a yard ahead, two at the maximum. Traffic crawled, and if you had to go out, you felt along the curb and groped your way across the pavement.

We needed money—and a warm destination. By happy circumstance an old friend supplied the latter. I need to say more about Garry Davis here. Garry Davis had flown a bomber during the war and had emerged a pacifist—and was determined to do something about his beliefs. He burned his American passport at the United Nations, which was then meeting in Paris, and had declared himself the first "citizen of the world." This action drew international attention and soon he was leading the world citizen movement. At one time we had shared an office in New York and it was there that I had designed the World Passport. The passport was a nifty green job that faithfully copied the American passport. It was in English and Esperanto and I still have mine. Garry used his to travel around the world, causing government officials a good deal of grief. He had gone back to Europe just about the time we went to Mexico. We kept in touch when we went to England; now he was in Paris. He wrote that he hoped to go to Italy soon, southern Italy. He had world citizen friends there who had arranged a place for him to stay. Perfect; we would meet him there. All we needed to do this was some more money. I couldn't face another confession so it was time to call on the old boys' network again. When I had edited pulp magazines and Hans Santesson was unemployed, I had commissioned articles from him. Now he was editor of a new SF mag, with the shy title of *Fantastic Universe*. I sent him the outline of a story titled "The Robot Who Wanted to Know." I said it would run to five thousand words. Unlike *Astounding,* Hans could only afford to pay a penny a word. But, also unlike *Astounding,* he paid in advance to prevent our death by freezing and starving. Fifty dollars was more than enough to get the camera out of hock, pay the rent, and buy some food—and leave a bit over. The robot story went out by airmail—along with an outline for another story, to be titled "Arm of the Law." This would also be five thousand words in length. And, unbelievable as it seems now, the fifty dollars it earned would pay for our train tickets to Italy.

The famous footlocker was shipped ahead to Naples. We would pick it up before we departed for Capri, where we were to meet Garry. John Blomshield, my painting teacher, knew the island well and had once loaned me a copy of *The Story of San Michele,* written by a Scandinavian super con man who settled there. I didn't remember much about Capri from the book, other than the fact that oranges grew there. It had to be warmer than London.

We said our tearful good-byes and headed for Victoria Station.

9

The footlocker had gone on ahead and should be waiting for us in Naples station. We were saying good-bye to London—and hopefully to winter as well. When we reached Victoria Station, there, standing at the platform, were the gleaming black-and-gold coaches of the world-famous train, the Golden Arrow. As an old rail fan I had read, with some envy, about this elegant way of traveling from London to Paris. A one-class train—first class of course—that sped nonstop to Dover to the waiting ferry, where the coaches would be uncoupled from the locomotive and rolled aboard the ferry by puffing, coal-fired donkey engines. Should they care to, the passengers could enjoy the pleasures of the Channel ferry during the crossing—or remain in the dining car, where the champagne undoubtedly flowed. The coaches of the Golden Arrow would of course be first off in Calais, to be coupled quickly to the Paris train—and away, an elegant and comfortable way to travel.

However, this first-class train was far too expensive for us and we weren't going to Paris, not yet. We passed by the gleaming delights of the Golden Arrow and on to the next platform, to the dusty second-class coaches of the stop-everywhere local that eventually trundled its way to Dover. By the time we had arrived at the coast the sun had vanished and a cold rain was falling. I grabbed up the suitcases, Joan took Todd by the hand, and we hurried to the waiting ferry.

It was still raining in Calais and our first view of France was the sodden railroad yard where we stumbled across the wet tracks as we followed the signs leading to our train to Rome. This proved to be an elegant—and clean—French Wagons-lits. Our spirits perked up. This was more like it. We were in France, on the continent of Europe, ready to cross it to Italy and—hopefully—the sunny south. We found which one of the glossy black carriages was ours and climbed aboard. The waiting conductor welcomed us—in English. He was equally facile in greeting our fellow travelers in French, German, and Italian; a polyglot who appeared to speak every known language. He consulted our tickets and showed us to our compartment, bowed slightly, and left. If this was second class—what luxuries could there possibly be in first?

A long couch to the right stretched the width of the compartment; a large window filled the far wall. A sink, all dark wood, gilt plumbing, and engraved glass, was built in beside the door. Among its practical fittings, we quickly discovered, was a concealed potty. This was a tribute to French practicality and design. When the hinged door below the sink was pulled open, the chamber pot was revealed. It resembled an immense gravy boat as it hung there in its fitting, pouring-spout down. After utilization—at night, in the dark, with no witnesses, of course—it was slipped back into place. When the supporting door was closed its contents were decanted onto the tracks.

After dinner in the splendid dining car we returned to find that the train staff had been busy while we were away. The back of the couch had been lifted up, another cot swung down, and the entire thing converted neatly into three berths, now made up with linen and blankets. The perfect count for our family. Todd on the bottom complete with teddy bear, I with my nose to the ceiling, Joan in between where she could keep a watch on us both.

We slept—and slept so well that we almost missed our connection. We were in the station in Zurich, Switzerland, where we had to change trains for Italy. Unlike the more easygoing parts of the world that we had grown used to, here everything ran on time. And run is what we did, following the porter with our bags, down the stairs, through the tunnel, and up to a different platform. To watch our train pulling out, an almost tragedy but not a disaster. It appeared that a new train was being assembled from bits and pieces from all over northern Europe. There was some rapid muttering by the porter in German, consultation of a wall chart, a guttural oath, and another dash through the tunnel. Only two-year-old Todd seemed to enjoy all this.

This time we made it, safe harbor at last. No sleeping car now because this was a daytime trip, but rather a compartment for eight passengers who appeared to be right out of a Graham Greene novel. Whistles blew, trainmen waved flags, and we moved slowly forward. Rattling through the switches in the station and out onto the main line. Dark buildings slipped by, faster and faster—until we were in the suburbs; trees and white houses. Then the countryside with the mountains beyond, with the snow-covered Alps brilliant against an electric blue sky.

Inside the train we were the objects of great attention. Hard as it is to believe now, there were no visible American tourists in Europe in 1958. The jumbo jet had yet to be invented, while the few Super-Connies, the three-tailed Constellation transport that we crossed the Atlantic in, thrashed their propellers for twenty hours to get their passengers between the United States and Shannon. It was not a popular form of transport. The rich and well-off Americans took the liners across the ocean and stayed at expensive hotels after they arrived. If they took the train they went first class. Hippies hadn't been invented yet; guitars were for bars, backpacks for the mountains. We were a novelty. All the European eyes sparkled with curiosity at the sight of this American family group.

It was the Italian mother who cracked first. A little girl sat on her lap and motherhood radiated from her as from a maternal nuclear reactor. She had been clamping her lips shut, not wanting to be the one who broke the silence, while looking admiringly at Todd's fair blond hair. Finally, no longer able to control herself, she leaned over and asked Joan, *"Quanti anni il bambino?"*

Italian is close enough to Spanish for Joan to make out the

meaning. Plus—what is the first question a woman asks about a child? How old was he? Just over two years. And your little girl, she's very pretty, how old is she? Joan was speaking Spanish, the other woman Italian, no barrier at all to concerned maternal conversation.

Of the eight of us in the compartment, there were four, possibly five different nationalities. (One silent, dour man never spoke, never looked up.) It was our first introduction to normal European linguistic convention. Speak the language you know and hopefully it will be sorted out. It soon became Italian, Spanish, French, and English. Someone tried German and did not get very far.

We discovered that the man next to the window, in a smartly cut three-piece suit, was a trader in gemstones. We must have looked an honest lot—particularly since we were graced with the presence of the Italian army officer hunchbacked under the weight of medals and decorations—because after discussing the fortunes of international sales he actually produced some of his product wrapped in tissue paper. There was appreciation on all sides.

We had some food with us—and apparently so did everyone else. We unwrapped our sandwiches and hardboiled eggs; a bottle was opened and wine shared around. Then some incredibly delicious salami appeared. When we reached Rome late that afternoon it was like the end of the party.

After the linguistic chaos of the train I looked forward to some good Esperanto communication. I had found the address of the Hotel Montenegro in the *Jarlibro,* the Esperanto yearbook that was filled with names and addresses of clubs, businesses, and hotels. The ad had promised cheap and clean accommodation. I had written and reserved a room for the night. I had not received an answer but was not worried. Mexico had been an education into the Latin mind and since it was now winter, Rome suitably chilled, there should be room at the inn. A taxi, a little difference of opinion over the fare, settled amicably—again after Mexican training— and a ring on the door and the affable owner who spoke only Italian appeared. Yes indeed, the room was ready, enter, enter. An explanation that of course he didn't speak Esperanto, Italian was good enough for him. But he advertised because all Esperantists were poor but honest, clean and willing, good customers. He led us to our quarters, opened the door, and proudly waved us in.

He had something to be proud about. I am sure if we had slipped back in time and had rented the room in 1858—or 1758 for that matter—I don't think we would have noticed the difference. Only the single feeble electric bulb, hanging shadeless over the bed, spoke of the twentieth century. The bed, the curtains, the giant dark wardrobe, all were a part of history, as were the washing arrangements. Hot water brought in a pitcher and poured into a bowl. Toilet down the hall and shared by all on this floor. The giant bed, piled high with feather comforters, was more than big enough for the three of us. Comfort if not luxury, and a view of the Tiber from the window and five hundred lire for the night, eighty cents American at the time; I had a feeling that we were going to like Italy.

The next day we took the train to Naples, then a cab to the ferry that would take us to Capri. The short time we had been in Italy had been very heartening. No one we met spoke English—but they were happy to listen to our Spanish. And maybe we could find some Esperantists. It was a bright day and almost warm this far south. Some of the London chill was seeping from our bones. The island of Capri appeared out of the sea haze ahead, an incredible sight that we had not expected. It rose out of the water, sheer limestone cliffs with seabirds circling above the breaking waves. Our ferry pulled into the tiny seaport of Marina Grande and we disembarked with the others. What would we find here?

Our ancient Fiat cab ground up the hill in low gear, to the village of Capri on the hill above, driving through the narrow streets, growing ever narrower, until we stopped at a dead end. Apparently our pensione was not approachable by road. The driver picked up the footlocker that I had retrieved at the Naples station, and led us down a paved path between the small rocky fields, to a low building very much like a converted barn. Which is exactly what it was. Interior walls had been erected, fascinating plumbing and cooking apparatus installed, furniture put into place. Garry Davis was not there, but there was a message to see Violet Rawnsley, who was staying right next door. She was English, ninety-five years old, a vegan, and confirmed world citizen. She made us welcome. She had corresponded with Garry but had never met him, and was more than happy to be of help to him and his friends. She talked to us about the island.

It was roughly a mile wide and two miles long. The village of Capri, world famous, was situated in a saddle above the marina. Further along the island was the other village of Anacapri, where she had her home. Apparently the sun caught the Capri part of the island better and she was spending some days here for the warmth. She would be going home in a few days and we must visit her.

When there were no more messages from Garry—and he didn't appear—we took her up on her offer. A dinky little bus took us down the hill, to the Piazzetta in Anacapri. While Capri was all glitz, hotels, and expensive restaurants, Anacapri did not have a tourist feel to it at all. Here is where the locals lived who worked in the hotels in Capri, as well as fishermen—and there were still even a few farmers. Violet made us welcome and introduced us to Michele Ferraro. She had the word circulated that we were interested in a rental. Good news indeed for the locals in midwinter since all the tourists had been long gone. Michele was the owner of the *pasticceria* where he baked all the cakes and sweets that the Italians—and the tourists—love. He also owned a house where his newly married daughter lived—and it had a vacant ground-floor apartment.

We looked at it and instantly said yes. There was a large bedroom, bathroom, and living room, with a kitchen built into one wall. There was even a small patio at the entrance. It was just a matter of settling the price and moving into Il Nido—the Bird Nest—as the hand-painted tile by the door proclaimed. Within a week our little nest almost killed us.

Like all of the island's houses, Il Nido was made with stone walls two feet thick, built to a design that must have been a thousand years old. In the older houses in the village you could easily recognize a Roman course of triangular stone sitting on an Etruscan foundation. We later watched one of these solid structures being built and understood more about our new home. First a deep cellar-like hole was chipped and blasted into the volcanic rock that formed this part of the island; it is just a few feet under the surface wherever you start to dig. This large hole in the rock was then lined with cement and became the water cistern. The boulders that had been pried out of the hole were reduced to fist-size chunks of stone in a portable motorized grinder that made an ear-destroying noise, then mixed with concrete to build the floor and walls. The roof, plaster over concrete, was flat, with a drain at one end. During the rainy season the water from the roof filled the cistern below—and had to last the entire year. The windows were metal framed, as were the doors.

The thick walls kept the house delightfully cool in summer—but brutally frigid in the winter. There was not only no central heating, but no heating at all, we soon discovered. During the winter months in the south of Italy you put on a lot of clothes and looked forward to spring. Some homes had a charcoal brazier that produced a trickle of warmth, but that was certainly not enough for us. The three of us spent our first freezing night with all the blankets, and most of our clothes, piled on the bed on top of us. The next day I sought out our landlord. With a great amount of effort and rushing about, a small and ancient gas heater was produced. This was connected by a yard length of rubber hose to a portable tank of gas. We were used to this arrangement because our stove in Cuautla had worked the same way.

With one important exception—the Mexican tank had been outside the house. A copper tube for the gas had been brought into the kitchen through a hole in the wall. But in Italy the tank was comfortably accessible inside the house. I turned the gas on at the tank, turned the handle on the gas heater, and lit the fire. We basked in the warmth. Of course I was very careful to turn it off before we retired, but not careful enough. I was still a creature of American civilization, so I had turned the gas off with the valve on the appliance—and never noticed that the rubber hose connecting the heater to the tank was so ancient that there were cracks in it. With the valve on the tank still turned on, the faulty hose was kept filled with gas.

With all the windows and doors closed Il Nido was practically airtight. The leak must have been a small one or Joan would have smelled it. Not me, of course—after a lifetime of hay fever I have almost no sense of smell at all. Comfortable and warm, we fell asleep.

Sometime during the night I was awoken by a sound. It couldn't have come from outside the house—with two-foot stone walls and sealed windows nothing could be heard. It was a smacking sound, not loud, almost barely audible in fact. Then I realized it was the baby smacking his lips. Why? I couldn't understand it, had difficulty working it out. Difficulty in thinking for some reason. At least I could wake Joan. She stirred and sat up.

"I smell gas!" she said. The stove was leaking! I had enough working brain left to understand that. I also knew that I had carbon monoxide poisoning and had to do something very quickly. Air, oxygen, that came first. I pulled on the handle of the bedroom window, opened it, and found myself lying on the floor. I had blacked out. My thinking was fuzzy, confused, but I knew one thing—I had to go on.

I did. It seemed to take forever, although Joan told me later that it had been less than a minute from beginning to end. I could not stand very well but could do a shuffle on hands and knees. Struggled the bedroom door open, managed to close it behind me. Fumbled with the gas heater and tank, could not figure out what to do. Had just enough sense left to know I had to get rid of it. Dragged it to the front door, unlocked the door, pushed it through and fell down again. Joan managed to get me back to bed and that was the end of that.

The doctor came next morning and took my pulse, looked at the color of the inside of my eyelid, and advised me to drink lots of black coffee and left. A realist, that doctor. Since I wasn't dead I would eventually recover. That's the thing about carbon monoxide poisoning. The CO molecules lock on to the hemoglobin molecules in your blood—preventing oxygen from reaching the brain and body. Too much and you can't absorb oxygen and you die. If you are still alive after the gassing all that you can do is take it very easy. If you are not dead then it means that at least the minimum oxygen for life is reaching the body. Taking it very easy is very much in order. Very slowly, new blood platelets will replace the old ones and eventually all will be well.

I was glad that I had written so many men's adventures, written about so many guys holding on and surviving in extreme situations, cutting off their own arms, going down with their ships. It was a question of life imitating art for a change. When I found myself on the floor I knew—since I had written the scene many times—that I had to get up again and carry on, no matter how I felt. So I did. My knees were bruised and bloody from falling; I had felt nothing at the time. Even now I don't think there was anything very noble or heroic about what I did. I just stumbled along as best I could to keep myself and my family alive. We also never bothered mentioning it to any of our parents. Cowardice perhaps—we could easily imagine the recriminations without experiencing them. After Todd's malaria in Mexico, now this! Maybe they had been right about our leaving New York. Instant guilt—and instant anger. No! Joan and I had made a decision and we would stick to it. When I mentioned my doubts to her she dismissed them. Accidents, not to mention muggings, could happen in New York just as well. We had made this decision for very good reasons. We would stick with it and soldier on.

It would take a good bit of soldiering. Things were not going that smoothly. I recovered quickly enough. Just in time to face the eternal menace of the freelancer: money. There just wasn't any. My agent never answered my letters. And the cash was—all too quickly, really—running out. I was physically well by this time, but emotionally coming to bits. Since I was worried about money I couldn't write. The process of writing intelligent prose requires a certain stability in life and a modicum of peace of mind. I had neither. Since I couldn't write I could not earn any more money. Since I worried constantly about money I could not write. There was temporary salvation at least. A trip to Napoli to the hock shop with the gold bracelet and the camera once again kept the wolf at bay for a bit.

A word of sage advice for any young writers or artists who are in this position: hock the bourgeois gear. Art comes first. If you are not committed completely you do not deserve to succeed. Harsh but true. But don't lose your precious assets. Not only for emotional reasons—you may be down on your luck again and need to visit the pop shop just one more time. So if you have a five-hundred-dollar camera, never hock it for full value. You will never raise enough to retrieve it. Hock it for twenty-five or fifty dollars. Then retrieve it when the first check comes in. He who hocks and gets it back, hocks again when things get black.

We now reached the very bottom moment, the blackest night that we had ever experienced. This moment came when we were down to exactly sixteen cents—one hundred lire. The price of one more airmail stamp to my agent or a liter of milk for Todd. These are the kind of moments in life that one really does not need, but we had walked into it with our eyes wide open. Making this decision had been much harder for Joan than me. I had known that I wanted to write, needed to write, had stories and books that needed doing. I hoped that I would succeed. Joan did not hope. She felt very secure in her knowledge that I would do these things, create art, create literature—and support our family with earned income. I had no such assurance: she was rock-steady in her belief. She had put everything on the line and she would not waver. So she solved this one as well. Since I wasn't doing too well as a good provider she realized that she had to go out and do it herself. She talked to the two brothers who ran the grocery store. In Spanish-Italian she convinced them that it would be a wise thing to extend us credit. An acknowledgment to her tenacity, and their kindliness. This was done.

I sit back and look at these words, written fifty years later, and marvel. That I could have got my small family into this desperate state on an island in the Mediterranean in midwinter was no small feat. That Joan could approach the grocers with such determination was a marvel of an equal and opposite dimension. No credit to me for getting us into this dreadful situation; all credit to Joan, the most wonderful woman that ever existed, and of course the grocery brothers as well. They were really on our side, as was their culture. Before we left Anacapri we began to understand more about these hardworking and very independent people.

It must be realized that, for the most part, Anacapri was a peasant village, which meant that cash money was incredibly tight. A workingman earned about two thousand lire a day—$3.20. A ten-thousand-lire note, $16.00, was referred to as a *pezzo grosso,* a big thing. Our maid, Anna, who earned seven hundred lire a day, had never even seen one before and marveled at its size when I finally got my hands on this formidable sum of money. But it was the locals' attitude toward the arts—and toward the middle class—that I found most reassuring. One they loved, the other they loathed. Opera was a part of their lives. When they were in the trees, picking olives, they would sing arias back and forth to each other. One feast day a small opera company from Sicily performed highlights from *Tosca* in the town square. The performance was wonderful

and greatly enjoyed. The applause went on and on, rising to a cre-
scendo when the singers received their fees while still on stage.
Payment must not only be done—but it must be seen to be done. It
was a very poor world they inhabited, but some things are worth
paying for.

A little of that Italian pleasure and respect of the arts and artists
had even rubbed off on me. The grocery brothers always called me
by the honorific of *dottore* or *professore,* doctor or professor. Not
wanting to fly under false colors I used my dictionary and worked out
what I wanted to say before going to buy that day's ration of grated
Parmesan.

"Grazie, professore," the avuncular and financial-supporting
grocery brother said. I was ready with my prepared Italian speech.
"You must understand that I am not a professor." He raised query-
ing Latin eyebrows. "But you are a writer, are you not?" The village
was small and gossip constant; everyone knew who we were. "Yes,
I am. But I write fiction, articles. . . ."

"You write—and your writing is sold and appears in books?"

"Magazines, really."

"You write and your words are read by millions?"

"Yes. Though thousands might be a closer figure."

"Si, capito, professore." Yes, I understand, Professor.

Very nice people. But we were still broke and we now owed the
brothers in excess of thirty thousand lire. While forty-eight dollars
may be a laughable sum now, remember it then represented three
weeks' hard labor for a workingman. In desperation I turned again
to Hans Stefan Santesson. Swedish born, he had lived in the States
for years, but still knew his way around Europe. I outlined for him
another story entitled "War With the Robots" to go with the other
robot stories I had sold him, the standard five thousand words in
length. Although the story was not yet written, I asked him if he
could see his way clear to extending a small advance as he had with
the other stories.

He did better than that. Being a European he understood the

frailties of international financial transactions now that we had left the Anglo-Saxon civilization of England. A few weeks later I received a letter from him, ordinary airmail. In addition to his letter the envelope contained part of a sheet of carbon paper cut to size. So that if the envelope was held up to the light its contents could not be seen. Its other contents were a U.S. fifty-dollar bill.

An advance on my story at one cent a word. Thank you, Hans, wherever you are now, in some Viking Valhalla hopefully, thank you for coming through in a very pressing hour of need.

Cash in hand, some of our grocery debt paid off, food in stomach, wineglass filled, I could relax and write the story. (Local wine was cheaper than bottled water at this time—sixteen cents a liter.) I wrote not only this story but a dozen more for Hans, all on the robot theme. Most of them paid for in advance. Eventually I gathered all these stories together into a collection titled after the first of the stories, *War with the Robots*. The collection is still alive, although, unhappily, Hans is not.

At last we had word from Garry Davis. He was still on the way to Italy—but there had been problems. For the moment he was staying with American comic artist Dan Barry, who at that time lived in France. Serendipity. I had never met Dan—but his reputation went before him. He had been the top artist in comics, drawing the top rate per page. His name was apocryphal among the other comic artists. He had been known to tear up a thousand-dollar check because the rate per page was less than he had been promised. Now he was working for King Features, drawing the syndicated science fiction comic strip *Flash Gordon*. I knew about this because an old friend in New York, Larry Shaw, had written scripts for Dan for a while. Since Larry was no longer doing this I felt free to apply for the job.

I wrote to Dan. I was still not entranced with comics and had absolutely no desire to stay in the comic business forever—but my family had to eat. I pointed out the fact that I was an ex-comic artist who had not only drawn the stuff but had written a mountain of scripts. I was also a selling SF author. And where else would he find this combination in Europe?

Dan's reply was instant and firm: write some scripts. This was the beginning of a mutually profitable relationship that continued for ten years. For all those long years I wrote all the daily and Sunday scripts for *Flash Gordon*. The payment wasn't much, but it was tax free and enough to pay most of our daily living expenses.

I was just getting started on my first scripts for Dan when one wet and rainy night there was a knock at the door: there at last was Garry Davis, carrying a folding rubber boat.

Joan made coffee, I poured some wine, and he told us the latest chapter in his war against the evils of nationalism. The French would not honor his World Passport and French authorities had kicked him out of the country, pushed him onto the bridge on the Côte d'Azur that connects France to Italy. The only problem was that, without a passport they recognized, the Italians would not let him in. So, for some days, he had camped on the bridge in no-man's-land, a modern-day man without a country. Sympathizers brought him food, but this was a no-win situation. It persisted until a more practical world citizen brought him a folding rubber boat and a bicycle pump. In the dark of night they had launched Garry into the ocean and he had paddled to Italy. He had deflated the boat, boarded the train, gone on to Naples. There he had taken the ferry, found out where we were staying, then arrived at our door.

But not for long—there were no secrets in Anacapri. He had visited Violet Rawnsley and the word was soon out. A few days later we were visited by the marshall of the police, a polite but very firm man. We translated his ultimatum. Garry had a few days to rest up, but at the end of that time he would be arrested and taken to the prison camp in Frascati just north of Rome. There was no choice. We thanked the *maresciallo* and very soon said good-bye to Garry yet another time. The rubber boat was confiscated.

This adventure had an interesting finale, which we heard about some months later when Garry wrote to us from New York. It appears that the prison of Frascati was a former German concentration camp—scarcely changed since its Nazi days. The rusting barbed wire was still in place, the accommodation miserable and unheated, the food slop. It was filled with displaced people, passportless men from all over Europe. These poor creatures had to suffer this imprisonment, unable to appeal, their sentences unending. They had no hope, no future, their world bleak, uncomfortable, and hopeless.

For six days a week, that is. The Italians, with very Italian logic, allowed them out for the day every Sunday. The result was obvious. As soon as a prisoner had enough of the camp, enough of Italy, he would escape and cross the Italian border and would become somebody else's problem, a very Italian answer to a solutionless problem. Garry wrote to his father, who was very rich. Meyer Davis controlled all the East Coast society dance bands. Meyer sent Garry a ticket for a ship bound from Naples to New York. Garry made a daring escape from the concentration camp and went home.

I was now writing the *Flash Gordon* scripts and Dan himself had rented the vacant apartment above us in Il Nido. After an almost vegetarian six months, meat was beginning to sneak back into our diet. Once a week, before Dan arrived, we would buy an *etto* of hamburger meat, one hundred grams—about three ounces—and Joan would make spaghetti bolognese with it. Dan enjoyed her home cooking and grew nostalgic for the food we had all left behind. Europe had never heard of the hamburger then—though an incredibly greasy and disgusting burger called a Wimpy was on sale in Britain. Why didn't we have a big American hamburger fest! Dan would pay for the meat if Joan would cook it. Right on! Next day I bought *quatro etti,* four hundred grams of hamburger meat, almost a pound in all. The butcher was most cheerful as he wrapped it. "You must be happy to be entertaining," he said, suddenly seeing me as possibly a big-time spender. "Family or friends? They surely must be a dozen at least."

He had never heard of a hamburger. All he saw was an even bigger bowl of pasta with bolognese sauce.

Friends had been so easy to make. Like Franco, who worked at the customer window in the post office. We talked a great deal while he was leisurely putting stamps on my mail. He was from the Abruzzi, as alien to me as my New York origins were to him. We talked home and family. Then tragedy loomed. An uncle was visiting from America, a bishop no less, who had to be entertained— but no one in his Anacaprese family spoke English. So Joan and I were drafted as translators and were quite happy to join the family for a meal at Gracie Fields's restaurant in Capri. A pleasant hostess, a pleasant meal, a pleasant bishop who enjoyed meeting his relatives, though unhappily, none spoke English. Not your usual evening with your friendly post office clerk.

I'm happy to report that the evening went very well—and Uncle Bishop proved to be a most charming and interesting man. He was kind enough to thank us for our aid; this was the first time that he'd had a chance to talk to his Italian relatives.

Since there was no private place in Il Nido for me to write I had rented a room above a shoe shop on the *zocalo,* the town square. The shop belonged to Ernesto, a most genial man, who quietly ignored his bad leg that gave him a severe limp. We grew into the habit of lunching together in front of his shop. I usually bought a piece of Edam cheese, *formaggio holandesa,* from the *salumeria;* I had that and a handful of olives. We sat in the sun and discussed the new pope, the American Seventh Fleet, and other topics of current interest. This did wonders for my Italian. When I told Joan about my growing friendship she instantly invited Ernesto to dinner. Instead of flowers he most graciously brought her a pair of his handmade shoes.

We even made friends with the chef in the local pizzeria, though I doubt if we ate there a half dozen times in the year. Todd's blond hair always broke the ice; there were of course no Anacaprese blondes. The chef's wife appeared from the kitchen, complete with young daughter; she and Joan talked family while I talked pizza with the chef. He had some dried red chili peppers hanging beside the oven, mostly for show. Since American pizza is always accompanied by crushed red pepper he cheerfully diced one for me. On all future visits he waved when we entered, and reached for a hot pepper.

Even in the summer of 1958 when the restaurant was filled with tourists, the red pepper was chopped even before we had sat down and opened the menu to discover that prices had trebled for the short tourist season. We smiled boldly, but a glimpse of worry on Joan's face echoed mine. I hoped I had enough money with me to pay the bill. We ate well as always, enjoyed the gossip—and I tried to smile when the waiter brought the bill. Then I really did smile. "Family prices—not tourist!" I told Joan. My pizza was one hundred lira, sixteen cents, the winter rate. With all of the other dishes priced to match. It would be hard to leave this island, yet it had to be done.

10

Despite all the pleasures of Capri it was time to leave, but leaving
would not be easy. Yes, we had very good reasons to return to New
York, but leaving the life we had built up in Anacapri would be
difficult—since we had no idea when, if ever, we would return. It
had been a very good year—well, not really. It had been a year with
some horrendous ups and downs. Too many downs at times, but it
had all worked out in the end. Would we have stayed in Italy? Perhaps if things had been different; certainly we were quite happy
there. It is hard to say—since other pressures were building.

First, health. Joan was pregnant, which was a good and happy
thing, but she had some health problems that the Italian doctor
could not track down, which meant we needed a better doctor,
which in turn meant either going to Switzerland—or back to the
States. Neither of us had any particular desire to return to New York
at this time, but there was another factor

My agent. He had been a good enough agent in New York, han-
dling my submissions and sales—which was really not the world's
toughest assignment. Apparently it was for him now. He never answered letters and never sent checks. I was sitting at the very end of a
long, thin branch that stretched from New York to Anacapri and he
was sawing the branch off. Outside of *Flash Gordon* I was writing
for only two specific markets, SF and men's adventures.

Most important to me was science fiction. Any story that I wrote
was submitted first to John W. Campbell and *Astounding,* which
by this time paid a massive three cents a word. If John didn't buy
the story and returned it—then the agent had only to consult a

submission list that I had prepared for him, with all the SF magazines listed in descending order of price per word. Any returned story should have been submitted to the next market on the list. Apparently said agent could not rise to the challenge of submitting stories in this manner. There was no news—and no money. While SF was important to me personally, as a writer, just as important—or more so—was staying alive. Before anything else I had to see that the family was fed and clothed. To do this I had relied quite heavily on the men's adventure magazines. I was not thrilled to write these bits of fiction parading as fact but they were easy enough to grind out and they did pay the rent. I had prepared for my agent a similar submitting schedule for this market. Best-paying ones at the top were up to $250 or even $500 in some cases (rare cases). What I really counted on were the salvage markets, which averaged around $75. These were dreary, badly printed magazines that nevertheless had to fill each issue. My copy was far better than most of the articles they contained so I could count on, eventually, selling everything that I wrote.

One would think that this kind of agenting was not very hard to do. You put the story in the envelope with a covering note, slip in a stamped return envelope, seal it, then drop it into the mailbox. Either the story or article would come back—to be submitted to the next magazine on the list—or in case of a sale a check would arrive. Deduct 10 percent and mail a check for the balance to the happy author. The sort of thing that anyone with an IQ over fifty-five could do; hard to screw up. My then-agent did. With my life, future, and career in his hands he managed to get everything wrong. He did not answer letters. He sold nothing that I knew of, for no money was arriving. So this became the deciding factor. Get to New York and find a doctor for Joan and fire the agent while resisting the impulse to beat him to death.

So it was across the Atlantic for a second time, but now there was no friendly Dave Kyle or cheaper-than-cheap fan flight. So how were we to get back to New York from the middle of Italy? Plane travel was still a novel—and very expensive—form of travel.

"We go by ship," Joan said. "There must be ocean liners that sail between Italy and New York. After all—Garry went back that way." I nodded agreement, although neither of us had ever traveled on anything bigger than the Staten Island Ferry. This meant a trip into Naples, which was a full day's adventure in itself. I had to rise at dawn, shave quietly, then sneak out without waking Joan or Todd. Then the two-kilometer walk up the hill to the bus stop in Anacapri. Over the hill to Capri and another bus—or walk if there were time—down the hill to the harbor of Marina Grande where the ferry left for Naples, an ancient diesel that putt-putted majestically across the bay. It took all of an hour and a half to sail the eighteen miles. I had done the trip before, going to American Express to cash checks or more often to the Monte de Piedad, the religious hock shop, to pop my camera or Joan's gold bracelet.

This time I hoofed it around the city looking for a travel agent, stopping only when hunger struck, to dine at one of the outdoor stalls near the American embassy. They served an incredibly delicious bowl of *pasta e fagiolli,* a peasant soup of vegetables, beans, and macaroni, thick enough to walk on, with crusty brown bread and a glass of red wine. It was 150 lire for everything; twenty-four cents American. There were still some compensations in life.

Selection of a ship would be determined by the price of the tickets; at this time money was basically our main consideration. There was little cash available—it was now a year since we had flown the Atlantic and my total income had been three thousand dollars for the entire period since we arrived in Europe. When I read this I realize how faulty my literary research had been before we left New York. I had read with relish Hemingway's memoirs, his and those of all the other authors and artists who had moved to Paris after the Great War. What joy! What freedom! Even my painting teacher, John Blomshield, had told us stories about the glorious days in France. But he, like the others who wrote about the period, never supplied much detail about how they found the money to stay alive on some alien shore. I knew they had done it, but did not know how they had done it. So I had to improvise, as I have written here.

Much time would pass before I discovered the truth; perhaps it was better that I had not known it at the time or I would not have put myself and my family at such risk. I got by, barely, on my own terms. It was years later that I found out why the American expatriates in Paris had not worried about money—they had brought it with them.

But now it was time to return to the States. I did a quick survey of the prices and it was a very easy decision to take the cheapest crossing on offer. We were to travel with the Home Line—which had a lot going for it. It was a Greek company, which meant that they were well crewed and prices were well squeezed by the owners, and it had an Italian kitchen, really Neapolitan, which meant we would eat happily in a manner to which we had quickly become accustomed. The ship itself had been American, originally the *Matsonia,* so there was a good chance we wouldn't sink.

I booked passage for three, two and a half really, on the next sailing, which would be in October. The first ferry of the day from Capri would not reach Naples until our ship had sailed. This meant an overnight stay in an inexpensive hotel. We said good-bye to our Italian friends, with some tearful farewells, and I promised Dan that I would write more scripts soon, and we were off. The hotel in Naples was old but clean. We had a meal out, and retired early. Everything went very smoothly until after we had checked out and I put our bags into the cab in the morning. I reached into the inside pocket of my jacket for the wallet that held our tickets and passport. It was gone. Naples, city of thieves, they had done it. This was it, the end, finito. This was undoubtedly the lowest moment that I had ever experienced in a life that, face it, had contained some really low moments. I was barely aware that Joan was talking. "The room. Maybe you left it in the room?" A chance, anything. It took some furious and heated argument to get the key back from the front desk. I hurried to the room, looked in all of the drawers, behind the bed, nothing. My jacket had been on the back of the armchair—could the wallet have dropped out? I bent and looked— and saw it lying in the shadows behind the chair. The sense of relief drained the tension and energy from me and I collapsed, sprawled full length on the rug. I stretched my fingers out and re- trieved it. Everything was there; it was all going to be okay.

The ride to the dock, the boarding, finding the cabin, all of this passed in a haze of relief. We left the bags on the bed and hurried on deck because she would sail soon and Todd certainly had to see the entire technical process of getting under way. It was only when we made our way to the rail that we realized that we were living in the middle of a scene from a real-life Italian opera. A band was on deck playing off-key and lachrymose Italian songs. People were struggling up the gangway, holding on to each other, reaching out, crying openly.

What was happening in front of us must be placed correctly in time. Remember, this all took place in the days before travel be- came commonplace and cheap. It was certainly an extraordinary once-in-a-lifetime occasion for our fellow passengers. It was obvi- ous by their clothes that the people boarding were working-class Italians, not very young, gray-haired for the most part. There were even grayer, older people in the crowd below.

This was Italian reality, the raw material for an Italian opera. Those boarding the ship must be immigrants who had left for the New World well before the war. They had worked hard, saved what they could, and had returned for a once-in-a-lifetime visit to the families and relatives they had left behind. But the joy of their visit had now turned to sadness, even despair. It would be years before they could return again—if ever. They were looking at aunts, un- cles, cousins, whom they would probably never see again. This was a final parting, an anguished and permanent separation. Some of the black-garbed women on the shore clung desperately to parting relatives. They had to be physically separated from their loved ones. Oh, how they wept. No wonder they were weeping. The band played tender, sad songs and I realized that Joan was crying as well. Who could blame her if she found it impossible to stay dry-eyed at this moment? I blinked at my own tears. Only Todd unreservedly enjoyed the scene.

People waved and called out as the gangway was pulled up, the moorings cast off, the ship pulled slowly away from the dock. And as the ship slowly moved along the length of the dock the people below ran alongside, waving and crying, until they had reached the very end, where they massed together, plump, elderly women in dark dresses for the most part. It was almost too painful to bear, the dock getting smaller and smaller behind us and the waving crowded mass slowly vanishing from sight. Joan went below to unpack and I stayed on deck for a time with Todd, who was greatly enjoying the mechanics of our seagoing adventure.

Our departure may have been an unhappy one for many of the passengers, but it was a holiday for us. It proved to be a delightful voyage—as long as we were in the Mediterranean. We had glimpses of the first-class dining room as we passed and we were not impressed. Our second-class one was far superior, with a carafe each of white and red wine on every table, part of the meal of course, and a real Neapolitan kitchen. The food was varied and wonderful, our eight Italian companions at the large round table friendly and talkative. Once the tragic parting was behind them they remembered the joys of their visit and we did as well.

We stopped for a few hours in Barcelona. I found a post office, where I took the *Flash Gordon* scripts that I had written since we had sailed and mailed them to Dan in Capri, with just enough time to gawk at the mad Chirraresque cathedral, then back to the ship. We left behind the calm Med at Gibraltar and sailed on into the overwhelming discomforts of the stormy autumn Atlantic.

We were seven days crossing from Barcelona, the storms and heavy seas bringing misery right up until the very last day. Seasickness struck down our table companions, one by one, until we had the table almost to ourselves at meals. Todd and I were zonked on Dramamine so we could function; Joan has never been seasick in her life and one can only admire that with awe. Our one surviving tablemate was an Italian seaman who was totally indifferent to the rough seas.

Not so his wife, who stayed below in her bunk until the storm had blown itself out. Finally, days later when the rolling had almost stopped, wan and pale and wrapped in her dressing gown, she appeared and took her chair. The waiters, happy at last to see their customers returning, loaded the table with food. She grew paler— nor was her husband, the hearty sailor, of any help in her misery.

"Mangia!" he said enthusiastically, reaching for the heaped bowl of spaghetti. "Eat!"

"Una mele," she begged. An apple, just an apple.

"Mangia!" was his hearty response as he heaped pasta on her plate. *"Mangia!"* She stared with saucer eyes, and as every dollop of spaghetti hit the plate her skin grew paler and cold sweat broke out. With a weak cry she fled and her husband stared uncomprehendingly after her. We put our attention on our plates and made no attempt to explain to our friendly co-passenger what he had done. Since then, with good reason, the cry of *"Mangia!"* has become a family password.

The weather grew better, which we hoped was a good omen. Our fellow passengers appeared at the dinner table—speaking English again: Italy unhappily left behind. The good weather continued and the sun was shining clearly through the smog when we entered New York Harbor. Well over a year since we had left. We were two hours late docking and, when we emerged from customs, we were delighted to see the round figure of Avram Davidson, who had been patiently waiting for us all day. If the delay had disturbed him he was too much the gentleman to admit it. He had a book to read and had brought us a hot pastrami sandwich, now cold, as a welcome-home present. It was wonderful.

We were back in New York. There were very important things

to do, such as find a doctor for Joan at once, and pay a visit to the agent to cheerfully cut his throat or something. And after that? We had absolutely no idea. First things first and then we would decide. Our health worries vanished after Joan's first visit to the doctor. She was anemic, and iron tablets took care of that. It was one of the most commonplace complications of pregnancy—and the Italian doctor hadn't recognized it? We took a silent oath never to be ill again in Italy.

We stayed with Joan's parents in Long Beach while we looked for a furnished apartment. There proved to be plenty of them about, and very cheap too since the holidaymakers were long gone and the cold, green Atlantic was already pounding the beaches. We had to sign a contract agreeing to leave by May first or pay a thousand dollars a week rent, which was a simple way of assuring that the apartments were available for well-heeled vacationers when the summer season started.

The literary agent question resolved itself simply. When I went to see him I realized, a little belatedly, that he was both incompetent and stupid and not worth venting my ire on, a pleasure to fire and forget. I remembered what Conrad had written in *Nostromo* about a certain villainous character. "Let him live, for he is his own damnation." As long as I was in New York I wouldn't need an agent, but I would have to find one before we left the city.

And the science fiction novel was still there. Never forgotten; looked at—but put aside far too often while I did the bread-and-butter work. I was still grinding out comic scripts for Fleetway in London, and of course *Flash Gordon* scripts for Dan. I polished off the current assignments as quickly as I could and did another chunk of my novel, *Deathworld.* I was perhaps three-quarters of the way to the end by this time, but was still very insecure about this, my first novel. I sent what I had written so far to John Campbell, editor of *Astounding,* who summoned me to his office.

He was not pleased. He had assumed that after all this time I had sent in the complete novel. He wanted it done, through, finished as soon as possible. I left his office sweating and knew that the time for completion was to hand. Or else. But other equally important—or far more important—events were happening. On January 9, 1959, Joan woke me a little past midnight. I blinked rapidly when I saw that she had her coat on. "I've timed the contractions," she said, "and they are now two minutes apart. I've called the cab and it's on the way."

At last a hospital visit with some good results! Moira was born later that night, and has blessed us with her presence since that day. She is now Dr. Harrison and teaches diabetes to pharmacy and medical students and carries out research into Type 1 diabetes at the University of Brighton, UK. Todd works for a gas ana- lyzer company in California. We have always been proud of our children—with very good reason.

I had finished writing the book. John Campbell had had the *Deathworld* manuscript for what felt like a very long time— though it was only a matter of some days. All the other copy I had submitted to him had been done through an agent. So I had no idea at all how long he took to report, or what I should do if the delay stretched out much longer. The tension was beginning to get to me. I tried to work ahead on the *Flash Gordon* scripts but couldn't concentrate. Then the letter came. Street & Smith Publications was the return address. Why was my hand shaking? Because it was a letter of rejection? What else could it be? I tore open the envelope, which proved to contain no letter at all, just a check, made out to me, for the sum of $2,100.

John was certainly parsimonious with words once he had ex- tracted what he wanted from a writer. But what could a covering letter say that the check didn't? Seventy thousand words at three cents a word. Two thousand, one hundred dollars. An incredible sum considering the fact that I had earned very little more than that during the entire previous year. We had money ahead for the first time in our life, real money. We could plan our future and not stumble on from circumstance to circumstance. And I was almost a novelist. I had sold the serial rights to my first novel, to the most prestigious and important magazine in science fiction. For once everything was coming together perfectly.

"We can go back to Europe now," I said.

"I would like to live in Levittown," Joan answered.

We had been to Levittown to see Ed and Carol Emshwiller. He was the top artist in SF, she a fine new SF writer. They had children—and they were both creative artists while living in the comforts of suburbia. So why couldn't we? If not Levittown on Long Island, then why not Levittown, Arizona? These were tracts of inexpensive and attractive houses built mostly for returning GIs. That excellent writer Cyril Kornbluth had lived in one and died of a heart attack while running for a commuter train. There were both good and bad things to be said about them.

I could fully understand how Joan felt. At times it was not easy schlepping around the world with an infant. And now we had two children, which made life that much more complicated. Distant countries did not compare well with a clean modern house, a garden for them to play in, the English language, nearby schools and friends. It certainly looked attractive.

I hated to even think about it. We had made the big move, escaped the clammy clutch of suburbia and middle-class existence. The thoughts of returning to them made me break out in a cold sweat. I had to make Joan understand. Having lived in that big and fascinating world out there I could not bear the thought of sinking again beneath the surface of this society I had known all my life. Far fields were still hideously attractive. We were at loggerheads. We both knew exactly what we wanted to do and why. Except that for the very first time our needs and desires were diametrically opposed.

Details of married arguments are bitter at the time and distasteful to recall. But I must mention the ending of this one, because it has to go on the record.

We couldn't compromise. I couldn't make her understand what

Levittown would do to me. My anger was rising. Once in school, and later in the army, I had been so angered by a situation that I had blacked out with rage. For just the third time in my life over- whelming anger washed out intelligence and I raised my fist. But, furious as I was, I could not hit a woman, especially my wife, lying tiny and pale on the bed. It wasn't a conscious thought. But this kind of rage needs an outlet so I twisted about and slammed my fist into the closet door, with sobering results. I had punched right through the thin wood. I pulled my hand out and saw that my little finger was hanging down; I had broken it when I struck. Laughable by hindsight—shocking at the time, in context.

This is when Joan made one of the major decisions that affected our lives. My actions had delivered a message that logic and rea- soning had not. The gravity of my feelings was more than obvious. "Of course we'll go back to Europe," she said calmly. "I didn't realize you felt so strongly about it."

Our traditional sexual roles had been reversed; man the logical, woman the emotional. It was I who had exploded with uncontrol- lable anger when logic no longer worked. While it was Joan, whose perceptions of emotions were far more understanding than mine, who had seen clearly how I felt. She had her desires and needs, but at that moment she put them second place to mine. When I saw the doctor I discovered that the little finger is too small to splint by it- self. It was taped to the ring finger, then all my fingers immobi- lized in plaster in a sort of curved hook shape, very handy for picking up boxes when we packed.

We made our plans in private. Parental lamentations would be great when we announced we were leaving for a third time. But where should we go? Not back to Mexico, certainly. Not with the endemic malaria and a small baby. England? Memories of smog and cold still bit deep. Italy? Thank you, no. After Joan's experi- ences with the medical profession there we were not going to sub- ject an infant to their ministrations. By happy coincidence I was still in touch with Preben Zahle in Denmark, and a visit to the travel agency revealed the fact that the only nonstop flight to Europe was SAS to Copenhagen. Why not? I had sold articles to a magazine there and Preben would help us find a place to stay. We would take the Anglia car out of storage and ship it by sea; it would arrive a month after we did. By which time we would have made plans to move on, stay, or whatever. It seemed a sound and logical plan.

Of course seeing it typed out like this, half a century later, it carries more than a whiff of utter madness. How could we have thought we were being logical and practical? Flying off to an unknown country where they spoke an unknown language, with a few hundred dollars and two tiny children? Why hadn't Joan forced me to go to Levittown? There are some questions that can possibly never be answered. Except to say, yet again, that it seemed like a good idea at the time.

Under a cloud of double-barreled parental guilt and scathing recriminations, we boarded the SAS plane for Denmark. One half of the *Astounding* money had purchased our tickets. We sat three in a row in tourist class with four-month-old Moira asleep in the bassinet mounted on the bulkhead before us. Todd, a seasoned transatlantic traveler by the age of two, stayed glued to the window.

It was the summer of 1959 and Copenhagen was warm and sunny. Our room in the Pension Gotha was comfortable and charming and the city fascinating. If we could find any fault at all it was the almost perpetual daylight. The sun moved slowly across a cloudless sky then most reluctantly dropped behind the horizon close to midnight, shuffled along below the twilight horizon, only to pop up again about two A.M. One needed heavy curtains to get any sleep. We rented a car and explored the green countryside that began at the city's gate. Everything we saw we liked, and by the time the Anglia arrived we had determined to stay here for a while. We had found a house to rent and moved in.

We might have reacted differently if we had known that this was the warmest summer in Danish history. Across from the Pension Gotha was the Botanisk Have, the botanical gardens and museum. Deep in the museum's multilayered depths were storerooms. Including one containing bulbs brought back to Scandinavia by Linnaeus himself in 1730. For the first time since they had been placed there, centuries earlier, warmth had penetrated to the cool chamber and these bulbs had germinated. We were too uninformed to get this message. We thought every Scandinavian summer would be like this!

By the time autumn and the first chill nights arrived we were settled in and had no desire to move. Modern and sprightly, Denmark really was the human paradise that Britain and the States aimed at. Clean, organized, socially responsible. The schools were incredibly good and the socialized medical system human and reliable. In America we have been brainwashed to believe that socialized medicine is creeping communism. In reality this is just big pharma and medical business propagandizing us in order to continue with their incredibly expensive private health insurance profits. But socialized medicine really works—and works quite well. We, as consumers, were more than pleased. As foreigners we had to pay something toward the universal health insurance—but just a few hundred dollars a year. After that everything was free. Prescriptions had to be paid for but half the sum was returned and government control meant that medicine was fairly priced. The doctors and nurses were well paid and enjoyed the work. We were beginning to realize how lucky we were, that the workings of chance had brought us to a country where we could raise the children in safety and comfort.

And I was now a novelist. My new agent, Bob Mills, had sold *Deathworld* to Bantam Books for the then astonishing sum of $2,500. I was financially secure for the first time in my life, as well as emotionally secure, savoring the fact that I could write, in fact had written, a salable novel. It was time to get back to work. I started my second novel.

11

Our first house in Denmark was newly built in Bistrup, a suburb of Birkerød. This was a dormitory town for Copenhagen, which was some twelve miles away. We were at number 10 Bregnebakken. *Bregne* means fern in Danish, and a *bakke* is a hill. Bregnebakken was dead flat; but "the fern-hill" still had a romantic sound. As we began to settle in we started to learn more about the culture in which we were being immersed.

I wouldn't say that the Danes are the direct opposite of the Mexicans—but they sure came very close. One northern, the other subtropical; a Germanic language, a Latin language; one very organized, the other very laid-back. Take the Bistrup sidewalks—or lack of them. Since this part of Bistrup was newly developed, with houses still being built, there were no sidewalks. Or rather there was a gravel-covered path that was separated from the paved road by a row of cobblestones set on end. This made good sense since all the utilities, water pipes, sewers, gas, and electricity were laid under the gravel path, which meant that the paved road was never dug up to make utility connections to a new house. In the fullness of time, when all the houses had been built and utilities connected, the gravel would be replaced by preformed concrete slabs. If, at some later date, some of these pipes needed attention, the road would still not be torn up. The slabs would be lifted aside and repairs done. Nothing could be simpler or more practical.

And all the gravel looked quite attractive, smooth, and neat. Except in front of number 10, where it was bumped and pitted. I assumed that the city took care of this sort of thing until I noticed that all the householders were raking their gravel smooth every day, voluntarily. Not a bad idea; I would have to get a rake pretty soon and take care of my stretch of gravel. I put the day off until a scratching woke me up one morning just after dawn. Our neighbor, Herre Larsen, had raked his patch smooth then had done mine as well. I bought a rake the same day.

The Danes like to be organized and exact great satisfaction from doing everything the same way. This was proven a short time later when I made a new number for the house. The small brass 10 on the front door was very hard to see from the road. Coming back one evening from the post I passed a pile of the brick-shaped granite cobblestones that were put into place to separate the gravel path from the road. I had learned all about moonlight requisitioning in the army. The moon was indeed up, no one in sight; one of the stones made its way to my garage. We had some blue paint left over from decorating the kitchen. I painted the face of the stone blue, and when it was dry painted a neat 10 on it in white. I buried this at a thirty-degree viewing angle in the grass next to the gravel sidewalk-to-be. Now visitors could find our house.

Not only ours—but they could find everyone else's house as well. Within a month most of the houses on Bregnebakken had a half-sunk cobblestone with a number on it prominent in their front gardens, undoubtedly obtained from the same supplier that I had used. What I found most appealing was the fact that they were all sunk into the grass at a thirty-degree angle—and had white numbers against a blue background. The same color as our kitchen walls. The Danes are a very, very organized people.

I pointed this out to a reporter from a Copenhagen newspaper who interviewed me for an article. There were very few foreigners living in Denmark in 1959 and they found the idea of an American author immersing himself in their economy and culture most interesting. I was queried at length about national differences and, as an example, I mentioned that when the lunch hour whistle blew in an American factory everyone downed tools and left. But from our pension window when we were in Copenhagen I had watched two tall cranes that were working on a new building. At quitting time the crane operators, instead of simply turning the things off and leaving them, took the time to line the cranes up end to end so that they formed a straight line. I found this quaint and amusing and the reporter wrote it all down.

The article duly appeared and a friend translated it for me. The American factory and the Danish cranes were there. But the slightly smug conclusion was: look how much better at organizing things the Danes are. Not like the lazy Americans. I was beginning to like the Danes.

All of the Danes seemed to speak English—but we were determined to learn the language. A retired translator was happy to tutor us at home. Although she was Danish, she had worked for the war crimes trials doing simultaneous translation between German and English. She had a nice linguistic story from the trials when she was translating for a colonel in the judge advocates department who had previously been a judge in the American South. During the trial he queried her.

"Ma'am, you seem to be having some difficulties there. I note that you begin to say something—then change your mind."

"I'm very sorry, Your Honor. You see, in German the verbs come at the very end of the sentence and I sometimes have to guess what is coming in a long sentence. I'm sorry if I guess wrong."

"Not your fault at all, ma'am. I understand. Now you just tell these Germans to put their verbs in the middle of the sentence just like the rest of us do."

It was time to get back to work. I had sold John Campbell a short story entitled "The Stainless Steel Rat." It had been fun to do, the villain as hero, what Kingsley Amis had called a picaresque hero. Cheered by the feedback I wrote a sequel, "The Misplaced Battleship," which John also bought. But the character of the Rat himself, Jim diGriz, would not lie down. I adapted and expanded the two short stories into a novel, also called *The Stain-*

less Steel Rat. I sent it off to Bob Mills, who duly sold it to Pyramid for fifteen hundred dollars. A financial step backward from Bantam—but a sale was a sale.

We were making friends—and so was Todd. Muriel Overgaard was English and married to a Danish marine engineer. She and Joan became the best of friends. The Overgaards' three sons spoke English at home and Danish outside of it. Thomas was just Todd's age and they became very close. Todd listened to all the Danish around him, but spoke only English. Although when he talked with Thomas we heard more and more Danish words getting mixed in. Within six months he was talking Danish as well as the other children—with a North Zealand accent just like theirs.

The money wasn't exactly rolling in, but we kept our heads above the water. The Anglia worked as well in the snows of Denmark as it had in the deserts of Mexico—though it needed a little TLC. A blanket over the hood at night kept in the heat from the kerosene heater under the sump. A few turns of the hand crank in the morning, to loosen the oil, and away it went.

And I was still writing *Flash Gordon* strips (I did the daily and Sunday scripts for ten very long years) which meant that I could turn my back on the men's adventure and confession magazines and be a full-time science fiction writer. Probably only the second one in the world at these pre-boom times; Bob Heinlein was the other. (Every other SF writer edited, taught school, worked at some other job—or lived off his wife.) The money from the *Flash Gordon* scripts was just about enough to pay the rent, plus a bit of the food bill. It took me about three months to write a year's worth of scripts; which meant I had nine months annually to write SF. Dan Barry and I kept in touch by mail and in person when it could be arranged. He had left Capri not long after us, had upgraded his Škoda for a Mercedes, and Kitzbühel was the proper place for him. He drove to Denmark for a visit; we stopped off in Kitzbühel on the way to Italy in the summer.

Looking back through the telescope of time I am amazed at the amount of work I got done—and the busy life we led on what was a very small income. Of course we spent every cent as it came in. Americans living abroad were exempt from United States income tax up to some impossible figure like fifty thousand dollars a year. If I made five thousand it was a good year. I developed a specialty of avoiding excessive income tax and, best of all, the dollar was strong in those days. We went to Italy in the summer; I took the typewriter and banged out my *Flash Gordon* scripts. We even managed some skiing trips to Norway in the winter. We traveled overnight on the ferry from Copenhagen, the four of us in a compartment well below the waterline with ice floes banging along the hull outside as we made our way up the fjord to Oslo. Then we took the train to Lillehammer or Donbos and seven nights there, with full room and board. A week later we took the ferry home. Today's skiers will see a lot of dollar signs rolling by when they estimate the cost of this trip. In the early '60s it was one hundred dollars, all-in, for an adult, including ferry, train, hotel, and meals. Half price for children, or three hundred dollars for a family's weeklong skiing holiday.

We made one trip to Lillehammer at Christmastime on a Christmas Special that was really fun. Santa came in a horse-drawn sleigh with gifts for all the kids. The ski instructors took care of all ages. Moira was just starting to learn with miniskis—like all the others in her class. And no ski poles! Eye-poking was out. And I did admire the young instructor's sorting-out technique. When one of them fell—not far to go!—she would grab them by the back of the collar—then lift and shake. Eventually skis, arms, and legs came right and she put the ski-let back on the ground.

Every room was taken, every table full with a mixed clientele of Norwegians and Danes. After hundreds of years of Danish occupation Norwegian sounds very much like Danish. So we all talked away in our own language and had a wonderful time.

To complete the international scene the waitresses were English, student nurses hired in to fill the seasonal gap. All went well with these international arrangements until one evening in the middle of dinner. The nurses were talking to each other—and the last thing they were expecting to find was a bilingual four-year-old. They talked in English about the evening meal and they were overheard. A moment later a terrible cry of pain went up—

"Jeg vil ikke spise Bambi!"

I won't eat Bambi!

A moment later and a concerted cry of agony went up from the united non–Bambi eaters. There were parental pleadings, the thud of an occasional blow. We shrunk in our seats. Eventually the screams died down and peace was restored but it was definitely our daughter's day.

In addition to all the fun and games there was the work—and I was writing like fury. Only SF now, and selling everything that I wrote. A novel every year, hopefully serial rights sold to John W. Campbell before book rights. My third novel was serialized as *Sense of Obligation* in *Astounding* in 1963, and a year later by Bantam with a jazzier title, *Planet of the Damned.* In those days not only didn't the author have the right to pick the title of a book—but many times never knew the title until the book was published.

Deathworld had worked very well and a companion volume with the same cast of characters seemed very much in order. I wrote it at the usual sixty thousand words—to be broken into a three-part serial. John bought it and titled it *The Ethical Engineer.* I was happy indeed when Bantam bought the paperback rights and, after much suffering, and first considering bringing it out as *Planet of the Slaves,* they published it as *Deathworld 2. Deathworld 3* was written and sold on the same terms. All four of these first novels—the Rat book and the Deathworlds—were fast-paced, futuristic action adventures.

I even did a bit of ghostwriting. Hans Stefan Santesson made me an offer I did not want to refuse. He was editor of *The Saint* magazine and they were inaugurating a new department. "We're going to start reviewing new detective novels. Are you interested in writing the reviews under Leslie's name?" I surely was. A regular supply of new thrillers to read, a short review of the good ones under Leslie Charteris's name, a small check to cash. Plus a smaller check from a bookseller who bought the still-mint book.

I had ghostwritten plenty of fiction—and nonfiction—so was no stranger to this kind of supernatural writing. Writing the reviews was fun and my work with Leslie expanded. There was also a syndicated Saint comic strip and, considering my comic background, I began writing the scripts as well. The stories were quite long, up to twelve weeks, just about enough plot and action for a complete novel. I soon discovered the open secret that a French translator was expanding each comic story to novel length, in French.

This relationship continued for a number of years—until the syndicate killed the strip. Leslie—with good reason—was grumpy over the decision. I agreed with the syndicate—although I did not say so out loud. The stories were just too long to keep the comics readers' attention. Leslie and his wife, Audrey, were living in Windsor Great Park at the time. When I visited London on business he invited me for dinner at a very good restaurant in nearby Maidenhead. (He was ever a good host—and always picked up the tab.)

We had been working ahead on the comic and an outline for the next adventure was well plotted out. With the comic strip dead it would be a shame if all this work went to waste. It was then that Leslie asked me if I could write a Saint novel from the plot—in English!—to ghostwrite a novel for him. This took some thinking about. I had ghosted a lot of things in the past—but never a novel. It was something new for me, if not for Leslie, since the last Saint novels had been ghostwritten. It would be cash-on-the-line and no credit for the writing given.

I talked to Joan about it and we soon nodded in agreement. We could use the cash—and I had plenty of writing credits for my SF novels now getting into print. Thus began *Vendetta for the Saint*. My debut mystery novel; always start at the top, I say. And it really was fun to do. I bought all the Saint books I could find and had a massive read-in. Leslie wrote simple, declarative prose, which would be no problem to emulate. Nor did he tend toward the purple—which would be a pleasure after my labors at the galley oars of confessions. And I could use the same descriptive phrases: the Saint's "teak fist" and "teak brown fist" did manage to mash many a villain's jaw. He was a good, solid commercial writer and a ghost job should present no problems.

Thankfully his politics did not have to be dealt with, because his firm stance was somewhere to the right of Genghis Khan. My faded liberal beliefs presented the worst kind of commie liberal— which he often told me I was. Leslie did not like Italy or things Italian; I had lived there and loved the place, which worked out fine. The Saint was a great traveler so this Italian trip filled in a possible gap.

Writing a book—particularly a ghosted book—is not easy. Problems in story come up which entail story conferences. This was always fun with Leslie, since they involved meeting at a new restaurant each time. There were gustatory failures—Leslie had heard that a new hotel at Heathrow Airport had an excellent restaurant. We went, we ate: it was terrible. And it was always a pleasure hearing Leslie telling the manager just what was wrong with the meal. He was a good cook, wrote a restaurant column, and really knew his beans. As recompense later in the week we went to the carvery at the Piccadilly Hotel in London, which proved an excellent feast.

Our working relationship lasted a good many years and covered many countries. Circumstance found us both in New York City in 1965 when the World's Fair opened there. There was a brand-new Thai restaurant that Leslie had to try out; Joan and I joined them. It was very ethnic with clanking gamelan music in the background, the waiters all wearing Thai longyis. An aperitif to start, of course, and we raised our glasses in a toast.

"*Salud*—or *skol*—doesn't fit in here," he said.

"Or *nazdarovya*."

We had to know.

"Waiter," Leslie said to the olive-skinned attendant. "What kind of a drinking toast do you use in Thai?" The waiter stopped and frowned. "I don't know, sir, I'm a Puerto Rican myself."

I would like to say that we fared better, linguistically, in France. It was the summer in Cannes and boiling hot. I, and my family, had traveled south from Denmark and were staying in the Pension Esperanto on a hill above the city. We soon discovered that the Esperantist who had founded the pension was long vanished and the present owner only spoke an incomprehensible Provençal dialect. Luckily his wife was from Madrid so our Mexican went down very well.

With the arrival of the cocktail hour I joined Leslie in the superposh Georges V Hotel on la Croisette. He was waiting in the cool bar. "What do you usually drink in France at this hour?" he asked.

"Dubonnet."

"Filthy stuff. You can't really like it."

"I don't."

His quick temper flared. "Then why on Earth do you drink it?"

"Because I really like a digestif called Byrrh but whenever I order it I get a beer."

He sighed tremulously at my linguistic failing. "The accent, you must always watch the accent in French and you'll stay out of trouble." He made sure that I could hear the difference between be-AIR and b-rrrr. Then demonstrated how it should be done. *"Garçon, s'il vous plaît. Je voudrais un Campari avec un Byrrh."*

I did my best to remain invisible when the waiter brought the Campari—and a glass of beer.

I was very pleased when Anthony Boucher wrote a review for *The New York Times* calling *Vendetta for the Saint* the best Saint novel yet. There was plenty of action—and a plot, for a change. So in addition to being a science fiction novelist I was now a detective novelist as well.

In the back of my mind there was a book of a totally different kind itching to get out—my army novel. I loathed—and still loathe—the military, the military mind, and everything to do with militarism. This wasn't any abstract feeling, but something that had grown stronger every year that I had spent in the service. Although I hated the army I had done my job very well. I was a sergeant when I got out of the army—and I hated it all the more. I had read all the relevant and satiric military novels, back to *Candide* and up to the Erich Maria Remarque books. Also *Good Soldier, Schweik*—and then, in 1962, I read *Catch-22* when it was published.

This was it, the clue I needed. Black humor and surrealism, that was the way to write about war. The realistic war novelists had shed gallons of blood, hung miles of entrails from the trees—and had said "shit" and "fuck" so often that the reader was bludgeoned and numb. This was going to be a new writing experience for me, and a disquieting one. I was a writer of action and adventure. At least that was the only kind of fiction I had written and sold so far. But I reminded myself that I was also a novelist who had sold five books. I experimented. I wrote the opening chapter of a never-to-be-written novel entitled *If You Can Read This You Are Too Damn Close*. I thought it was new and funny—and the technique sure was experimental. Joan read it and agreed.

What next? Of all the editors that I knew, only Damon Knight was interested in the avant-garde in writing. Why, hadn't he spelled his name "damon knight" for years, in the style of e. e. cummings? And wasn't Damon now working as consulting editor to Berkley Books, buying SF for them? I would do it! I wrote some character sketches and a rough outline for my planned novel, gave it the title *Bill, the Galactic Hero,* bundled it up with the *Too Damn Close* copy, and sent it off to him.

Damon liked it. On the strength of the copy and outline he extracted a contract and a $1,500 advance from Berkley, $750 on signing and the balance on delivery. Only $750 for a year's work? My spirits sank when I realized I was going to tie up all that time writing a book that might not even sell. My last novel had been serialized in *Astounding* and published by Bantam and had brought in $3,700. But reality had to be faced. There was no possibility of submitting the planned novel as a serial for *Astounding*. John Campbell and I got along very well, but our politics were light-years apart. With no serial sale in sight—and the chance the new book would be bounced as unsuitable—we were on the way to the poorhouse if I did not change my mind. I was about to write a novel that, if accepted, would earn $1,500 for a year's work. If it bounced I would have no money at all, other than the Flash income. I quail back as I say this. . . .

Nevertheless I started the novel. What a pleasure to do! I would laugh all day at the witty copy I was writing. Then suffer all night realizing it was not funny at all. And it was a hard slog; I couldn't get more than fifteen hundred words done a day of first draft— some days only a thousand, whereas I could write a steady two thousand words, sometimes three thousand, a day of adventure. I was sorely tempted to give it up and write *Deathworld 4* and continue right on through to *Deathworld 69*, which I knew I could sell. I would have too, if Joan hadn't had the faith that the book was good, that it was working, and it would be great when it was finished.

Some months later, with a happy sigh I typed THE END, and sent the book off to Damon. Who, fulfilling my gloomiest thoughts, instantly bounced it. No good, he said. Not funny. You are an action writer, Harry, and an ex-comic book artist, not a humorist, and this is basically a war book. Go through and take out the jokes and then I will buy it as an SF war novel.

Depressing news indeed and money was running short. Should I do what Damon said? No! I couldn't agree. The book, good or bad, was a unit and would not be changed. I rejected his advice, withdrew the book from Berkley—and ignored their pleas to return the advance. Writers do not give money back to publishers, never.

Some fingernail-biting months later I was more than pleased to discover that I was not the only one who saw some merit in the book. Fred Pohl was now editor of *Galaxy* and *If.* I had sold him some short stories. I knew he didn't buy serials but I sent him the book anyway. What did I have to lose? There was also Mike Moorcock. An old friend and drinking companion, he was now editing *New Worlds* in England and had turned this very staid and old-fashioned magazine into a journal of the avant-garde. Mike also didn't print serials, but what the hell, maybe he could find something here to use. I was getting desperate and the bank balance was hitting the bottom. I sent him a copy as well and lightning struck. Joan was right and Damon was wrong. Fred would publish a large chunk of the book in *Galaxy,* retitled (by him) "The Starsloggers." (Unfortunately when he ran an ad for the story in the issue before it was published, a typo crept in and the title became "Starloggers." Sort of interstellar lumberjacks, I guess.) Blessedly, Mike Moorcock liked the book as well and wanted to buy it. Since the novel was already divided into three parts, the last two being "$E = mc^2$ or Bust" and "A Dip in the Swimming Pool Reactor," he pretended that they were three different stories and used those titles in separate issues. It was good news for me that, in those days of literary provincialism, Americans did not read British SF magazines and vice versa. When, horrified, I realized they would both be publishing at the same time, I wrote the two editors and warned them. Gentlemen, as well as editors, they brushed my worries aside and soldiered on. I cashed their checks and we kept on eating. And they were both right about their markets being completely different; not one letter of complaint was ever received.

I hadn't been back to New York for some years and knew how important it was in publishing to press the flesh, get the latest gossip—and remind the editors that Harry was alive and well and still writing. I counted the pennies and found enough for plane fare as long as I flew Icelandic Airways. This was a bargain airline in those days that managed to take twenty-four hours to flap its way across the Atlantic. At least they fed you continuously and kept you drunk with unlimited free cognac so no one was sober enough—or awake enough—to notice how long the trip was taking. Of course I had no money for a hotel once I got to New York. I had to rely yet once again on the Old Boys network. Bob Sheckley had stayed with us in Mexico. Now he had an immense apartment on West End Avenue that boasted a tiny maid's room behind the kitchen. I moved in. I couldn't sponge food off Bob so I made it a point of having lunch with a different editor every day. I made sure I stuffed myself at lunch so I could last until the next day. I didn't have enough editors I had sold books or stories to to fill the week— but I always could rely on Don Wollheim. I had never sold a book to Ace, where he was editor and publisher, but our friendship went back to fan days. Still a fan at heart, Don wanted to hear all the fan and publishing news from Britain. I simply wanted to eat. So, lodging with Bob, eating off editors' expense accounts, I got through the week seeing as many editors as I could—manuscripts under arm. At that time Doubleday was putting out a successful SF line and I submitted the Bill novel to the new editor, Tim Seldes. I had never had a hardback book published in the States and thought it was about time. So did he and it was accepted. And the editor at Berkley, Tom Dardis, who had bounced the book on Damon's say-so, now agreed to publish the paperback edition, his spine and his resolve strengthened by Doubleday's acceptance.

Life was looking very sweet and I didn't want to make any more literary experiments for a while. Back in Denmark I started another action adventure, titled *Plague from Space*. By this time Seldes was gone and there was another new SF editor at Doubleday. Larry Ashmead had taken over while *Bill, the Galactic Hero* was still in production. He had enjoyed the book and was nice enough to tell me so, and he bought *Plague* as well. A long publishing and personal relationship began. Unhappily John Campbell did not purchase the serial rights. Though *Science Fantasy* in England did, at a much lower rate of course—thus the joys of freelance.

Sometime after it was published I got a horrified letter from Larry saying that some new writer had stolen my plot outright and had written a book called *The Andromeda Strain* and would I sue? Never litigious, I said no. Of course as the years passed I rather wished that it had been my original book that had been made into a film; but that is life.

We moved home twice in Denmark, first to Rungsted Kyst where Karen Blixen was our neighbor, although we never met her. Then the final move north almost to Elsinore, to the little fishing village of Snekkersten, or "ship stone" in Danish. The story was told that ships used to take on ballast at the harbor here. Our house was on Rortangsvej, "pipewrench street"—but the name had no history that we could discover.

Life was very peaceful and satisfactory in Snekkersten. Moira was going to nursery school in Helsingør and Todd attended the primary school just up the street. The family had grown too large for the faithful Anglia, particularly since we wanted to take a Danish babysitter with us on our summer trips south. With great reluctance I traded the still-functioning Anglia in on a Volkswagen bus. This had been a Copenhagen taxi and the tiny engine was reaching the end of its working life. The flimsy engines in these primitive vehicles weren't worth repairing; you simply traded a clapped-out engine in for a rebuilt one. The VW van—called a *rugbrød* by the Danes, because it was shaped like a cubical rye bread—was primitive and basic beyond belief. It had no gas gauge. When the engine spluttered and died you knew the tank was empty. Before the moving vehicle lost way you groped for a handle and pulled up on it, opening an auxiliary five-liter fuel tank. If you were lucky the thing coughed back to life and you looked for a filling station.

We tore out the old seats and rebuilt the interior as a camper.

There were bench seats and a table, while Joan cooked on the ledge over the rear engine, on a Primus stove, when the back door was opened. At night everything was rearranged as a large bed, big enough for three, with a bunk for Todd above.

Life was very peaceful and satisfactory in Snekkersten. With growing children the benefits of socialized medicine have to be lived with to be believed. We were quite happy here and settled in well. After our first year in Denmark we were all bilingual, but talked Danish most of the time because Todd and Moira usually had their friends in the house. We had settled in nicely and the writing was going smoothly and selling fine. A novel a year, some short stories, an anthology or two—and of course the weekly *Flash Gordon* strips. This steady output meant that we actually had a bit of money in the bank, so it became possible that we could budget a summer holiday. Europe was at our door and we wanted to see more of it. By the summer of 1962 Todd was six and Moira three and a half—a good age to start traveling.

We started out on a not-too-ambitious first day for a shakedown trip. Across the island of Sjaelland to the Storbaelt ferry to Jutland, the northern, Danish part of the peninsula, to a grassy campsite. After a good meal at the campsite restaurant and a night's sleep we were prepared to see the rest of Europe.

Neither Joan nor I were happy at the thought of spending a night in Germany. So after an early start we headed south across the German border, had lunch in the camper, and well before dark were across the border and into Holland for the first time, heading for a campsite.

It was wonderful country—and very much like Denmark. There was a grassy field to park in, spotless toilets and showers, a cheap and very good restaurant. Camping was a very middle-class form of holiday at this time, mostly in tents of various sizes and grandeur.

Now the years of speaking Esperanto were paying off. The yearbook, the *Jarlibro,* listed clubs and facilities in every country.

In Paris, on Ile de la Cite, we stayed at the Pension Esperanto. It was one room thick and seven stories high; good for the legs. A good French breakfast included—in Esperanto of course. (*Bonan tagon sinjoro—ĉu vi havas kafon kaj kreskanta?* "Good day, sir— will you have coffee and croissants?") Very civilized.

After Paris a leisurely camping journey across France was followed by a frightening trip from Switzerland to Italy by train. The underpowered VW made slow going through mountain passes, churning away in low gear most of the time. When I discovered a car-rail link I thought I was onto a good thing. I wasn't. We drove the bus onto a flat car and the wheels were chained into place. There were no passenger coaches on the train—we had to stay in the car! Rattling and swaying we passed through the pitch-dark tunnel and were occasionally doused by water leaking through the stone ceiling. We were very glad when sunlight and Italy opened out before us. Never again would we subject ourselves to this tunnel torture.

Reaching Italy was like coming home. We were speaking Italian again and basking in the warmth of the country and the people. Italians are mad for children, and captivated by *picole bionde*—little blondes—which both kids were. When we entered a restaurant they would be swept up and carried into the kitchen. They were sat onto a table and fed bits of food like baby birds. We poured a glass of *vino locale* and relaxed.

During the previous few months I had been in correspondence with the Ravenna Esperanto Club. I was going to speak to the group—the first American to have visited them. They had even found a most reasonable month's summer rental for us. It was near the beach at a very good price. I spoke to the group, made new friends, and enjoyed the hospitality and home cooking. The small house we occupied was owned by a widow who rented it out during the summer—and moved into her garage until autumn.

We settled into an easy routine. Joan and the kids would spend the morning on the beach while I hammered out *Flash Gordon* scripts on the portable. They returned for lunch and, if I had done my quota of work, we would all enjoy the sun and sand for the afternoon. We would shop for the makings for dinner on the way back and an early night after a long day. These summer trips across Europe—ending up in Italy—became a happy annual event. The work went well—we actually had money in the bank for a change. The children were happy in school and out of it. We were well settled into Denmark.

Perhaps that was the problem, the nagging feeling that something was not quite right.

12

There was one trip to Italy that I was actually paid to take. Life has few riches as fine as this one. It seems that the Italian Tourist Office had decided to hold a film festival, to encourage the summer tourists to come to Italy for their holidays. As usual there were science fiction enthusiasts working away in the background. Anyone can throw a plain old film festival. So why not beat the ordinary and have an international festival of science fiction films? And hold it in Trieste, since, frankly, there is little else to attract tourists to that international city at the top of the Adriatic. The thinking was that, since there was nothing else like this on the world scene, all the countries would be happy to contribute films to this showcase for free. As a further temptation, some big-name SF pros would be invited as judges—and getting them would be the only expense that would be needed to get this festival off the ground.

The invite was like gold. A week in the best hotel—with all expenses paid. What could be bad?! (The films were; but that could be suffered through.) And, with infinite wisdom the sponsors had also invited two old mates, Brian Aldiss and Kingsley Amis, to be judges as well. Not only that—my entire family was included in the invite.

We drove from Denmark across Europe in our decaying VW camper. It was a dusty VW that drew up at the luxurious entrance of the Grand Hotel de la Ville, but a client was a client. The porters whisked our bags into the hotel and a driver took the car to the garage. Joan and the kids went to have a restorative drink in the lobby bar, while I did all the passport and ID paperwork so dear to the Italian heart. Then to the room! In reality, it was a suite, with a Mussolini balcony where one could give speeches to the masses. Our bags were there ahead of us so Joan unpacked and we settled in. I rang room service for more drinks and some sandwiches, and signed for them. I was running a tab with all expenses paid. Luxury!

Brian and Margaret Aldiss arrived later that afternoon with Kingsley and Hilly Amis soon after. We all joined in the lobby bar then went in for an early dinner in the hotel restaurant, which proved to be a first-class Italian meal. There was an impressive wine list that we did great damage to. The judges had to attend the opening ceremony that evening; the ladies opted out, sensing correctly that the Italian ceremonies would be long and boring.

The festival formally opened in the Castle San Giusto, in the Roman theater in the castle grounds. The sky was clear and it was a pleasantly warm Italian evening. The introductions were boring, but boredom was alleviated as the moon rose over the battlements—it was in partial eclipse.

The opening film began and, it can be said, this put a bit of a damper on the occasion. It was *The Man with the X-Ray Eyes*. A Roger Corman film starring Ray Milland. Now Roger has made some notable films, but most tend to be low-budget potboilers. Ray Milland must surely have made some memorable films—but they are now remembered only by film buffs. I am forced to say that this film was less than memorable. Since we were judges we lived through it, making scurrilous comments to ease the pain. We had had plenty of wine with dinner, which fueled what we thought were humorous remarks.

All would have been well, and normally we would have found the hotel bar and the ladies. But the lights came up and there, sitting just in front of us and well within easy earshot were—yes, fate's cruel design—Roger Corman and Ray Milland. Much shrunken we crawled out and headed for safety. I regret to say penance was not done. By hindsight it was just too funny. And it was a really bad film.

After that first night we attended special advance screenings of the films for the judges, held in the mornings. This worked fine because we then had the afternoons free. So we all decided to do a little exploring. We visited the market and museums, and the aquarium with its leaking tanks, where the children grabbed the tail of the long-suffering resident penguin, Marco. The city of Trieste is tucked away right at the top of the Adriatic Sea and is less than a mile from Yugoslavia. None of us had visited that country—which became suddenly possible when we discovered that we could make a day trip by simply showing our passports.

A trip was planned for the next day. Since we would be missing our midday meal at the hotel, Joan had the hotel prepare a picnic luncheon. We were off as soon as the morning films ended. Notching up one more country on the VW's record. A quick look-in at the border, stamps in the passports, and we rolled into Yugoslavia.

It was pleasantly rural and undeveloped, a rocky countryside with small farms. The one we saw was being tilled by a one-horse plow. Foreign tourists were still a rarity in those days and we felt like explorers in a new world. We stopped at a gas station to buy a map and it was a pleasant surprise to discover that everyone spoke Italian, which made it easy to make special arrangements when we stopped at a country hotel with a restaurant garden. We were the only customers there and they were only too happy to please. They brought out the menu—unhappily in Serbo-Croatian. We did not want to experiment with some dodgy food—not with the fine Italian lunch waiting in the basket in the car.

"Strike a deal, Harry," Brian said. "Tell him we'll buy plenty of drink if we can use his garden for our picnic."

"I second that," Kingers added.

A deal was struck. I didn't have to exaggerate the amount of drink we would need and the waiter—probably the owner—hurried away. He was back soon enough with a first drink course, a pitcher of slivovitz. It was the size of a water pitcher and cost about what water would cost in a restaurant back home. There was red and white wine, a beer or two, and imitation Coca-Cola for the kids, called tsokta-tsokta.

Then there was the packed lunch—which proved to be more than a simple picnic lunch. There was pâté and caviar, a whole roast chicken, three kinds of salad, a variety of cold meat, pasta salad and rolls, giant black olives and assorted pickles.

It was paradisiacal. All of the food, and a good deal of the drink vanished. Then it was late afternoon and time to cross the border before dark. The gents went to pay the bill, which was more than reasonable. While we were splitting it up Kingers, ever one with the eye for drink, drew our attention to the row of bottles behind the bar.

"I say, chaps—look at that!"

The bottles all contained products of the ALCO distillery, and featured drinks labeled in English. There was cherry brandy, port, sherry—and ALCO REAL SCOTCH WHISKEY. This could not be passed by. We all ordered a shot and toasted and drank. It was strange, different, not scotch. Then you belched and it was a blend of slivo-vitz, the local plum brandy.

We drove back to Italy with most of my passengers enjoying a nice sleep.

We made two more Yugoslavian luncheon runs. On the second one the border guard accused me of running unlicensed tours. I had to buy him off with Todd's ray gun water pistol—replaced under duress.

There is something else I must record. Brian Aldiss often talked of doing a book: *The Worst Toilets in the World*. At this Yugo-slavian hotel Margaret, Joan, and Moira had to go and pee—girls always go together, as you know—and went into the hotel. They came running out: "Oh, it's terrible, it's terrible!" Brian and I ran in: "Let's see it!" We had to see how terrible it was. "That's *noth-ing*," Brian said. "I went into a toilet in India which was so dark that I had to feel my way, and when I sat down on the toilet I found myself on an Indian's lap, and he said: 'Excuse me, sahib, but I was here first!' "

We had incredible lunches, different every day. Italians don't just make a sandwich, there'd be meats of all kinds, salads and what have you, and huge black olives. And we'd have the best local wine, which was more than drinkable. Then after the lunch we'd go and have a nap on the beach we found there, and the kids would play in the sand. I remember once we were trying to find our way back from this beach to the border. We stopped the VW bus near a little barracks and Brian was trying to get some directions from the policeman. He was having no luck, and finally Kingsley shouted out:

"Oh Brian, do tell him to fuck off!"

These guys couldn't speak any English, but "fuck off," *that* they understood! "Fook off?!" they roared. This was not the time for intelligent discussion. Brian ran back and jumped into the open door of the camper and slammed his head into the doorframe, almost braining himself. We laid him down and drove away.

We had all sorts of jolly times that week and all in all it was a successful festival with an interesting aftermath. The festival lasted for a week and featured some truly desperate films. In the mornings we at least had a chance to weed out the most awful endeavors. There was one French film that gave avant-garde a bad name. The only good thing about it was that it only ran for ten minutes. It consisted simply of a man carrying a human-size replica of a plastic toy soldier over his shoulder, walking through the streets of Paris. We assumed it was Paris, but it was so dark it was hard to tell. That was it. There was also the German submission. This was clear enough—too clear, if anything, when the lovely heroine is stretched out on a dissection table and cut open—with a real corpse dissected and bloody. We convinced the Italians to drop it. Not family entertainment.

Luckily these were the exception and there were some outstanding films. The Czech contribution was excellent, *Ikarie XB-1,* which was based on the novel *Magellanic Cloud* by Stanislaw Lem. This was a world-class film that alas, never gained general release. The rest of the films were dogs that deserved their early demise.

All in all it was a worthwhile endeavor that was repeated the next year. We went but, alas, our mates weren't invited. At least Arthur Clarke was there, a writer I have always admired. His novels are among the best ever written while his short stories are so memorable that I can quote from them from memory. Now I would be sharing a drink alone with Arthur!

Would that our expectations lived up to our dreams. The first low blow was a corker. Arthur didn't drink. After deadly pressure he did accept a small sherry, but he did no more than touch it to his lips. I looked at it with mean depression and went in search of a large whiskey.

Worse was in store as he lived up to his fannish reputation. SF fandom has a vocabulary all its own. "Gafiate," for example, means get away from it all. And truefen have fan names. Arthur's was "Ego Clarke," a name assigned—not chosen. I was soon to find out the truth of Arthur's fan name. No matter how I tried, the conversation had but one topic. Arthur.

I soon admitted defeat and went with the tide—and enjoyed it. There were endless tales of conflict with Stanley Kubrick. They had just finished shooting *2001: A Space Odyssey*. And it was great material. I looked at the untouched sherry, sighed—and knocked back a restorative whiskey. *De disputant non disputant est*. Or, you can't argue with taste.

Brian fell in love with Yugoslavia. He liked it so much that he planned an extensive visit, and arranged to write a book for Faber called *Cities and Stones,* a travel book about Yugoslavia. His wife, Margaret, was going to collect recipes for a Yugoslavian cookbook. One of the porters at Trinity College in Oxford was a Yugoslavian, and Brian and Margaret took private lessons until he could get by in the language. Then they took off to Yugoslavia. They had an ancient Land Rover, which Margaret drove because Brian couldn't drive at that time. A few months into their trip we arranged to meet them. We made an appointment by postcard, to meet at this campsite that I found in an Esperanto travel book. Serendipity; we arrived there within an hour of each other.

Brian weighed about ten stone, 140 pounds. He'd lost so much weight he was ghostlike. Apparently the Yugoslavian food was the worst food in the world, once you got away from the tourist areas. There was nothing to drink and nothing to eat, and the idea of doing a cookbook was quickly abandoned. Open another tin we'd brought.

We were just tourists here, way down in the foot of Yugoslavia, practically in Greece, and Brian was right. Every restaurant we went to had nothing on the menu, and we'd say, "What do you have?" And they'd say *ćevapčići,* minced pork on a skewer, served with tomato and onion. Not bad. Or we have *raznjići,* which are pieces of pork on a skewer cooked over a charcoal grill. But that's all they have. Period. It's good the first time you eat it, but as the sole item of a diet . . .

Later I learned two words. We went to this very charming tourist spot, Plitvice, which is a series of natural springs. There was a lovely dining room with white tablecloths and a thick menu. They had everything on the menu that you could possibly want. I went through the whole menu with the waiter and I learned two words: *neiman*—we're out of it—and *odma*—we never had it in the first place.

I had found the campsite in the Esperanto yearbook, and I brought a lot of tinned food from Denmark, tinned herring and pâté from France. As we were driving down I'd buy some more food for him. It was greatly appreciated. We ate it all, Brian finishing every last crumb. Then rain cut the trip short and we had to get out of the campsite and head home. Some time passed before I saw Brian again. We reminisced about our Yugoslavian adventures.

"You know, Harry, we had a good time there—and we had some really good wine. Including a very black wine called *dingac*. But it was nothing but very bad food and I spent the whole time looking for those big black olives and I never found them."

Sadly I spoke: "Brian, I've got some very bad news for you . . . we took those across with us from the hotel in Trieste!" We still occasionally refer to those black olives.

Yugoslavia really was a broken-down country then, but while I was there I got the idea for a "first contact" story—"Rescue Operation"—which I grew out of that landscape.

There was a friend we knew from the science fiction meetings who we used to call Joe the Jug; his real name was José Dolnicar. He was a physicist, an astrophysicist from Ljubljana. We had planned to meet him in this little town, but found him pulled off by the side of the road. "Harry, I'm so pleased to meet you." He was a scuba diver and he'd found a two-thousand-year-old wreck. He had dived on the wreck, which had been carrying amphorae of wine. Alas, all broken. When he opened the boot of his car it was filled with broken amphorae. I took two, still covered with seaweed, back to Denmark and gave one to Brian.

José became the hero of the story I wrote as a result of this chance encounter. Within two hundred miles there is an advanced physics institute and here, only the superstition of the miserable peasantry. They were the most *peasant* peasants I met in my entire life.

Harry, 1972.

Far left: Harry's maternal Irish grandmother.

Left: Harry's mother, Ria, as a young woman in the early 1920s.

Harry, aged 3, with his parents, Ria and Hank Harrison, in 1928.

Harry, or Bud as he was known to the family (second from the front), aged 3 in 1928, with his cousins in Oneida, New York.

Harry, aged 13 in 1938,
in unknown location,
most likely New York.

Harry, aged 13, taken by
his father.

Harry, 1938, taken by his father,
Hank, also known as Leo.

Harry with his mother, Ria, around the time he was drafted.

Harry in the army in Laredo, Texas.

Harry in the army in Laredo, Texas, holding a raccoon.

Harry and Joan on their wedding day, June 4, 1954, at the Society for Ethical Culture in New York City.

Harry and Joan's wedding day, posing with Harry's parents, Ria and Hank.

Harry's father, Hank, appeared in a New York newspaper in Oneida in June 1953.

Harry and Brian Aldiss being funny, as usual. Location unknown.

Left to right: Alan E. Nourse, Ann Nourse, Harry, and Joan. Taken in the early 1970s at the Nourse home in North Bend, Washington.

Harry and friends and family at one of the many famous pool parties at the California house on Palm Avenue.

Harry in his tux outside the Palm Avenue house in California.

Todd and Moira and family dog, Gumpy (named by Harry after Andy Gump), in California in the '60s.

Young Todd and Harry in a field in Denmark on a rare sunny day.

Todd and Moira jumping in the garden at Palm Avenue, California. The road in the background was known as Suicide Hill, and all the local kids used to ride their bikes down it at breakneck speed, with dire consequences.

One of many long Italian lunches in the '60s. Left to right: Kingsley Amis, Margaret Aldiss, Brian Aldiss, Joan Harrison, Harry Harrison, Hilary Amis.

Harry and a host of SF writers and professionals at the first World SF meeting in Dublin, 1976. The four in front are Alfred Bester, Sam Lundwall, Brian Aldiss, and Harry. See if you can spot Theodore Sturgeon, Anne McCaffrey, Tom Doherty, and many other professionals.

Harry in Dublin in the '70s.

Harry and Brian Aldiss
outside a favorite haunt,
The Rose Revived, Witney,
Oxfordshire.

Harry in the
campervan being
loaded onto a
small Italian ferry.

Harry was guest of honour at the first science fiction convention in Denmark
to be held outside Copenhagen, Dancon 78, in Odense, August 1978.

The American slide-on camper, complete with toilet
for the kids, that Harry bought in California.

Josef Nesvadba and Harry in Bromma, Sweden, in 1979.

Harry posing with his John W. Campbell Memorial Award alongside great friend Sam Lundwall in 1977.

Harry admiring himself in a bookshop window.

Fred Pohl and Harry in Fanano, Italy, in 1985 for the World SF annual meeting. Fred was the president of World SF from 1980–1982.

Peter Kucka and Harry in Fanano, Italy, in 1985 for the World SF annual meeting.

Left to right: Brian Aldiss, Harry Harrison, Fritz Urban Gunnarsson, and Sam J. Lundwall at La Genoa restaurant in London, 1991, during Sam's 50th birthday celebrations.

Harry, Peter Weston, and assorted others at Intervention Eastercon 1997 in Liverpool.

Harry during a visit to Japan. He wouldn't eat raw fish again.

13

It was late afternoon. We were all in the sitting room being very laid-back. I had finished my quota of writing for the day and had crawled out of the studio and into a very dry gin martini. Joan had a glass of wine. The kids had a few friends over but they were on the way out now. We were talking Danish. But why? I realized suddenly that the Danish children were gone. "Speak English!" I said, and there was an unexpected sharp edge to my voice. The kids didn't notice this—just shifted gears out of Danish and went on with the Lego machine they were building, talking in English. Joan raised her eyebrows. I apologized and put my attention back to the gin for a bit.

We talked about living in Denmark at some length, then broke for dinner. We picked up the thread later that evening when the children were in bed. One thing was painfully clear; we were Americans, not Danes, and we should be speaking English, not Danish. We were being absorbed by a culture that was not ours. The children spoke and thought in Danish. As fine as this was—it was not English. They were Americans and it was time that they saw something of the land of their birth and spoke a language with a little more international appeal than Danish.

The words come easily enough when I look back now, but it was very difficult facing up to facts at the time. It must have been cooking on the back burner of our brains, because suddenly there was a lot to think about. As we talked around the problem we realized that here was a major decision that had to be made, but we weren't sure just what had to be done. The kids went to their Danish schools here and worked hard. They seemed to be enjoying their circle of friends. The same with me and Joan. Life was smooth and sweet. We went out in Copenhagen lots of evenings; we had just seen the Bolshoi on tour from Russia. We had friends over for dinner and enjoyed dining at their homes.

My work went well. The future was ordered, smooth, and clear. We could relax and do nothing. Or uproot the family in a major move that would see us leaving Denmark: a very major move whatever way one looked at it. We would be leaving and destined never to return. There could be no turning back. It had been seven years since we had made the big move that brought us here, but now it was time to leave.

However—for a lot of reasons—we weren't ready for the big trip back across the Atlantic; we weren't emotionally prepared for it. We decided then—for better or worse—that we should move to England for a trial year. Years later, with Moira an adult, we mentioned it; she agreed that she was not ready at the time to face a major change to the United States. She agreed that the year in England had been a good decision.

Looking back at it now, decades later, I believe that it wasn't the wisest of decisions—it just postponed the significant move back to the land of our births. But it seemed like a good idea at the time. And Moira approved of the move as it worked out.

Once the decision had been made we acted upon it. All the furniture, the shelves and books, the whole lot—went into storage. We rented a furnished house in Sutton, Surrey—the stockbrokers' clerks belt. Packed up, said a tearful good-bye to friends, and drove to the ferry to Harwich.

What can I say about that English year? Joan and I enjoyed it, that was clear. Seeing all our English friends, enjoying speaking English full time. It was hardest on the kids. Moira was young enough to go to a little Dame's school right across the road, a sort of kindergarten where she made out pretty well. But not Todd. He had left all of his Danish friends behind, particularly Peter. They had cried when they parted. He made no friends in Sutton; he was in the wrong culture there and kids can be very cruel.

Then the twelve months were up and it was time to leave. This time it had to be to the United States. We would stay in Joan's parents' house; the welcome mat was always out there. The next step would be decided after we settled into Long Beach, New York.

But we had to cross the wide Atlantic first. How we did that requires more than a little explanation. It starts with an old friend and collaborator, Leon E. Stover. Leon was a cultural anthropologist and sinologist—and a good friend of many years' standing. We later collaborated on a novel together, titled *Stonehenge: Where Atlantis Died*. Leon was a professor who taught at IIT in Chicago. One of his students was Georges Pappadakis. We discovered that Georges was a student there at his father's command. He had also worked as a fisherman on an Italian boat learning fishing—and Italian—the hard way. I'm not sure what other travails he undertook at his father's orders—but the deal was surely worth the price. For Georges's father was a shipping magnate and, upon completion of his seven labors, Georges would be master of his own ship. Not a little yacht for putt-putting around in.

He got himself a full-sized freighter, of which he was the new owner and master, and was based in London. I used to visit Georges when I was in London and we became quite close friends, so much so that when I mentioned our planned move to the United States—including shipping the loyal VW, he said, "If you are moving to the States you must go on my ship."

Just like that. I opened my mouth—then closed it: I could think of nothing to say. It is not every day that one hears this kind of offer. It was then that he insisted that I see his ship. He was visiting her that same afternoon and he took me along. It was an easy drive to Harwich and a warm Greek reception was waiting for us when we boarded the ship; paternalism personified. All of the sailors were from the same Greek village and Georges was treated like the elder mayor. The very first thing he did was hold an informal court where they brought him their problems. With the crew's troubles sorted out we finally got to meet the officers.

They were quite a mixed lot. The captain had been an officer in the Greek navy, while the electrician, Sparks, was Dutch, a young man already on the fat side, with good reason. His cabin was stacked wall-to-wall with cases of Dutch beer. He had the endearing habit of checking to see if a circuit was live by bridging the poles with his index finger and middle finger. If the circuit was hot there would be a crackling and the smell of burning flesh, he would chortle and hold out his scarred fingertips for inspection. The kids were very impressed. I noted he had thick rubber soles on his shoes.

The radio operator was a gloomy Yugoslavian named Vladimir. This was at the time of the Vietnam War and he was fascinated by the war in every detail. Yugoslavia was communist—of a sort—so I asked no questions. Until one day when we were talking about the war and Vladimir was at his gloomiest. Finally he sighed heavily and said, "I would like to fight in this war."

"On which side?" I said.

"Don't care about side. Just want to fight."

I opened my mouth—but there was really nothing I could say.

In later discussions I found out some of the reasons for the international flavor of the officers. It seemed that the Dutch had excellent electrician technical schools and graduated—still young—well-trained professionals (for "young" also read "lower salaries"). The same went for Yugoslavia, which turned out well-educated, English-speaking professional radio operators, who sent home, by Western standards, a smallish salary—that was a small fortune in that now post-Soviet country.

The elderly German chief engineer was really chief engineer of all the Pappadakis ships. He had had some minor surgery and was now recovering with a seagoing—working—holiday. And so it went. Expenses were pared to the bone in one of the most competitive fields, benefited by Georges's most unusual education.

Tramp steamer is an unfair appellation to this corner of the maritime field where ships competed for cargo. Some of them went to the wall; Georges's ship survived and profited.

Georges, in his role of village elder, dealt with the many small problems, mostly family matters of the crew. Then he consulted with the captain and engineer about repairs—putting them off once again; "save money" was the motto. It seemed that the propeller had been bent when it touched bottom in the River Plate. Repairs were not that urgent and would be delayed. But the vibration was doing no good to the shaft bearing, which needed replacement in the future. The delay made financial sense although the bearing was slowly beating itself to death. Later I was to discover that the highly efficient, naval-academy-trained captain had left the navy after some disagreements concerning a personal relationship with one of his young sailors.

With all the minor problems solved and out of the way, Georges was faced with the major question of what next. "Unloading is complete and I want to get to the States," Georges said. "There are a number of cargoes in the USA that we could pick up once we are there—but I hate the losses from an Atlantic crossing in ballast to get there."

He paused, rubbed his jaw in thought—then laughed and hit the table with his fist. "Your car—that's the answer. Of course you can bring it—along with a load of stateside-bound MG sports cars. The ship will still be in ballast with this light cargo—but the costs for the trip will be covered." He reached for the phone. "I'll get onto the shipping agent right now."

The paperwork for our voyage was done that very day. I was signed on as crew—a supernumerary—the family boarded as that—family. After that it was a flurry of packing, saying good-byes, then a swift drive to Harwich one final time. Just as the first of the jazzy sports cars was being winched aloft and dropped into the hold.

Then the crew—it was a familiar meeting, an encounter with a new family. Like all the Mediterranean peoples, the Greeks were mad for children and here were two blond ones! They and Joan, and our bags, vanished from sight. I watched the VW go spinning into the air then drop into the hold. The sun shone and the ship buzzed with activity. This was going to be all right! There was nothing but good vibes emanating from this little maritime adventure.

I joined Georges in the wardroom where I enjoyed an excellent sherry and chatted with the officers, a mixed and cheerful lot. We all said our good-byes and Georges was off. The first officer showed me our quarters. "You'll be here just behind the bridge. That is the captain's quarters. Right next to it is the owner's cabin. Mr. Georges insisted that you have it." It was more of a suite than a cabin, luxuriously fitted out. "It is all officers' country back here," he said. "The second mate is joining the ship when we get to the U.S. so the children can use his cabin." They certainly could. It had been a long and trying day and we retired soon after dinner.

Next morning I woke early and stepped out onto the bridge. Not early enough—because the kids were up well before me. Todd was there, engrossed in the ship's technology. A sailor was updating one of the charts and he was a silent but attentive observer.

"Is my son bothering you?" I asked the officer on watch.

"No! He is always welcome. He's learning to be a watch sailor." In Greek culture no child could ever be in the way. But where was Moira? I need not have worried. In fact I had to get out of the way. Back in the passageway one of the sailors hurried by with her on his shoulders, wailing loudly, imitating an ambulance. He went right to the mess hall where her skilled attention was badly needed. I only then noticed that she was wearing her nurse's outfit, Red Cross cap, and carrying a plastic hold-all of toy medical equipment. One of the plump cooks was stretched out on a table, groaning loudly. Stethoscope and thermometer were employed, candy medicine administered, the cure quick if not miraculous. I went in search of coffee to take to Joan. Moira kept her human ambulance running for hours and had no shortage of victims to cure.

The weather was perfect, the trip paradisiacal. The food in the officer's mess was of course Greek—and all the better for that. We sunbathed during the day, played cards in the evenings. The captain was partial to a game of canasta, probably because he cheated so outrageously. No one else seemed to have noticed: the chief engineer marveled at his good luck. The stakes were low, my losses minuscule—I looked on it as some small payment against our passage.

We never had to worry where the kids were, with countless eyes always on the watch. Moira was showered with gifts that the seamen undoubtedly were bringing back to their own children. Joan insisted that they must stop spoiling her so and returned most of the expensive stuff. Todd was in mechanical heaven. He was happiest on the bridge—and I soon found out why. That was the day I found him standing on a beer crate in order to see the compass, which he had to do since he was steering the ship!

This was a little too much: he was only twelve years old. This could not be right, and I felt I had to protest. But to whom—the first mate was standing right behind him, a seaman next to him. The officer saw my gaping jaw and smiled. "He is a very conscientious little boy—and a quick learner. We are here to watch him but there is little we have to do. As soon as he learned to compensate for the turning factor of the ship I knew he would be all right. This is a long ship and any course corrections take a while to be felt. Novice helmsmen always tend to overswing, so the ship follows a snakelike course. Not with your son. He caught on right away." He smiled down at his new sailor, then spoke quietly. "Frankly I have some teenage seamen who don't do as good a job. They never seem to catch on."

The sun was shining, the sea empty in all directions. I stood back out of the way and watched awhile. The officer was now busy with a chart, the sailor was polishing brass. The ocean was empty.

The officer and the crew were well aware of the ship's steering wheel. If they were happy with their new unpaid employee I couldn't complain. The beer crate raised Todd to steering height—and no farther. On future sunny days when I stood at the ship's bow and looked up at the bridge—and saw no helmsman—I knew that my son was at the wheel. I could say nothing—but I still found it disconcerting.

It was a slow crossing if you measured it in days, but all too fast for us. Joan and I talked about the future and it was none too clear. One thing we emphatically agreed upon was that we would not be staying in New York. Nor could we think of any reason to stay in suburbia or anywhere on the East Coast. We had heard nothing but good about California and we thought: why not? The climate was right; the film industry there was industriously booming away—and we had friends who worked in it. It had the added and attractive fact that it was hooked on to Mexico. Yes—California it would have to be.

Then we were just one day away from New York Harbor. Being a freighter we stayed away from the Manhattan passenger wharves and instead plunged into the massive commercial dock area on the other side of the Hudson River. A tug eased us up against a dock in the Port of Newark. Cables were thrown and secured and we were now home. Officially and physically. We put down the anchor in the outer bay, in a spot designated by the port authorities. In the morning a pilot and other harbor authorities would start boarding. As a native-speaking American I was asked by the captain to aid with officialdom and I was more than happy to oblige.

At seven in the morning the pilot came aboard; a number of pencil-pushing types were close behind him. There were some bottles of scotch open on a table in the officer's mess and we were soon busy with the paperwork there. There were some sealed full bottles as well, which soon vanished, helping to lubricate our paperwork. Customs came and went with unbelievable speed. There was a tall pile of passports for the crew. These were opened, stamped, and returned. Since the Harrison family would be leaving the ship here it got a little more complicated. A few questions were asked, the passports riffled through and stamped with unbelievable dispatch. The same applied to the VW for which I had produced all the relevant documents. Ancient vehicle, personal use only, a few thuds from the official stamps and welcome back to the United States.

I think that the crew turned out en masse to see us off. It had been a fun crossing for all of us. After many a cheerful good-bye we disembarked, our bags were brought ashore for us—and we watched as our bus was lifted from the hold. A veritable antique in the sea of gleaming sports cars all around her. We loaded her up, more waving and good-byes, and then we were threading our way out of the endless dockland.

We finally found the exit and showed our passports one last time, and we were home, if you can call the roaring trucks and cars passing us on the New Jersey Turnpike home. Nor was it any better when we had crossed the river and joined the solid phalanx of traffic on the Cross Bronx Expressway. White-knuckled, I squeezed the steering wheel and felt very much the country rube in my native land. I relaxed only when we crossed the bridge into Long Beach and put the brake on in front of my in-laws' house. Joan's mother was waiting. No father there, for this was a working weekday. The arrival of his daughter and grandchildren was not reason enough to miss a day at the shop. His first heart attack was soon after this.

As quickly as I could, I slipped away and back into the VW, where I cracked one of the five-dollar bottles of scotch that the captain was happy to sell to me from the ship's store. A short time later Joan joined me.

"Whisky," she said.

"You never drink whisky." I gaped.

"Cut it with water. She's already correcting the way the kids speak."

"Did you expect anything different?"

"No. I had just forgotten."

"California, here we come."

"Roll on the day!"

She laughed and everything was all right.

Except that it wasn't. Days became weeks and we fled Grandma's house and rented a furnished apartment in Long Beach: California wasn't that easy to reach. The children went to the local school and hated it. Moira's teacher stood her up before the class and, with her newly acquired English accent, she was told to speak so the other children would listen and learn how to talk properly. One can easily imagine how popular that made her with her classmates.

We had to get out and find someplace to really settle down, for all our sakes. All the globe-trotting had been fun, but it was time to call a halt. I finished all my assignments, signed contracts, and promised delivery soonest for all the rest. I had the VW tuned up and ready for our heroic drive from ocean to ocean. However I had one slight trouble with the gearbox that would cost a fortune to repair and so would have to be endured. There was no reverse gear.

"You can't drive to California without a reverse," my father-in-law said.

"I'm only going one way and not coming back," was my feeble response. The silence that followed was deadly.

Came the day we were all packed and ready, time to go. I scraped the ice off the windshield, then we boarded and said all our good-byes. Not for the first time did our parents think that we were mad—and were quick to tell us so. We waved good-bye, I put the VW into gear, and we were off. In more ways than one if you were to believe our in-laws.

14

Autumn had arrived and we had the first frost on the day we left Long Beach.

We headed south, not west as yet, in order to find the southern sun. We rolled through Pennsylvania and gaped like rubes at the difference that time had worked on the American highways. Some ten years had passed since our earlier trip south to Mexico, and America was now one interconnected freeway. Gone, but not missed, was the two-lane blacktop. Gone also were the Bates-style motels. As European yokels we gaped ever wider at the high-rise chain motels. By late afternoon we had enough of the driving and left the freeway for one of those palaces of delight, only to discover that we were going to have some parking problems. All the cars of the clientele were parked in a row, up against the curb in front of the motel. Nose in. This was fine if you had reverse gear and you used that to back up and out in the morning. What to do?

What I had to do was make a U-turn in front of the curb. Then it was all hands—except the driver—to push the VW so it rolled back down against the curb ready to drive straight out in the morning. This produced some raised eyebrows among our fellow motelers, gaping at Joan and the kids pushing and getting the VW rolling. But it worked and they got some needed exercise!

The kids wanted to head for the pool and, after persuading Joan that the unpacking could wait, we headed for the poolside bar where we could keep an eye on them. We ate at the hotel, hamburgers and fries all around. The kind of junk food we rarely ate at home. If we treated the drive as a rule-breaking holiday it might make the trip that much easier. It was going to be a long way to California: I had a vision of a row of hamburgers smoking away into the sunset. I insert here a small word of advice to those who are thinking of undertaking a transcontinental drive. Don't. If you still feel that you have to do it, then get some kind of vehicle that can wind up to a decent speed. Don't do it in a decrepit van with a top speed of fifty miles an hour. That is a top speed downhill with a tailwind. You will eventually get there and you surely won't get any speeding tickets: that is about all that can be said for it.

Once we were on the road, Brian Aldiss had the dubious pleasure of receiving a daily postcard report, so that he could share in the heady joys of our trip. While we were refueling each evening the kids went through the local postcards in the gas station, finding a classy one for Brian.

"Is this one bad enough for Brian?"

"You can do worse. Keep looking."

When a blurry pic of the local hash house, or a gem of a local sight—a plaster dinosaur, or the world's largest doughnut—was found, we would buy the card and list that day's roadkill:

2 sparrows
1 furry blob
1 something bird

These were the feeble reports from the populous states like Pennsylvania. Things improved the farther west and south we drove, where the wildlife roamed suicidal and free. Like:

3 rabbits
1 hedgehog

1 rattlesnake
1 skunk

The latter detectable by smell, well before—and well after—we had passed the flattened corpse. It took us three days to cross Texas alone; the panhandle seemed to stretch, unchanging, forever. That's because it did. We lost track of the cardboard-thick jackrabbits, though we did pass the flattened remains of a big dog, which we hopefully listed as a coyote.

Mexico was close to our road and a trip across the border for memories' sake could not be resisted. We parked and walked across the international bridge and into the third world. The food stalls smelled impossibly good but were easily resisted, with memories of gut infections still strong. A clean restaurant tempted us, *Mi Casita,* and this we did not resist. When done, if it is done well, Mexican food can be the best in the world. Moira dived in and tried everything, from the guacamole to the turkey molé—Todd wolfed down only the handmade tortillas. How children can be so different . . . ? Filling was the word, and we walked it off, only stopping at a booze shop to buy a tax-free bottle of Cuervo Tequila Añejo. Next to the cash register on the counter were some Mexican cigarettes, including one pile that was tastily labeled HORSESHIT CIGARETTES. You don't often get a chance to buy this particular brand. On the front of the pack was a drawing of a horse producing the labeled contents. On the back there were health warnings. *Not fart in carload* and *Real horseshit no donkey shit.* Delightful.

I peeked at the package and saw that the printing was on a wrapper covering a normal package of Mexican cigarettes. I bought them, knowing who would appreciate them. That night I put the Bible from the nightstand to good use for once. With my buck knife I hollowed out an opening in it that just fit the pack of barnyard cigarettes. When it was done I wrapped the Bible with wrapping paper so the ends of the innocent book showed. In the morning I mailed it, book rate, to Brian in England with the return address of

A. Einstein at Princeton. In case the Brit customs found the doubly illicit contents.

This story had a happy ending. In the fullness of time the package arrived in Oxford. It seems that Brian was then the literary editor of the *Oxford Mail*. He dissected the Bible when it crossed his desk and greatly admired the cigarettes inside, then he took them to the office and passed them around, so his coworkers could enjoy an exotic foreign puff or two, showing them the packet only after they had inhaled deeply—and coughed out mightily.

We were still crossing the endless miles of the USA. The road rolled slowly but steadily by. We took warning at the promised hundred miles to the next gas station and filled the tank. We trundled on across the desert and back to what passed for civilization in this part of the world. We drove past the last of Arizona and crossed the border into California, land of our dreams. We had made it. There were cheers all around and we cracked the still-cool California Cabernet Sauvignon we had purchased that morning and had a glass. The kids preferred Coke.

We were heading for San Diego. A friend of ours from Cuautla, Adam Glass, had moved there after leaving Mexico and we had stayed in touch. He said that we would like the city. We probably would if only we could have found it. Somehow I missed finding San Diego, ending up miles south of it, which is hard to do when you consider the fact that it is America's eighth-largest city. We ended up almost at the Mexican border. Heading back to civilization we came down a very steep hill and into the community of Imperial Beach. Once again destiny took a hand. Our comments as we drove down Palm Avenue are imprinted forever in my memory.

"What a lovely house," Joan said as we whistled by it.

"Did you see the For Sale sign?" I answered.

It was getting late and there was a grotty motel nearby. We checked in, then went exploring. The street we had come down was Palm Avenue; when it crossed the railroad tracks and under the freeway, it became the four-lane road to Coronado with shops, gas stations—and restaurants. Since we were only about five miles from Mexico there had to be a Mexican restaurant—and it turned out to be a pretty fair one. We tucked in—and promised Todd a takeaway burger and fries on the way back to the motel. It had been a long day and a tiring one. We fell asleep watching television, ending our first day in California.

I was dragged awake in the morning by the sun streaking through a rift in the ancient curtains. I lay there, possessed by a feeling of darkness, that life was repeating itself in a most unpleasant way. Here I was at the end of the road, in a broken-down motel. Just like Mexico these many years ago. No road ahead here, for it ended in the Pacific Ocean. Or go south a few miles and you end up in Mexico. Maybe we should continue on into Mexico, back to Cuautla? We certainly knew how to live there. The kids would pick up Spanish in a few months. There was a pop as I punctured this particular daydream. We were in America, 100 percent. We would stay here and the kids would go to American schools and we would all swim in our native culture and then? Then I would turn the coffeemaker on and face the new day.

It had been a long trip and no one argued when I decided to take a day off. After breakfast I went to the drug store for tomato juice and gin—America would take some getting used to—and picked up limes in the utility store. The kids splashed into the pool and we had Bloody Marys—in plastic glasses—at a table poolside. "Well, where do we go from here?" I asked in what I hoped was an enthusiastic voice, meaning the big picture, the many problems.

"We find a better place to stay than this fleapit," Joan said, eminently practical.

"Right," I said, and went to get the yellow pages; still used in those precomputer days.

Funny, with the ragged end of Southern California all around us, we never considered changing our locale—taking a look at Hollywood, for instance. Fate had landed us here and we wanted to check it out and we both wanted to see that for-sale house on the hill nearby.

Coronado, right down the road, was one gigantic naval base, which meant sailors and their families and rental units galore. We found one nearby, checked it out, and moved in that same day. Then we called the phone number on the house on the hill and went to see it that same afternoon. The owner, Willy, was there ahead of us. With a liter bottle of Booth's gin and a bag of ice cubes.

"Let's try this gin, then we can look around at the house."

"None for me," Joan said.

"Maybe a small one," I said, surprising no one. "With a squeeze of lime."

"You look around," Willy said to Joan. "I'm sure the children would prefer a run in the garden."

Well done, Willy—who proved to be no dummy. He was a school superintendent—good job, as well as pouring a good drink. Joan returned after a bit and wanted to show me the joys of the en suite bathroom. Once there she closed the door and whispered, "I love this house. Can we buy it?"

"I hope so," I said as cheerily as I could. "Let me talk to Willy."

It really was exactly what we wanted. A spacious, modern California house with three bedrooms and a giant living room, opening out on a patio and garden, with a large lawn. The lawn ended in a row of trees and beyond this was a typical California half-desert landscape, almost three acres in all. I had another gin and asked the vital question.

How much?

I swilled down some more gin and tried to remain calm when I listened to the answer. I kept my cool. I had only limited funds in the bank so I must now hit the bank for a mortgage. With what collateral? I crossed my fingers and snuffed in the gin. This was not going to be easy. It wasn't. Joan's parents came through with a loan. And . . .

And who cares about the boring details of buying a house? I shudder as I write this. Basically—we started from nowhere and ended up with this jolly, happy home. More important is—what was happening to the people living in it?

Having bought the house on the hill we now had to turn the house into a home. Getting our furniture out of storage helped. Along with the prints, amphora, bits of sculpture, the odds and sods that make a house a home. We picked from friends as well, but this was a more difficult process. Joan was lucky in that she met Dixie Preese soon after we moved in. Dixie proved to be a loyal friend—keeping contact by correspondence long after we moved away. Dixie was married to Verne, a very unlucky guy. He only had one leg; the other was blown off by air force pilots who bombed the safe bunker with Verne and some generals instead of the target.

An interesting fact: it wasn't until some time later that we found out that the locals called this stretch of Palm Avenue Snob Hill. Imperial Beach itself was covered with acres of low-cost working-class and military housing. Out on the fringes of this was the Chicano housing. There were just a few large houses here on Snob Hill, each with plenty of grounds—including one with a barn and some horses. Our house sat at the bottom of a steep hill christened Suicide Hill by the locals. Kids used to ride their bikes down it at speed, start to wobble, and crash at the bottom in front of our house. Cars would also fly down too fast and deposit their hubcaps in our front garden, much to the delight of the children, who amassed a fine collection over time. The local ambulance crews were on speed dial to respond when kids came off their bikes and broke their arms.

We were settling in, the VW was snorting and groaning and not really worth repairing so I shopped around and discovered that

Toyota was trying to crack the American market. They did so with a very nifty little Toyota Corona. I bought the first one—but not till after they accepted the VW as a trade. Poor thing! They could never unload it on the secondhand car dealers and I watched it sink slowly into the dirt of the back lot. The tires went first and it settled onto its rims at a jazzy angle. For all I know it's still there—a tribute to German *arbeit*.

Joan zipped around in the Toyota, chatting up the other moms in the school run. Todd was too grown-up to be seen with his mother, but she did manage to see his principal and his home class teacher. Their first shock turned to interest since most of the other moms were navy wives or Spanish-speaking Chicanos who carefully avoided him. Todd seemed to be fitting in okay, mostly ignored by both groups. Moira enjoyed school and settled right in. In fact she wrote about it:

> The school I first went to was Sunnyslope Elementary. It was very different from England, much less formal and much bigger. It was so sunny as well, not grey like England! I loved the lady who helped serve the lunches and I joined the Brownies like a proper American child. I loved my teacher Mrs. Morrow and all the lovely books that we were given. They were so incredibly new and shiny. Being a true writer's daughter, I used to stand them up on my desk just to look at them and smell them!

Living in California was an experience. I was hammering away on the typewriter and my ancient Rheinmetal portable seemed to have reached the end of its days since it had suffered a twisted carriage, crunched in transport. I felt that a new machine was in order—I had never had a new one before—relying instead on secondhand machines of dubious origin, meaning possibly stolen. So

I took a deep breath and bought a new IBM Selectric, just released on the market, which had a rotating silver ball with the letters on it, which we soon called a flying matzo ball.

There was no room in the house for an office—so I moved out. There was a grand two-car garage facing the front garden and I seized it. I nailed the large up-and-over door shut and put in an air conditioner and was right at home. I filled it with yards of shelves for my books. Its back door gave access to a breezeway to the house. All was well in Southern California.

But I did get a small whiff of the culture I was now living in. I hated waste and I muttered and felt the bent carriage on my Rheinmetal portable. There was a large stationery store in the next town and they had a typewriter department that had a display of antique typewriters. I grabbed up the Rheinmetal, put it in the car, and made a visit to the repair department. The mechanic came out and listened to my story, nodding in agreement.

"So that's it," I said, pushing over the typewriter. "Can it be fixed?"

The mechanic took his time, turned the machine over, sighting along the carriage, then testing it with a steel straightedge, then putting it down between us.

"No problem," he said. "Easy to fix."

"That's great," I said. But I spoke too early.

"But I'm not going to," he added, pushing the machine across to me.

My jaw dropped and I asked the important question. "Why not?"

There came a simple answer to a simple question.

"It's a commie typewriter," he said, and went into the back of the shop and closed the door. It had been made in East Germany, not West Germany. This was before Glasnost, and the two Germanys were still separate countries. American politics had taken a strange turn in the years we had been away.

This—and much else—got me up the nose. I was looking for an end to it all, but there was no end to it. I was just plain overworked, which got me down. And I just was not happy in America, that's all. The politics got right up my nose too. That part of the world where we were living was very right wing—they're all ex-navy and it's in their blood. It made for an uncomfortable environment. On an earlier visit to America, my cousin Debbie had thrown a party. She was an accountant and all her friends were in the same trade. I was chatting with one, an ex-navy man now employed by H&R Block. Which says a lot. The conversation went:

"So you're Debbie's relative?"

"First cousin."

"Great to have relatives you get on with. You still live back east?"

(The following conversation is quoted verbatim.)

"No. In fact I live overseas. In Denmark."

"So you're a commie."

"Sorry . . . ?"

"You have socialized medicine, don't you?"

"Yes, but—"

"So you're a commie."

He turns about and leaves. No attempt to listen to the benefits of the Danish medical system. How happy we are to use it. How capitalism and socialism mix easily to all our benefits. What had happened to my country? Had big drug and big pharma worked such a mind-blowing change?

There were other reasons for my dissatisfaction with living in California. I missed going to Italy every year and talking Italian. I missed the endless variety of Europe as well as the Esperanto people. There was no Esperanto group in San Diego—what a surprise! Maybe if I'd lived in a different city I'd have been happier there. But Joan loved every minute of Imperial Beach life. She had many friends there and she enjoyed the life, which made me pull back my neck and not complain for a bit.

Not that we didn't have some good times. Brian Aldiss and his wife and small son made their first trip to the United States—and stayed with us. We did have some great fun! I rented a trailer, hooked it on behind the camper, and headed for Mexico and Baja California. We swam, sunbathed, barbecued, ate glorious Mexican seafood, and returned, most reluctantly, to the United States. There was the time when Brian explored the joys of American supermarkets. This was many years ago and the first limping supermarkets were opening in England. Brian curled his lip at them. He pointed to an American employee who was cleaning up a broken jar. "In England it would be there for a week," he said. He was wide-eyed at the endless variety displayed and the sheer mileage of shelves. In the very center of all this food was a little snack bar for those stricken by sudden hunger. Among the items on offer was an English Burger.

"What," Brian asked, "is that."

"Haven't the foggiest. I'll ask . . ."

"No, don't—because I know! It's a burger which, after cooking, is cooled down on a chiller plate—then served with a cigarette butt crushed out in it." He wasn't being kind to the English that day.

I had taken Brian to the various beer bars that stretched the length of Palm Avenue. They served bottled and draft at exactly the same price and they all appeared identical. They weren't—and the stranger soon felt uncomfortable and left. Each bar had a very exact clientele, with no exceptions. The one next to the supermarket was for wives of petty officers who were at sea. Strictly female, with the occasional much-striped sailor home on leave.

Around the corner next to the post office was for younger other ranks—no ordinary seamen. It goes without saying that Brian helped me with my research—his English accent confusing them when he ordered the beer. Then there were the ordinary, rough-and-tumble California tough bars. Brian was specially fond of the one where the murder had taken place. It was only a bit of a punch-up between a navy chief—out of uniform—and a Mexican-American. It would have ended at that—torn shirts and a few black eyes—had the chief's date not taken a revolver from her bra and passed it over. A single shot, a dead Mexican. The chief handed her back the gun and ran out the door but he was back just when the police and the MPs showed up. He had changed into uniform. What Brian liked most about the story was the busty girlfriend. Who when asked why she had the gun explained that she always had a gun in her bra . . .

Brian enjoyed the frontierlike quality of Imperial Beach but, sadly, it was time to leave. Brian and I were enjoying a last beer when he hesitated—then said with feeling, "I've enjoyed every moment—so don't get me wrong . . .

"But I do feel that you are knee-high in a waist-deep culture."

He didn't elaborate.

He didn't have to.

Living in California meant that, inevitably, I was going to get involved with films. But this was from left field. I was contacted by Alex Cox, the most creative of the new generation of filmmakers. He had made the classic *Repo Man*. Now he had squeezed a twenty-four-hour option out of my agent for *Bill, the Galactic Hero*. We met for breakfast at one of the delis and took it from there. There was a lot of interest in our pitch, followed by a positive maybe. Depressing on one hand, but exciting for me to make all these contacts.* The best was Roger Corman. We talked a lot about film, and it was a revelation to me to listen to two real pros. No sale was made but Roger called me in a few days later and asked me to write an SF screenplay for him; I replied with an instant yes. I would get five thousand dollars for the script. Whether the film flopped or was a big success that would be my fee. Working for Roger was a gamble.

---

*Harry Harrison's sense of chronology failed him here. As written, it appears that his contact with Cox was in the 1960s, when in fact it was decades later. The filming only just being made in the twenty-first century.—ed.

Many big directors and actors had owed their success to Roger—and his fixed-fee contracts.

I read through the proposed outline and there were opportunities. But the walking through the forest inside giant wooden wheels wouldn't fly.

"The backer wants big wooden wheels," Roger said.

"I've just thought of a way to make wheels work!"

I wrote the script and sent it to Roger. Who called me in a week later.

"Not a bad script, though it requires some work."

"Happy to do it."

"You won't have to; the project goes back into the file cabinet." I kept the five grand and it would be some years before I wrote another script.

Not that my name wasn't known. *Star Trek* was in its early weeks and already hitting the charts. So I should have been flattered when Gene Roddenberry called me in.

"You know, Harry, this show eats ideas, zipping round space and all that."

"I know. And I'm here to help. How about some bright new twists? Two, maybe three of them, new and applicable to your show."

"That's what I want!"

"Three ideas at a time and they'll only cost five hundred dollars each, a bargain."

"Well, I don't know . . ."

Well I knew. Ideas are gold in Hollywood. He could have afforded it ten times over. But he was just a schlock merchant who would always think cheap. It would be some time before my film career took off. Meanwhile I wrote my books for a growing readership.

15

Brian Aldiss and I got to know each other in the 1960s through our common interest in good science fiction. Brian was literary editor at the *Oxford Mail,* and at the same time was writing very classy reviews for the British Science Fiction Association magazine, *Vector.* I wrote for the same magazine. We corresponded and found that we had very much in common, and the friendship grew bit by bit. Out of this came the idea of having a magazine devoted to intelligent reviews of science fiction. Along with Tom Boardman and his publishing know-how we created *SF Horizons,* the first serious critical magazine about science fiction. We did only two issues of reviews and articles and—an idea pinched from *The Paris Review*—interviews. It cost you nothing to get a guy talking about his work. Kingsley Amis interviewed C. S. Lewis in the first issue. Jim Blish was a great fan of William Burroughs and went to interview him. There was a good variety in there.

Traditionally, for about ten or twelve years, I would work like crazy all year round and Easter would be my time off, at the Eastercon in England. Joan would see me out of the house and I would go and stay with Brian. We'd have a few drinks then we'd go off to the Eastercon by train and do some serious fanac, which would usually end up with us doing the Harry and Brian act. One fan asked us if we did much rehearsing. Another compared it to Flanders and Swann. They wouldn't believe that it was all spontaneous. Then it was back to Brian's neat little house in North Oxford, with a pub located just across the road, a mucky duck (Black Swan) if I remember correctly.

There's a moral story of some kind lurking here. Brian had bought this house with the income from his first novel sale. I had bought four one-way tickets from New York back to Europe with the income from my first novel. But safely ensconced behind glasses of strong drink we let the ideas flow. We started a novel together but we were too different as writers. We hit pay dirt with anthologies. We started off with *Nebula Award Stories 2* for 1967, doing it for a miserable editorial fee from the Science Fiction Writers of America.

This started the blood stirring. Why didn't we bring out a Year's Best? There were other annual anthologies, but they all closed in December when the last magazines came out. I realized that we could close in November, because the magazines dated December actually come out then. By closing early we would have two months' lead on the other guys. Not only that but we would have the whole book done and set in type except for one story. We would put in the best stories from the December mags and publish in February of the new year and beat them all to the bookstores. It was a grand idea, except the publisher managed to screw things up and it came out eight months later, after all the other Year's Bests.

But our anthology earned out and was quite successful and we were very cheered. At this time there were three or four annual anthologies—Judy Merril had one, Terry Carr and Don Wollheim did one as well. But our tastes were completely different. I checked each year, and I was very happy that we never overlapped with any of them. Every story we had was completely different from theirs. I like to think that ours were intelligent, up to date, and fun! We got a fan letter on a postcard from Tom Disch saying it was the only intellectual annual anthology.

At this time I was reading *The Humanist Annual*—the atheist annual—and I found a short story called "Mary and Joe" that really worked. It was written by a Naomi Mitchison. I wrote and got permission from her, and I put it into the Year's Best. We began a correspondence and she sent me a copy of *Memoirs of a Space*

Woman, an English hardback novel. It was quite good and an American publisher agreed to buy it. Only when we met later in London did I realize who she was: Lady Naomi Mitchison. Her husband was in Parliament, her brother the noted scientist, related to the Huxleys. In later years we would visit her in her fabulous home in Campbeltown, Scotland, where we had the chance to mingle with the Huxleys and end up feeling like intellectual pygmies!

I came to know Anthony Burgess in a similar way. I anthologized one of his stories and we began a correspondence. We met in New York over a curry that he cooked. This began a friendship that lasted a good number of years.

We were still churning out the Year's Best. We looked at what we had and figured that by December, if science fiction magazines hadn't filled three-quarters of the book, we were going to put in stories from elsewhere. Brian was a great guy for justifying the use of a story. I remember we had one where this guy is hit by a car, and he's lying unconscious on the ground, paralyzed. But he can hear people talking about him. I asked, "Brian, how can we justify this as science fiction?" He wrote back, *This man, trapped under this car, is as far from humanity as he would be if he was on one of the moons of Jupiter.* Absolute nonsense—but it worked!

Brian and I also did the Decades series. We started with the "golden years," the '40s, which was the Campbell era. It wasn't planned that way but all of the stories were from *Astounding-Analog.* Then we did the '50s and the '60s. We couldn't do the '70s because we were still in the '70s. We were going to go back and do the '30s—but the stories were unbelievably awful, even those in the anthologies. Damon Knight did a pre-golden years anthology, Asimov did one—and I found all of the stories unreadable. We gave up on the decade idea and killed the series.

We worked well together but you couldn't find two more different writers in the entire universe—Brian and I had nothing in common in our writing—but we found out very early on that critically, as editors, we agreed 100 percent. In fact, we agreed never to disagree. Over all the years, in over a dozen anthologies with a dozen or so stories in each, there was only one story that one of us picked that the other didn't like. We just threw it out.

Publishers must have been eager for anthologies. They made money for everybody. I earned enough from them to give up writing *Flash Gordon*. I was still turning out a book a year. We'd get ideas for anthologies, and we'd just do them on the spot, such as *Hell's Cartographers*. One day Brian said we just get six of our friends to write ten thousand words on how they work and we have the book. "Who are the other four other guys?" I asked him.

Those chosen produced good copy, including Damon Knight, who sent in over sixty thousand words instead of the ten thousand. He thanked us for breaking a many-years-long writer's block.

Those days are long gone. I remember once I was staying with Brian at his house in Oxford, which was a charming old three-story house, very echoey. We had a bottle of Johnnie Walker that was providing us with inspiration. We were talking, remembering lost stories, putting together the anthology, climbing his shelves searching for the right stories. By the time the bottle was emptied, we had a pile of mags with bookmarks in them.

Next morning we looked through the pile of stories, and they made a very good anthology. The ones Brian had picked were quite good, and he enjoyed my selection. But there was one remaining story that I hadn't picked and neither had Brian. We figured Johnnie Walker was the only other person who could have picked it!

———

Brian has wider tastes than I have. Pamela Zoline wrote a story called "The Heat Death of the Universe," which Brian put into a couple of anthologies. I loathed it: nothing happened in it at all. Brian liked the avant-garde science fiction of the "new wave." Judy Merril invented the term for an anthology. I wasn't against it—I printed "new wave" stories, including Norman Spinrad's "The Last

Hurrah of the Golden Horde." But many so-called new wave writers just couldn't write very well. The best of the whole lot was Brian Aldiss's *Barefoot in the Head*. He read the French avant-garde writer Alain Robbe-Grillet, who inspired him. I read the English translation of Robbe-Grillet's book and Brian's was quite an improvement on it!

Brian and I agreed that stories in our anthologies had to be entertaining and they had to be correct scientifically. We had some odd items in there—like the computer-written short story and the complicated diagram that was Gahan Wilson's "How to Write a Horror Story." There were a lot of good writers who didn't get the attention they deserved. Jim Sallis, who published in *New Worlds*. Bob Shaw was a good writer, very subtle—he didn't write enough. He reminded me a bit of Jim White—sotto voce. Both were very quiet, soft-spoken, and very literate, but able to put the boot in when needed. The classic one from Bob was about "slow glass," a great story. Equally great was *The World Below,* a Jim White novel about a ship at the bottom of the ocean and the generations living there. Bob wrote Larry Niven's *Ringworld* idea before Larry did, in *Orbitsville.*

We both also believed that there's no reason why science fiction can't be well written, but it's hard to find. Some science fiction will never be well written—by the scientists and engineers who have fantastic ideas expressed in limping prose. We were so happy when people like Tom Disch came along, an author who would get a story right—and who could *write* as well.

Every year we'd end up with two or three or four stories from general fiction or "art" fiction magazines that were nothing to do with science fiction. Brian would write a justification that made it seem like science fiction. I dug a lot of Borges out that had never been published in the States. We did two or three of his stories before they discovered that fifty dollars wasn't what Borges should have been getting! They upped it to a thousand and we couldn't afford him anymore.

16

As well as writing and editing, I used to give lectures in the United States. I'd get five hundred dollars for a lecture. I had an agent, and I went from college to college—he'd line up three or four or five who were interested, and they'd put a lecture on and charge a dollar a head, and I'd get five hundred. It was the same lecture, on science fiction—I honed it, gave it a fine polish. It was full of gags and lightweight stuff and it almost killed me. It's very hard to get up in front of five to eight hundred people and give them a talk with jokes and everything else. The lectures were given at state colleges in the Midwest, and I used to drive from college to college, and I'd do four or five of these things. I'd go to one of the chain motels, which are all the same—when you got up in the night you knew where to go to pee. I'd have a bottle of gin, and a bottle of tomato juice, and I wasn't eating at all or sleeping at all. I'd have a hamburger or something and I'd try to sleep and then go on to the next one. I'd come off it really crashed, but five hundred dollars times five was more than you got for writing a goddamn book! I once gave a talk on international income tax to the American Society of Women Accountants. I was an authority! The chairman was my cousin, Debbie. They were all ex-army or ex-navy, working for H&R Block, which is a mass production company there, and people were retiring to Mexico. I gave them plenty of tips on how to do it, how not to do it.

I also began teaching, because I needed money. Greg Bear put me in touch with a guy called William Rupp, a young teacher. He wanted to run a course for high school kids with my help. We planned the course, but it fell through. But I had the whole course outlined, so I raised it up one notch to college level. There was one guy there who was taking it for graduate credit. I was doing a graduate credit course, and I'd never been to college at all! That tells you a lot about college education in the United States.

The students in my class were all high school teachers, so they all had a higher degree of some kind. And if you're going to have a course, you have to have a definition of it. To get over that one, I got them to come up with their own definitions. I gave them a book to read every week and they complained—a book a week? I said, "Yes, this is not philosophy, this is science fiction. Kids read it because they want to read it." So in the very first week I gave them *The Time Machine*—I figured anyone can read that, it's fifty thousand words. That was the first one, to drag them into reading it, and the second one was *Galactic Patrol* by "Doc" Smith. I figured that was what they really needed, a good dose of what science fiction is! The guys read it all the way through, and the women screamed and hated it and didn't read it. We came to the conclusion, after a lot of discussion, that the readers of "Doc" Smith were all prepubescent little boys, and not only that, but the Gray Lensman was also a prepubescent little boy—you take down his zipper and it's smooth, there's nothing underneath it at all! E. E. Smith had a PhD—he worked as a chemist in a donut factory. He was a fat guy with big daughters—I'd met them at conventions in the Midwest—he was a nice guy too.

I had authors come in to give talks to my class—I grabbed anyone who came through town. Philip José Farmer, James Gunn, Willis McNelly, and Fritz Leiber used to stay with me when he was down there. These were old friends coming through town who needed a bed for the night, and I made sure I got a lecture out of them. In those days they were all half bust—instead of going to a motel, you'd grab a friend's house, and you'd get free drinks that way as well! Greg Bear monitored the whole class. He kept saying he would pay; he never paid! I nudge him every once in a while,

Greg do you remember . . . ? It wasn't that much—twenty or thirty bucks, I don't remember. I made him work for his money. One of the books in there was *Odd John* by Olaf Stapledon, and Greg is a great Stapledon fan, so I had him give a lecture on Stapledon.

I couldn't offer the course for college credit until I had one guy, an engineer, who wanted to be a writer. He thought you had to go to college and get a degree to become a writer. Every week he'd come to class and he had a short story. It wasn't too bad. He gave me the short story to read, and I'd take it home and read it, and return it the next week corrected and he'd take it away and work on it, and after about five weeks he had the final copy. I said, "Why don't you send this to Damon Knight? It's the kind of thing he likes. I wouldn't buy it myself, I don't buy that kind of story." Damon bought the story. And the guy almost quit the class! He said, "I came here to learn to write, and now I'm a writer!" I said don't go, don't go. I made him stick around to get college credit. That's how we got a credit course.

The final examination was a party at my house and anyone who attended—and survived—passed with 100 percent. I think I did the course twice at least, maybe even three times. It's a lot of trouble getting a course together, but it's easier to repeat it.

———

There was a circle of young writers—neo-science fiction writers—learning in the "Harrison school of writing." There were two or three who had sold stories. There was a magazine being published out of an address where they were all living, in the Bay Area. There was one guy, Bruce McAllister—I put one of his stories in the Year's Best, and it was his first story. He lived in the Bay Area, and he sent me a letter saying he wanted to come round and see me. So I said sure, come on round, and he came with his mother and his father, who was an admiral. The next time he came without his parents. He ended up doing editing for me, on the Year's Best. He asked me how to do it. I simply said, "You read the stories as they come out in the magazine and you read the first ten words, and if you say 'This is shit,' then you turn it down and move on. We're looking for the best. You'll find out when you read these magazines that the editors have a very different idea of what makes a good story than I have, or Brian." Bruce had never read all of the magazines before, but he soon realized that so much of it was shit. . . . He was my first reader, and I really needed him.

Todd's teacher, Carol Pugner, wanted to do a science fiction course, so I worked with her on it and we wrote *A Science Fiction Reader,* a book for high school teachers to teach science fiction. Carol brought this girl, Joan, around to a party of ours. At the same party was Vernor Vinge, and she met him there. They got to know each other and eventually got married. My wife Joan was always trying to matchmake and was normally unsuccessful. This match had limited success as it didn't last forever—she went to New York and married an editor.

There is one anecdote that is almost too awful to print—a personal tragedy. There was a group of young science fiction writers there. One of them was a writer called Robert Taylor, who was a pretty good writer—this was during the Vietnam War when the draft was on—one day he said his problems were solved: he was volunteering. I said: "You're *volunteering*?"

He said: "I want to be a teacher and they've promised to send me to school and then I can teach in the military school."

"No," I said, "they're lying to you. It's the military: didn't you read *Bill, the Galactic Hero*?" I couldn't talk him out of it. I got a couple of letters back from him—he was in a bad emotional state. They lied to him and put him on the front line. He had a nervous breakdown, was cashiered out of the army, and it destroyed his life completely. That was one time when I couldn't say "I told you so." I may have exaggerated a little bit here and there, but I didn't lie about the military. It happened exactly like I said it would, but I hate being that kind of prophet.

I got a card recently with messages from fans, and one of them said "Best wishes, Harry, your book kept me out of the army." He wasn't the first to say that. I was at a convention and a fan said to me, "I had my papers for enlisting in the army, and that night I read *Bill, the Galactic Hero* and I tore them up." I said, "I saved your life, kid!" So it was a power for good in the world. I was at one convention and a combat marine came up to me, bad eye and an ugly-looking face, and he said, "Are you Harry Harrison?" I said yes. He said, "Did you write *Bill, the Galactic Hero*?" I said yes, looking for the door to make my escape. He said, "That's the only book that tells the truth about the military." That from a career military man!

Another of the things I did back then was to edit *Amazing*—I was editor of the magazine that started it all! I did it for the money. The publisher who owned it then, Sol Cohen, didn't have any great respect for science fiction. I knew him from my days in comics. He wouldn't believe I was an artist, so he sat me down in a room and gave me a penciled page and said, ink it. He should have stayed in comics. He was one of the more desperate publishers. When the bastard bought the rights to the magazine *Amazing*—the oldest SF magazine in the world—he got bound copies of the whole magazine, and he would tear stories out to put in for reprints. *Fantastic Science Fiction, Great Science Fiction,* and *Thrilling Science Fiction* were all reprint magazines from stories torn out of *Amazing.*

As an editor I was the first to buy a story from James Tiptree, Jr. "Fault" appeared in the August 1968 issue of *Fantastic,* which I was editing at the time. John Campbell also bought a story from her and his monthly publication schedule meant he was able to publish it first. But she was my discovery! I corresponded with her, not knowing that "James" was a she. I had her PO box number and nothing more. We corresponded for some years and I even got her an agent. Her secret was finally revealed when some fan noticed that the mother of Alice Sheldon had died, and that her address was the same address as this science fiction writer's mother.

When I got out of it, I'd been corresponding with Barry Malzberg, and Barry wanted to edit a magazine, so I said, "Why don't you edit *Amazing* while I'm in Europe?" I put him in touch with the publisher, Sol Cohen, and Sol contrived behind my back to throw me out completely and hire Barry.

The only thing I didn't do for money back then was write porn. I didn't join the Silverbergs and Malzbergs and all the others who wrote porn back then. I was asked, but I can't write fast enough. They would take two or three days for a book. They were only about forty thousand words. I forget the guy's name—he wanted me to go to work for him, and I was dying for money. At the time my mother was in a nursing home that was eating up money faster than I could earn it. This guy told me that most of his porn was written for him by middle-aged women. They would come down to the office and turn their work in. He said that the worst thing was that none of them could write—and he wanted to hire me to go through the first few pages of each manuscript and clear it up a bit, put in a few jokes or something and make it readable. It was a good offer. I told Joan about it when I went home, and I said: "Isn't that interesting?" And she said: "No!" I tried to argue for a bit. She said: "NO!" I couldn't get her to say anything except *no.* A couple of years later the guy who'd called me got arrested, and he didn't go down but his editor went down for a couple of years, for sending porn in the mail. Joan was right with that one word. I later heard from the children that they spent quite a lot of time teetering on ladders trying to reach the sample porn books that he sent me to read.

When I had moved over to the West Coast, I met an old friend who had been a publisher in Chicago. He was still interested in science fiction, and he took me out to lunch, and asked me about his old friends. Almost half the guys he asked about had been working for him doing porn, allegedly including Bob Silverberg. I didn't write porn, but I did write about sex in science fiction. Many years later after we had left California and moved to Ireland, a mad English publisher called Phil Dunn was originating books, and he knew I had been an artist and he said: "There is sex in science fiction illustration, but it's always subliminal in the pulp magazines." I thought about it and said: "Yeah, you're right." He said: "Why don't you do a book about it, sex in science fiction illustration, and call it *Great Balls of Fire!*" How can you refuse an offer like that? It was a lot of fun to write and to research, digging out things like old Krafft-Ebing.

Previously I'd done a lot of research at the British Museum but I discovered that every publisher has to send a copy of every book published to each of several "deposit" libraries—the British Library, Glasgow, Edinburgh, and, happily for me, Trinity University library in Dublin. It was great because there was hardly anyone doing any research there. I went down there to look for a book I had read many years ago that I knew I had to get hold of, called *Psychopathia Sexualis* by Krafft-Ebing, this horrible old mad Swiss who did research into symbolism, sexual depravation, and laying off sexual drives through mad fetishism. There was one mad glove fetishist who so loved gloves that he wore this great overcoat and when he opened it up he was nude underneath and he had about eighty pairs of leather gloves in there! He actually walked down the street with gloves on him. And if you ever wondered where the rubber fetish comes from . . . Krafft-Ebing has got all those things in there.

I needed to get hold of a copy, and I went to the shelves in Trinity for whatever the Dewey number is for sex books, and there was a big gap there! I thought they must be changing the shelves, reordering them or something. I went up to the guy at the desk and said: "I'm looking for a copy of *Psychopathia Sexualis* but it's not on the shelves, do you have it back in the stacks?" He said: "No, no, it's here." He reached under the counter and retrieved the book. I said: "Who gets to look at them? Undergraduates can't? You have to have gray hair?" He said: "I can't talk to you about that!"

It's great stuff. If you start looking at science fiction illustration, some of it's pretty obvious—there was a cover of *Galaxy* of a great big statue carved on a planet, with a guy in a spacesuit looking up at it, and the statue is of a woman sitting in a chair holding a great big rocket ship in her lap: it doesn't take Krafft-Ebing to figure that one out! And I found sadomasochistic torture and all kinds of things in those SF pulp illustrations. But the stories themselves were pure as driven snow.

Science fiction conventions were always a big part of my life and also the family's. The memories flood in. I have been invited to—or have attended—conventions in more than thirty countries: at a very rough estimate. At these cons I have talked with new writers, old friends, local SF writers. A movable feast indeed!

When talking about cons, with endless high points and very few low ones, the name Rio de Janeiro instantly springs to mind. This one had everything going for it. It was a science fiction film festival that had been tacked onto a world-renowned film festival. In addition to watching the films in Rio, we were going to have the pleasure of meeting SF writers who had been invited from all over the globe. Our plane fare was to be paid—first class!—which was a type of transportation unknown to most of us. On top of that we would have vouchers for our meals in a city that is filled with wonderful restaurants. It was almost too good to be true.

Which turned out to be correct—it wasn't quite true. The whole thing was a con arranged by two mad SF fans in Rio, one of them Austrian, Fred Madersbacher, the other Brazilian, José Sanz. They had talked the large film convention into tacking on the science fiction film festival. They thought they would just rent a few films, then invite a few guests. It wouldn't cost very much. Then, unbeknown to the main festival, these two organizers had gone overboard and invited every writer of note in science fiction. How could we not accept? We did, we did!

However, after the first rush of correspondence, not much seemed to be happening. Letters went unanswered, desperate phone calls were not returned. Then at the very last moment, just days before the festival, we all received cables to pick up our tickets at the flight desk in the New York terminal. The show was on! Only much

later, when the convention was in full swing, did I discover what
had happened. This was over a few drinks with Fred Madersbacher. It appears that he and his coconspirator had first invited all
of the authors—then had presented their bills for plane tickets to
the horrified festival officials. It quickly became a matter of international importance. The festival would lose face and respectabil-
ity if it didn't pay the invitees. We were not dead and we were
expected. Latin honor quavered and gave in. The con was on!

From the very beginning the entire affair had a surreal air about
it. I, and other American writers, met at the desk of Aerolineas
Argentinas at Kennedy Airport in New York. There were enough
of us to fill first class, a very good start! Until we saw our transport, the world's oldest 707—so bedraggled and oil stained that it
wasn't allowed next to the terminal and we had to be bussed out to
it. As we filed through its ancient portal, smiling stewards served
large drinks and things began to improve. However once we took
off the pilot greeted us and informed us happily that our next stop
would be Rio. Rio? An instant vision of the American hemisphere
filled my mind. We would be heading southeast over open ocean for
thousands of miles. Then the first land we would see would be the
jungles of Brazil. . . . If we didn't plunge into the ocean, the Mato
Grasso was slimily waiting. Would our ancient aircraft be up to
this? We discussed this in gloomy voices and ordered more drink.

Dinner cheered us a bit; lovely steaks, prime Argentinean beef
grilled over a charcoal grill in the nearby galley. At forty thousand
feet! I reached for another drink. It was an adventure. One I was
beginning to feel that I just as well could have lived without. Every
seat in the plane was taken. That was fine for first class—but what
about tourist class? Don't ask. We drank more, seeking oblivion,
knowing that we would wake up dead or in Rio.

We groaned awake in the first light of a new day, still alive;
bladders bursting. There was a long line for the single toilet. Alfie
Bester seemed to be in extremis and I suggested there might be
more toilets in the back of the plane. He opened the curtains and

stood, paralyzed. Every seat contained a crunched passenger who was eating from a plastic container, forks going up and down—since there was no space for sideways movement of the arms. Glassy-eyed, Alfie drew the curtains shut and said hollowly, "They're feeding the animals. . . ."

Alfie Bester was a good friend. When I came in from overseas I'd go and stay with Alfie for the weekend and drink, of course. He liked to drink and I don't think he knew how much he drank. He had gallon jugs of vodka planted around the house, with the lids off. As he was walking around the house he'd pick up a jug, balance it in the crook of his elbow, and glug, glug, glug. Then he'd put it down and walk around and do it again with another one. How could he know how much he was drinking? The answer was a lot.

I also knew him through magic. He was the writer, editor, and publisher of a magic magazine for amateur magicians. He wrote the whole thing himself, and through him I met Orson Welles, who was another amateur magician.

He wrote science fiction for fun, a little bit here and there. He made his money writing comics and radio, and later as an editor of *Holiday* magazine. He wrote some impressive stories, including one great one for *Astounding* called "Adam and No Eve." He never wrote very much SF, but it was all very good.

But back to Rio, a city of superlatives and designed for a science fiction convention.

We were expected and, happily, coaches were waiting, each destined for a different hotel. Normally, an opportunity for fannish confusion—but not in Rio. Toothsome, uniformed ladies had lists to see that we boarded the correct transport. Room keys were waiting at our hotels, along with program guides and meal vouchers for healthy sums, as we discovered when we looked at the prices on the menu. Not only that—the vouchers were good in the bar. Possibly a mistake; we hoped not. The healthy size of the vouchers worked out making the prices acceptable.

There were receptions, panels, and press conferences, which we loyally attended. There were lots of films, which we could avoid. When they were golden oldies, though, there were a few of us who positively embraced the golden age of old. At night Copacabana was a busy road of hookers and pimps, particularly the shore road, Avenida Atlantica. All the clubs were open for business from passing trade. I assume that business slowed by dawn, though I wasn't hanging around to find out. But it was midmorning that proved a winner. The knocking shops became beer bars, open to all. Brian Aldiss, Jimmy Ballard, and I sipped our beers and watched the passing parade. First to pass was Forry Ackerman, fan deluxe. I hailed him.

"Where are you going, Forry?"

"To see a film. *Forbidden Planet.*"

"Haven't you seen it before?"

"This is my thirty-fifth time."

"Forry, I want you to meet some friends of mine you may have heard of. Forry, this is Brian Aldiss and Jimmy Ballard."

"I've read every word these guys have written. Would love to talk but . . ."

"We know—art before pleasure."

Before Jim could finish scribbling a note for an article he had been commissioned to do, a large form passed on the pavement. "Hey, Van, a moment please. A. E. van Vogt, two friends of mine, Brian Aldiss and James Ballard."

"I've always wanted to meet Mr. Ballard."

"The same from me. I've been told that at your Dianetics Institute you can cure various kinds of cancer. . . ."

I will give you this much for the English—both Brian and Jimmy were able to keep straight faces and nod and say, "Oh, I say, is that true? That's very interesting. . . ." Van talked for about half an hour telling us how Dianetics was curing cancer, and neither of them broke up pissing themselves as they should have.

"Gentlemen—I must interrupt for an old friend, Bob Heinlein. . . ."

I did quietly ask Heinlein if he'd read *Bill, the Galactic Hero.* He said, "No, I never read other authors' novels." But after that he never talked to me again, so maybe someone read it to him.

Harlan Ellison—no, he was too quick for us. But Poul Anderson . . . Bob Sheckley . . . Damon Knight . . . Phil Farmer . . . It was that kind of a day and a place.

That afternoon was free and we all made for the golden sands of Copacabana, which was simplicity itself. We crossed the road in front of the hotel and spread out in the sun. The waves rolled in, large and thunderous, running far up the beach. They had rolled free the thousands of miles from Africa and had a wicked look about them. A few of the more foolhardy risked their pink flesh to the ocean's mercy. Brian Aldiss and I, both strong swimmers, found ourselves tumbled and half drowned, and staggered back to the beach and the security of the golden sands. Poul Anderson had found a shrinking sort of half-sized surfboard. We warned him that this was a wicked ocean—but his Viking genes took over and he plunged in.

"He'll drown," Brian gloomily predicted.

I looked at our fellow authors and saw salvation. Bob Sheckley was there, a strong body surfer and Poul's salvation. But he wasn't wearing his glasses and couldn't see if Poul was in trouble. The solution? We issued instructions: Phil Farmer, with eye of hawk, would alert Bob and send him to the rescue. Plans made and well in hand, Brian and I could get out of the sun and have a *chope* or two, the lovely local beer.

The sunburned swimmers trickled back to the bar, including an unhappy Poul. "I was all right," he said. "The lifeguard didn't have to come get me." His hand belied his words, shaking so hard he could barely lift his beer. Lifeguard? Drowning? What of our best-laid plan? Alas, it had gone awry—Phil, with his eye of hawk, had been watching the wrong swimmer!

The air of cultivated madness passed right through every function that we attended. The American reception was held in the museum of modern art. Not by chance, the film selected for the opening was *2001: A Space Odyssey.* Keir Dullea himself was shaking hands right next to the guy passing out large shots of Chivas Regal. Other than the nationality of the drinks being glugged down it was a pretty American affair.

It was early yet so we decided to see what other joys embassy alley held. The Italians were next and they proved their worth. The ambassador himself greeted each caller. He was a short and rotund man, his sparkling white shirt crossed by an elegant red, white, and green ribbon. We passed on from him to a waiter holding an immense tray of little pizzas. . . .

Clutching our drinks—a most acceptable red—we strolled out onto the balcony that overlooked the garden, where a string orchestra was playing some lachrymose Puccini. Tears in eyes, we resumed our ambassadorial stroll.

We ambled along, supping at the slowly decreasing edibles, until we reached the last—the Yugoslavian embassy, the poor man of Europe—and proving it. The curtains by the open door needed cleaning; the welcoming flunky gave us a wave of greeting and pointed at the drinks table. There were trays of glasses of mixed size and shape filled with some indefinable liquid substance that tasted as foul as it looked. One of our company spilled his drink on his shirt—which made a hideous stain. Some months later he reported neither smell nor stain could be removed; he had to burn the shirt.

It was still a paradise. When midnight approached we still had food vouchers left so we gathered at the bar, where the knowing washed down Beluga caviar with ice-cold Russian vodka. After a week we most reluctantly made our exits. We left with warm memories of a country and of a film conference we knew would never be repeated. The rickety 707 was an old friend now, the food just as good. The fact that we had actually survived one passage across the jungle meant we were old hands. Good-bye, Rio, good-bye.

17

In the mid-'70s, Joan and I left San Diego for England and were going to buy a house in London, but there were problems with the purchase. We decided to take a break and go to Ireland, to visit Annie McCaffrey and other friends. We spent two weeks there, laughing and drinking. The sun shone, we met a lot of people, and we had a lot of fun. Anne was already based in Ireland. On one of my annual visits to England I had stopped over in Dublin. I wrote an article for the Science Fiction Writers of America about being a writer in Ireland, and Annie read it and moved there on the strength of the article. She was the first of the science fiction writers to move to Ireland. More came afterward.

The deal to buy the house in London fell through. Many years later we did eventually buy a flat in Victoria, in Ashley Gardens, and kept that for god knows how many years, so we always had a foot in London. It was pretty tiny, but it was right down behind the Westminster Cathedral. And after going to Ireland for that short break, we weren't sure whether we wanted to move there or not. We found a furnished place on the shore on the other side of Dublin, and by the time the year was up we'd found a house in a condo. The first co-op in Ireland—that went bankrupt, of course, the week after we moved in. I spent years as chairman of the tenants' committee trying to get this thing back because no one could sell or buy. But it was very modern and very nice. It was on the shore at Sandycove, overlooking the harbor in Dalkey—the Forty Foot and the Martello Tower—I could see it right outside my window.

James Joyce's *Ulysses* opens there. I could look at it from my balcony every day and be inspired.

Before I went to Ireland I worked on *Skyfall* in London. We had rented a furnished place for four or five months, down the road from Gloucester Road tube stop. We were trying to figure out what to do next. The book had been sold to Faber & Faber, a very prestigious publisher. In it I needed to have a spacecraft crash into a specific place and blow up. I knew sod all about orbital mechanics, but I found a man who did, Gerry Webb. He was an engineer then on the British rocket program, which used American rockets from a Norwegian base for British packets. Very British, I thought. Gerry now runs a very successful business out of Moscow with Russian partners, selling packages for experiments on Russian rockets.

Skyfall involved American rocket guys and Russian rocket guys, training together, going up in a ship, a few little problems, and at the right time drop it in such a way that it would hit this one spot I wanted it to hit on the Earth. It wasn't too complex. But Gerry never uses one word when he can use forty-five! He was around for a couple of months—we were only there for a couple of months—and he was the world authority on high-altitude physics at the time. He gave me the plot device I needed for the whole thing. It was very simple: a proton storm—they hit the Earth, they disrupt communications, short out wires in the high-tension cables. What I didn't know—and what no one knew at that point except Gerry Webb—was that when they hit the upper atmosphere, which is very thin, tenuous, they are very powerful electrons, and would rise up to thirty or forty miles in five seconds. If a spaceship is coming around, and dawn comes, and the photon storm hits, it's like hitting a brick wall. So I could time exactly when I wanted to hit the "wall" and drop exactly where I wanted on Earth. Great, that was exactly what I needed from Gerry.

I also worked with Malcolm Edwards on a nonfiction book, *Spacecraft in Fact and Fiction.* I've known Malcolm for a million years; I knew him as a fan. The first time I met him was when he invited me to Cambridge, where he was an undergraduate. He organized the SF society there. I was a guest speaker. I was living in London, and they paid my car fare. I took the train up to Cambridge, and had a room in one of the colleges, with a bed and a chair and a light, and that was it. I asked Malcolm what he was reading at Cambridge, and he said, "Science fiction!"

He ran a convention a number of years later, in Coventry, and I was guest of honor. I hadn't been to Coventry before that. I went to see the cathedral there that got bombed in the war. It was a nice convention. Malcolm was always a superfan. He eventually quit academia and went to work in publishing, ending up as an editor. But before that he wrote this book, *Spaceships in Fact and Fiction,* and hawked it around, but no one wanted it. They said they would buy it if he had a collaborator who was a named science fiction writer. I said, "Sure, I'd be happy to collaborate on it. It won't be my usual fifty-fifty, because I didn't write anything of it, but I'd have to read the book if you don't mind, and make sure it's correct." I found the usual errors and things, and I changed the artwork where he had a diagram about how a thrust works to make a ship move in space—it was wrong, so I redrew that. That was our collaboration—I put my name on the cover. Why not? It wouldn't have been published otherwise and I got a bit of lolly out of it.

Around the same time I did some work for a publisher called Phil Dunn. He had found this artist, Jim Burns, who had done one magazine cover, in colored crayon of all things! But it was very good. And Jim had a great sample book. Phil recognized his talent and offered him a contract to do an illustrated book. The idea was to have an illustration on every other page, and I would write a story for him to illustrate. I suggested a couple of ideas. Phil was a railroad fan and I think Jim was too, and I said, "How about a railroad on an alien planet?"

I'd been an art director and an artist, and wrote a book I knew Jim could illustrate. I changed every chapter to a new scene to give him something new to draw, and wrote continuity between them. I wrote it like an adult comic book. I put in poo-bombers, and I made it mildly pornographic, with Styreen Fome undoing her zipper. . . . Jim used different media for the paintings and did a great job. It was called *Planet Story* and it was remaindered the day it was published, or soon after.

Phil was a sharp publisher and had a deal with a publisher in Hong Kong or Singapore for very cheap color printing. They would print by going five times through the presses, three colors plus black but *without* the actual text. The fifth pass prints the type in either English, French, German, or whatever. He had publishers lined up in each country and he sold them the book as a complete package, twenty thousand copies or whatever. The problem was that between signing the contract and the time of publication, the print costs would go up, and he'd lose a little bit of money. And every time he did a new book he'd charge a little bit more to try and recover his losses. Eventually his company went belly-up, but it was a great idea.

Jim Burns also got involved with another project I was working on. I wrote a screenplay for a film based on stories from *Heavy Metal* magazine. It was going to be animated by Halas and Batchelor. One of the stories featured a gorgeous nude woman, and a test animation was drawn. John Halas was one of the most skilled animation producers of all time—remember *Animal Farm?*—and he was not pleased with what he saw on screen: "Her breasts swing back and forth like two pendulums on a clock," he said. They needed an expert, and Jim was called in. He drew a three-second loop of her brushing her hair back over her shoulder with one hand. Her breasts rose and fell in what can only be described as a most attractive manner.

The film as we planned it was shelved: I got a "blow-off" check for a hundred and fifty dollars. The *Heavy Metal* movie that was made bore no resemblance to the one we had painstakingly envisioned.

We had been living in Ireland for a while when people said to us, why are you living in Ireland and not living in the country? We were living on the shore, only a few miles from Dublin—and we should have stayed on the shore. I was doing TV work, we had a lot of friends there, went to a lot of parties, and there was a lot of excitement going on. Then we moved out into the country to Avoca in County Wicklow, which was later used as the town for the television series *Ballykissangel*. I don't know how many years we were at house Kestrel Ridge, but Joan said, "We either move or I blow my brains out." It was a large and beautiful house set in the hilly countryside and was a perfect writer's retreat, but there was absolutely nothing going on there. Out above the Vale of Avoca, you could watch the water going by, and a train went by down there a couple of times a day. There were a couple of nice pubs, which we frequented, including one that still had a dirt floor. They pulled the pints from barrels. And when you wanted to go for a pee the guy opened the back door and it opened onto a field: there you are, a hundred acres, take your choice of anywhere to pee. That was probably the most traditional Irish pub I've been in.

But there was nothing happening—until it became Ballykissangel and then they'd come down in tour buses, but we'd gotten out by then. We bought a flat in Dublin, in Ballsbridge, near the rugby ground. There was a great Indian restaurant right around the corner, a relative novelty in Dublin in those days.

My daughter, Moira, had moved to a farm in Cornwall in 1984, when she was twenty-five, and had a small cottage attached where we spent our summers, or what passes for summer in Cornwall.

Mostly it rained. A few scant months after buying the working farm, Moira was diagnosed with type 1 diabetes. They took her to the hospital, and she called Joan. When a girl calls her mother and says, "Mum, I want you to come over and see me, I'm ill," she'll be out the door. Tell a *Jewish* mother that, and . . . I remember there was a knock on the door. Everyone knows not to knock on the door when I'm working. Joan came in all dressed up in her coat—"I've called the postmaster's wife to fetch me, I'm going to Cornwall." She had the plane booked, and all she needed was some cash. She said, "Moira called . . ." Bye-bye, she was gone. I went over in three or four days and joined her. We started spending the summers on the farm a couple of weeks later.

We always kept a place in Ireland, because I had family roots there and because the tax man there was kind to writers.

World SF—I can remember clearly just how the whole thing started. I was living in Ireland in the very modern apartment over-looking Bullock Harbor in Dalkey. I was sitting on my balcony, at ease with the world, relaxed, reading the London *Times,* and a news item caught my eye. It was just a few column inches about a literary event. It seemed that the Mystery Writers of America, the MWA, were meeting with their crime counterparts, the Crime Writers Association in London. Interesting but almost certainly dreadfully boring. I had been to meetings of both organizations and had found them a little on the dull side, nowhere near as much fun as a science fiction writers' function. As I read the report I thought, idly, that an international meeting of SF writers would be some-thing I would very much like to attend. I wished that someone would organize it, but who was stupid enough to volunteer to stage such a worthy enterprise? I looked in the mirror, turned away. No chance.

Thoughts like this lead to trouble. I was hooked—or rather I had hooked myself. I already had experience in running a conven-tion, having been chairman of one at the Henry Hudson Hotel in New York that the Hydra Club had sponsored. In addition I was personally acquainted with almost all of the American and British writers and I numbered a good many of European writers and editors as friends. Not only that, for some years I had been in correspondence with writers from behind what Winston Churchill called the Iron Curtain (a term not original with him; he borrowed it from Goebbels), the socialist countries under Soviet domination. I knew that I had had books published in the Soviet Union, since I had read reviews of them. At that time no money was ever involved, since the Soviets had never joined the international copyright agreement. The West stole their books—they stole ours. I had read some translations of Soviet SF so I knew they had a burgeoning SF literature of their own. Also, after living in Europe for over twenty years, I knew a lot of SF people there. My books sold well in Scandinavia, Germany, and Italy. We had camped through all these countries, meeting editors and writers. (Our children thought the world was populated only by SF writers. They were there at the end of any trip to any country.)

I broached the idea to Brian Aldiss and he was instantly enthusiastic. With his reassurance and aid I got the ball rolling for the First World Science Fiction Writers Conference, to be held in Dublin in September 1976. The fact that I was living in Ireland was a big bonus. Ireland was not a NATO country, that is, not a member of the North Atlantic Treaty Organization. The Soviets thought of NATO only as a group dedicated to the overthrow of the Soviet Union: the authorities there frowned upon cultural visits to enemy nations. At that time an Irish friend and keen SF reader, Fiach O'Broin, was working for Bord Fáilte, the Irish tourist board. He was not only an enthusiastic reader of SF but a good Irish civil servant who appeared to know everyone connected in any way with the government. Over a Guinness I broached the idea to him and I could not ignore the gleam of enthusiasm that glowed in his eye. Easily enough done, he insisted, not a problem at all.

Well it wasn't easy, nothing in Ireland is, but with Fiach's help an SF conference began to take form. All of the government agencies were behind me since this would encourage tourism in Ireland and bring in tourist money. Bord Fáilte would help with publicity. Hotel and travel bookings would be handled by the CIE. I also had an introduction to the Arts Council. This was vital if there were to be any Eastern Bloc attendees. In order to for them attend a conference abroad there had to be an official government invitation. The Arts Council of Ireland was official enough. They were shy at first, thinking I wanted them to shell out money.

Not at all! Not at all! What I wanted from them was a signed, official invitation. I would take care of printing more copies of the invitation. It was worded so that any writer could use it. Armed with this, the science fiction writers could get their various writers' unions to pay expenses.

For aid in contacting the different governments I went for assistance to the Russian embassy. Here I met the cultural attaché (who was also the commercial attaché), a very pleasant man named Romanov. A good omen. He would be happy to oblige—but his hands were tied. No cultural agreement existed between the USSR and the Republic of Ireland. He explained. "I speak to the Irish government. Sign agreement, I say. Then you send us harp player. We send you the Bolshoi Ballet."

This seemed like an offer that was hard to resist. We both knew why this lack of contact existed. Ireland was fervently Catholic and anti-Communist. Irish volunteers had actually fought for Franco against the Republicans in the Civil War. But times were changing. My tourist official allies were apolitical. A tourist from any country was gold. Sign! The pressure on the arts people was great. They bent—and broke. Very quickly after that cultural relationships were opened between the two countries. Score one cultural spring for science fiction. Ireland now admitted that the Soviet Union existed. The conference began to take shape, and thank goodness for the support of my family. Todd and Moira were both living with us in Ireland at the time and it could not have been done without their aid. The first writers began to trickle in from the States, mostly old friends; soon Joan ran a boarding house/ restaurant for penurious SF writers. It was all beginning to coalesce.

Memberships began to come in—and not only from writers. SF publishers were equally enthusiastic and I signed up many of them as well. The usual number of things went wrong that go wrong with any conference. We got past them. First there was the matter of gophers. Fan volunteers at any convention who will "gopher" anything. I hoped that the Irish Science Fiction Association would fill that hole. I told them they must wear suits, shirts, and ties, which led to moans of agony. Okay—borrow your father's. And all beards to be trimmed neatly, girls exempted.

Then the members began to arrive in the middle of September, 1976. Writers from the United States and the British Isles were well represented. Sam Lundwall, on a recent visit, came up with a photo taken at the conference and it is a bittersweet nostalgia trip to look at it. There, smiling and filled with life, are Ted Sturgeon, Gordy Dickson, Alfie Bester, Kyril Bonfiglioli, Jim White, Forry Ackerman, Bob Sheckley, Anne McCaffrey, Rob Holdstock, and Naomi Mitchison; all gone to the big conference in the sky.

Tom Doherty represented American publishers; John Bush, Toby Roxburgh, Nick Austin and Nick Webb represented Britain. Happily, French authors and publishers turned up. Sam Lundwall made it all the way from Sweden.

But no Russians. The one Russian I wanted to meet was Yevgeny Brandis. He had signed up—but unhappily died soon after. He was a world-renowned critic of English literature who had now turned to science fiction. (He had compared my work favorably to that of Jonathan Swift; I really did want to meet him!) In fact the only East Bloc members were Péter Kuczka and Peter Szabo from Hungary.

They must have given the con a good report because when we had the second conference eighteen months later we got not only Russians, but Hungarians, East Germans, Czechs, and many more from many countries.

The closing ceremony of the conference was a banquet where we enjoyed a very good Irish meal of smoked salmon, rib of beef, and dessert flambé—all at the unbelievable price of eleven dollars a head.

This first conference was a success—at least in Ireland. Press and television turned up and we had great coverage. The daily sessions were good and informative. Particularly a panel where writers told publishers what they should be publishing. While the publishers told the authors what they should be writing. Great stuff.

In fact things went so successfully and there was so much enthusiasm for another meeting that I bit the bullet and starting planning another one. Once we'd had a successful first conference, everyone who had missed it signed up for the second one. The venue this time was at the Royal Marine Hotel in Dun Laoghaire, the ferry port close to Dublin.

It was a resounding success. The Russians arrived. Yeremy Parnov came, the president of the SF branch of the writers' union—along with the president of the union himself. This was a great coup for SF because the writers' union ran publishing in those dark preglasnost days. They saw that only those authors they approved of were published. The Soviets opened the gates to the West for the party faithful. Hungarians, Czechs, East Germans, they all came. The Russians did not have very much money to spend and brought suitcases full of tinned fish to eat. Although Joan was in bed with a rotten cold, she took pity on them and their food and invited them to dinner. We did not have a lot in the house but a meal was cobbled together from packet soup and other fairly pedestrian items found in the cupboard. The Russian guests ate with gusto and were extremely flattering with their praise for the simple meal; I guess it was much better than having to eat cold tinned fish!

Attendees arrived from the West as well, authors and publishers from Germany, Italy, Sweden, Norway, France—they were all there, plus the Americans and Brits, of course.

And, oh, did we enjoy ourselves. This was cultural intercourse at its very best. (I will close the curtain on any other forms of intercourse. . . .) Deals were made, contracts signed. I met my Italian publisher, Gianfranco Viviani, and my German publisher, Wolfgang Jeschke, and we became the best of friends; still are.

Behind the scenes Moira was coping with the complications of people arriving from various countries speaking a variety of languages and communication not always flowing optimally. She thought she had everyone sorted and settled when an exhausted-looking man with a large suitcase arrived and stated loudly, "I am Russian and I am staying!" Eventually a room was found and diplomatic relations saved.

After the final session there was, by popular request, another meeting. Enthusiasm was high. How could we continue the good works started here? An organization was born: World SF. In a moment of madness I accepted the nomination as founding president.

For many years it grew and flowered. It was truly international, with meetings in many countries right around the globe, with officers from many lands. World SF became international. We had conferences in many of the member countries—then went right around the world. The conference we held in China opened that country to SF. I am much cheered the way my original idea has grown and very happy to see SF authors linking hands right around the world.

18

I was very ill and in April 2000 had to undergo open-heart surgery: I had a quintuple bypass operation. They cut my sternum in two and then wired it back together. For weeks it creaked when I breathed—the cardiologist told me this was normal and assured me it wouldn't break apart.

Nat Sobel, my agent, and my publisher, Tom Doherty, came up with two books to get me some money: *A Stainless Steel Trio*—an omnibus of three of my novels—and *50 in 50,* which I did do some work on after I left the hospital. I picked the stories after Paul Tomlinson scanned them all for me. The collection was published to mark my first fifty years as a professional science fiction writer. They say the first fifty years are the hardest. . . .

In 2004, Brian Aldiss and I were inducted into the Science Fiction Hall of Fame. He and I were the two living recipients, Mary Shelley and E. E. "Doc" Smith the dead ones. Not bad company to be in. The ceremony took place at the annual Campbell Conference in Kansas. We had agreed, Brian and I, that as we were being inducted into the SF Hall of Fame, we'd get all dolled up. Moira had purchased a new shirt, cummerbund, cufflinks, etc., and carefully packed it all up for me. When I got to my hotel I'd hung up my tux and thrown my shoes in closet. When the time came to get dressed, I couldn't find my shoes so I wore my brown sandals. The photos would only show me above the waist, so it wouldn't be a problem.

Brian came down in his tuxedo—and a pair of slippers: he'd forgotten to bring his shoes or lost them or something. Then a fan took a photo of us from the side showing our shoes! When Moira saw it she said, "Daddy, is that the best you can do?"

The Campbell Conference is also where they now present the John W. Campbell Memorial Award. Brian and I, along with a group of friends, created the award in 1972. Our intention had been to found a prestigious literary prize that was awarded for something more than merely the results of a popularity poll. It was to be awarded by a jury made up of authors and academics who taught science fiction. It didn't really work out and it was a foolish idea by hindsight.

We gave Barry Malzberg's novel *Beyond Apollo* the first John W. Campbell Memorial Award in 1973. It was a choice that caused a minor feud. Leon Stover thought it was a terrible book and the kind of book that John Campbell would not have bought. It was a very avant-garde novel, and the whole point of the award was to acknowledge well-written books of the kind John Campbell would not have bought. I didn't particularly like the book, but Brian and Will McNelly and others were all pretty hot about it, so we gave it the award. It was years before Leon talked to us again.

I have just sat back in my chair and have taken a good, long look at what I have been writing here. For all the very obvious reasons, I have been concentrating on my life in writing, my personal ambitions, woes, failures—and successes. I had the sudden realization that the most important fact of note in all this history is the momentous importance of my wife Joan in every bit of my existence. What my life and my career would have been like if I had not been married to her, I hesitate to think. Without her love and companionship my existence, not to mention my work, would have been quite different. Without her beside me at all times I would not have done the things that we have done together, been the places that we have been—nor would I have written the books that I have written.

So with her love and her unstinting aid I have become the writer that I am. Fifty novels later I pause to reflect. Writing is a solitary profession—but it should not be a lonely one. I can think of many people who have affected my career, aided it as well. Friends, teachers, other writers. Every writer needs support. A good agent must head any list of authorial necessities. Without a good, reliable, intelligent, tested, experienced agent, a writer has a built-in, lifelong handicap.

This is a truism that has proven itself time and time again. I knew one very well-known SF author who, to save 10 percent of his earnings, acted as his own agent. Early in his career an editor friend and I estimated that any fair agent would have doubled or trebled his income. By the end of his career he was out millions of dollars. (On the other side of the coin, there was another very good writer who stayed with a bad agent for his entire career; he was so lost in the agent's stable of second-raters that he received the same price for the last book he wrote that he did for his first one.)

As an artist, then as a writer, living and working in New York in the early days, I really had no need for an agent. When I first began working as an editor I began to have business contacts with most of the agents in the city. I was glad that I still handled my own work since I never hit it off with any of them except Bob Mills; Robert P. Mills. He was the managing editor of *The Magazine of Fantasy & Science Fiction* from its inception. He was also founding editor of *Venture Science Fiction*. When Tony Boucher resigned as editor of *F&SF* Bob stepped in as editor there as well. He liked my stories and bought them—but was a friend as well as an editor. It was my good luck to be in New York when he made a major career change from editing and became a literary agent. I happily climbed aboard his wagon. I think I was his second client; Gordy Dickson was the first.

Our business and personal relationship continued for a good

number of years. But I was living abroad when he became ill, and I knew nothing about it. When he died I found myself agentless and friendless in the cold world of publishing. What to do? It was panic-stations time.

Once a writer begins to sell seriously he or she *must* have an agent—this is a matter of fact, not opinion. A doctor who treats himself has a fool for a patient. The same is equally true of writers and agents. It was most depressing. I was living in Europe, pinned down to a writing schedule and unable to get to New York. And if I did—what would I do when I got there? After editing countless magazines, and over fifty anthologies, I knew all of the agents who handled science fiction. I could not see myself embracing any of them. For the first few years after Bob died, when contracts came up, I just renewed them, afraid to change a thing. But this was just painting over the cracks and had no future. Reluctantly, I scheduled a trip to New York, not really sure what would happen when I got there.

Then serendipity struck. A film producer friend in London told me that while I was in the Apple I should look up a literary agent friend of his. Yeah, yeah. I made a note of the name. But when I reached the city and talked to some friendly editors I began to realize that I had struck the mother lode. I wasn't acquainted with Nat Sobel, because, at the time, he had no SF writers in his stable. But he had many good writers, and even numbered English publishers and major magazines among his clients. He was a big-time agent, well known and well respected. But would he look at me and my specialty field? He not only looked—but he smiled.

We have been good friends since the moment we met. And he is tops in a very competitive field. Liked and appreciated not only by the authors in his stable, but by editors and publishers as well. Not only did joining Sobel Weber Associates seem like a good idea at the time, but it has been the prize-winner ever since. My everlasting affection and appreciation, Nat. Since you will read this first, allow me at least this little bit of commendation—knowing full well if I go on you will ruthlessly expunge all personal detail.

But you can't stop me saying . . . thank you! My advice to all writers is to get a good agent. Not just a good one, get the best. After that is done, take a deep sigh of relief and turn to the next big hurdle. Which is of course finding a good editor. I can happily report that I have been blessed with most exemplary editors, first in the magazines and then in the books. Head and shoulders above the pack was, of course, John W. Campbell, Jr. In his heyday he was the emperor of the SF world. His death did not diminish him; nothing could. He will stand forever as the editor who invented and shaped modern science fiction.

No hands will be raised in protest when I say this. If, like me, you grew up under the umbrella of *Astounding Science Fiction,* you were present at the birth of the world. The old *Amazing Stories* was a great read when you were six years old. If you had any taste at all, you began to have your doubts by the time you reached seven. I was twelve years old in 1937 when John became editor of *Astounding Stories* and the new age began. He retitled the magazine *Astounding Science-Fiction* a year later, and it stayed with that name until 1960 when it became the more sedate *Analog.* But whatever it was titled it was always his brainchild, his invention: the magazine that changed the world—our little SF world, that is. John knew exactly what he wanted to publish and worked his writers very, very hard to get them to realize that vision. The pulp hacks went to the wall and his band of accomplished writers prospered. Among their ranks are E. E. Smith, Robert Heinlein, A. E. van Vogt, Eric Frank Russell, L. Sprague de Camp, Isaac Asimov, Henry Kuttner and C. L. Moore, Clifford Simak, Theodore Sturgeon, Jack Williamson—even L. Ron Hubbard. Soon their ranks would be expanded by fans who read these first giants of the Golden Age, then became *ASF* writers themselves. Like James Blish, Gordon R. Dickson and . . . myself.

For me, like thousands of other readers, *Astounding,* or *ASF,* was the bible and the keystone to science fiction. However, unlike the Bible, it was reborn every month, fresh and new and filled with stories and ideas that titillated and inspired us. Since I grew up as a reader, it was the most important event in my professional life to meet John—then to become a member of his stable. This was not a matter of bending the knee and spine and submitting to his will and fancies. Rather it was a matter of hurling myself into the maelstrom of creativity that surrounded him, to listen to him, war with him, learn from John and the other *ASF* writers. I shaped myself as a writer, since we all must walk the final mile alone. But by god I was shaped in the annealing oven of John's genius—something that I will be ever grateful for. Late in his career he suggested that I should take over editing the magazine when he died. I recoiled, rejected the idea as honestly as I could without giving my reasons in too great detail. Because I knew that he was the magazine: the magazine was him. When he died that spirit that had created *ASF* for all those years would die with him. Yes, *ASF* is still a fine magazine. But it is not John's magazine.

A final note. When I was guest of honor at Devilcon 3 in New Jersey, I was interviewed on stage by Barry Malzberg. Barry is an old and good friend—and very much a historian of SF. He pointed out an interesting fact that I had not realized before. After the war, when I was writing stories and serials for *ASF,* I was most prolific. So much so that I had more words accepted and published by John than any other writer published by him at the time. Thank you, Barry. This is a warming and happy-making observation.

My first novels were all published first as magazine serials. Then they were sold as books. I was lucky enough to have the late Larry Ashmead as my first editor. I was also one of the first authors he published at Doubleday. He had been friends at college with another student who was one of the Doubleday family who later moved into the family publishing house. Since Larry had a degree in geology he was hired as a science editor—just when science fiction began to appear in books. Larry became science fiction editor because the word "science" was there. Sounds bonkers, couldn't happen. But if you know anything about publishing you will know it must be true.

Other editors came and went down the years until I settled with the happiest of sighs into the publishing embrace of Tom Doherty and his firm, Tor Books. Tom is an old and true friend who is absolutely the best in publishing.

I've been screwed blind by various agents around the world who wanted to sell my books. There was one I remember who was from India, and I remember his name to this day—Kunarumple P. Pernoose. How do you forget a name like that? And on his business card it said "Calcutta University, BA (failed)"! I sent him some books, and I told Brian about it and he sent some too, and he said: "It's probably a con job to get some of our books to sell." And it was, we never got a cent. But what I did do—I thought, what the hell, I'm corresponding with this guy—I said do you have any cookbooks in English about Indian cooking? I think I sent him five pounds or something, and he was honest about it, he sent about ten books that cost two-and-six each, paperbacks, in really crazy English. And with ads for the front cover. There was one thing I had to ask Brian about. This was about one of the measures of rice—it was a cigarette tin. He said that in India they had an oval tin. We finally figured it was about a cup or two or whatever. There were a lot of nice recipes, some of which Joan made, but that was all we made out of old Kunarumple P. Pernoose.

Once when I was in Europe a fan gave me a Spanish book to sign. I signed it but I'd never seen it before. It had my name on it. I opened it up, and it was published in Mexico City. I copied the details down and a couple of years later Mack Reynolds was living in Mexico, and I saw him somewhere at a convention and I asked him if he ever went to Mexico City. He said yes, at least once a month, it was only about thirty miles. I said, "Do me a favor, go by and see this joker who stole my book, and tell him I'd like some money—tell him you're my agent," and I gave him the address.

A couple of months later I got a letter from Mack, saying: "Listen, Harrison, next time you want to collect some money for yourself, don't ask me!" He went to Mexico City, found the address, went up the stairs, talked to the girl and went into the office: a nice guy with a necktie and jacket in a nice office, who spoke good English. Mack explained about Harry Harrison and his book, and he said, "Oh, yes, we published it. You want some money?" Mack said, "Yes." The guy opened a drawer, reached in, and took out a gun! He said: "I don't think I want to give you some money. . . ." Mack said: "I don't want to bother you anymore; I've got to go. . . ." That was Mexico.

It is these bad experiences that make you appreciate the good ones.

There are still many stories to tell, experiences that were lived. However, I will stop here. Science fiction has brought me a full life, along with my family—we have traveled and lived around the world. As well as my biological family I have had my science fiction family, where we have found a home away from home in nearly every part of the world. From these memoirs you will have glimpsed the things I feel most passionately about in life: my work, my beliefs, my enthusiasm for Esperanto and my family, especially my beloved wife, Joan. She lost her fight with cancer in 2002, an unimaginably horrific event. She left a hole in our lives that cannot be filled.

My daughter Moira has read and helped to edit my memoirs. She said to me the other day, "Dad, I thought I might be able to figure out the reasons we went various places and did various things by reading the memoirs but now I realize the truth. You did what you did because . . .

"It seemed like a good idea at the time!"

THE END

PART TWO

These essays were originally to be integrated into the main text of Harry Harrison's memoir, but Harrison died before he was able to do the work of weaving them into the body of the book. Because they were written separately, and in some cases repeat bits of material already in the book, they are being presented separately here, in approximately chronological order in relation to Harrison's career. Their importance to a reader of Harrison's fiction, and to his autobiographical efforts, is unquestionable, and they are entertaining and informative in and of themselves.

David G. Hartwell

JOHN W. CAMPBELL

When I was fifteen years old I thought John W. Campbell was God. I wrote that in the introduction to a collection of Campbell's editorials that I edited. I was of the generation that grew up reading Campbell's magazine. I read *ASF—Astounding Science Fiction*—and loved it. That was life everlasting! I read it before the war, I read it in the army, and I read it after the war. *Astounding* used to come out on a Thursday late in the month, and I found a subway station downtown that had them one night early, about a half hour's ride—an hour's round trip—and I read it on the way back. To read *Astounding* was a pleasure, while to be published in his magazine was a pleasure beyond measure.

I first met John in New York after I had submitted the idea for *Deathworld*. He had sent me back a long letter, seventeen pages in response to a one-page outline or something. So with that, I girded my loins and went up to his office and met him. As an editor he didn't need to be in the office, but he'd come in one day a week. He would read galleys in the morning. Then, after putting the magazine to bed, he would take invited authors to lunch, along with any other writers who were in the office.

He was a big man in every way. Six foot tall, and none of it fat. His head was shaved and he always had a cigarette holder in one hand, an inhalator in the other. Poul Anderson said that having a conversation with John was like throwing manhole covers at each other, but they were intellectual manhole covers. John Campbell conversation consisted of a series of pointed questions. I remember one day he looked at me and said:

"You're a medieval peasant and you're allergic to white bread, what happens? Speak up!"

I said: "Er . . . er . . . I eat white bread and I get sick."

"Right, and you fall down foaming at the mouth. Now where do you get white bread, eh? When would you ever see white bread? Only the landowner eats white bread, you would never see it."

"Maybe I get some that falls from his table. . . . Or he throws it out in the garbage."

"You're not thinking!" He'd crack the whip and make you think. I had about half an hour of this. My palms were clammy. I was wishing for salvation or for lightning to strike or something. Finally, reluctantly, he sits back heavily and says: "The answer is obvious. I said you were a peasant, remember? When would you ever see white bread? You'd actually be served white bread when you got the Host in church. When you got the Host you'd fall down and foam at the mouth—and *that's* the explanation for medieval possession! Go away and write the story."

I never did. If you want to write it and send it in to *Analog,* tell them John gave you the idea! In a conversation with John there'd be ten to fifteen ideas. He would infuse writers' little minds with Campbellian ideas. You could write them as stories for him, but he didn't demand that you wrote them, and if you wrote them, there was no guarantee he'd buy them. Randy Garrett made his living from John Campbell ideas; he used to write them all! Life was fun with John Campbell, I'll tell you! He made you work, and he'd make you sweat.

When someone asked John why he didn't write anymore, he said: "I have a hundred writers writing my stories now! If I have a hundred writers, I write a hundred stories a year!" He fed you ideas. With *Deathworld* he didn't tell me what to write, but he showed me new ways of approaching the material I had already developed. He brought new ideas out of my basic idea, expanding on it. It was an education to be with John Campbell.

John's office was just a few adjoining rooms at the back of a paper warehouse. When Condé Nast bought out Street & Smith, they kept *Analog* only because it was making money. But they had no office for it except in the back of this warehouse. He had one room where he did his correspondence, and there was a typing table where Kay Tarrant sat. She was the only other employee. She read the copy with the vigilant eye of a virginal old maid. She wouldn't allow curse words of any type.

This brought problems. I remember that in *Deathworld* it was very important that the word "damn" was in it. I asked John, "Is it okay to use the word 'damn'?" I could not tell him that Kay censored the stories after John had approved them. He said, "Yes, of course it's okay." But Kay took it out! There's the old story of George O. Smith being the only guy who ever got some dirty copy by her. He referred to a "ball-bearing mousetrap"—none other than a tomcat! She was so pure she couldn't catch the double meaning.

Lunch was the time when John talked to his authors. "Talk" is not the correct word—perhaps "destroy," "crush," "grind" might be better! He had appointments with some of the authors; the others just tagged along. John didn't care who came to lunch. You'd walk down the street with him and a bunch of three or four other writers. I remember once walking between John and Poul. Each was deaf in one ear. I had the good luck to be next to the wrong ear for both of them.

Lunch with John Campbell was a challenge, and there was really not much chance to eat. One day Randy Garrett was there and John was giving a lecture and all eyes were on him. Randy stopped the waiter and ordered a double martini, and I quickly said make that two. That's when I discovered that John didn't care what you ate or drank. Many times sustaining drink was the difference between life and death. It helped a good deal! He would ignore what you were doing, you could be getting drunk as ever, and he'd sit there with his cigarette holder in a world of his own.

The film *Lunch with John Campbell* is an attempt to capture one of those editorial lunches on camera. I was in New York having lunch and a drink with Jim Gunn—he was based at the University of Kansas and mentioned that he had some grant money for his students to do interviews with science fiction authors. He wanted to come to New York and do an interview with John Campbell. I said, "If you want to do a film about John Campbell, you should do lunch with John Campbell, because that way you'll see how John Campbell works and inspires his writers." Jim said, "That's a great idea, Harry, and you'll do it!" That's what you get if you open your mouth with a big idea. But I would get a free lunch out of it, and the chance to do the old verbal agro, which you always do with John, so it seemed like a good idea.

Gordy Dickson was in New York and I was talking to him about ideas that I could ask John about, and Gordy said, "You know, Harry, I always had a thought that the film *Lifeboat* would make a good science fiction story." I said, "Stop, Gordy, say no more. Let's present that to John Campbell, just that amount of material, and see where it goes from there."

We ended up doing lunch with John in his favorite German restaurant. Lighting was set up, there were two cameramen and a soundman. John couldn't care less what was going on around him, he was smoking his cigarette and nattering away. We started talking and like always with John, you mentioned the idea and he'd start with, "You couldn't possibly do it, it's a physical impossibility, it wouldn't work." Right away he would get your back up. And the film is full of us saying these wonderful things to move it along: "You know, John, you could do this and this. . . ." and John saying, "It wouldn't work!" And us saying, "Of course you're right, John, it wouldn't work. . . ." We'd instantly change gear. There was a lot of that. It's funny watching us bend our spines.

Within about five minutes, one of the cameras broke down. This made the whole film for me. When you see it, the one remaining camera is always on the wrong person. When John is talking, giving a lecture, there is Gordy knocking a drink back, or me pouring more booze.

We actually built the book on screen, plotted beginning, middle, and end, and then a few months later John died. Gordy and I felt driven to write the book and sell it as a serial to *Analog*. He flew out to California and we collaborated on it. Very early on we got a modus operandi. I write pretty much final copy, but Gordy was a wanderer and expander and he'd go back over it. We sat down and plotted the whole book very carefully, and then I wrote five-hundred- or eight-hundred- or thousand-word chapters, and Gordy would expand them to three thousand words. We had the structure absolutely dead right from beginning to end, and it worked well.

———————

I was in the middle of writing *Deathworld* or some book, and John Campbell wrote me a letter saying, "Harry, have you ever thought of war pigs?" I've thought of a lot of things in my life, John, but I've never thought of war pigs. He was very serious. Pigs have sharp feet, they use them to forage food. I know the whole glory of pigs now. But when you say "pigs," people think they're funny. They think bacon. And this was a very serious book I was writing. Who knows how long he went on about it. I was in the middle of a novel, and all I could think about was pigs, pigs, pigs. . . .

I had to cleanse my mind of pigs. I did that by writing the war pigs story, *The Man from P.I.G.* But it didn't exorcise them, because they ended up coming back over and over again, including in the last Stainless Steel Rat book, in which the porcuswine return. I got a lot of mileage out of the pigs! My daughter Moira must have been affected by this passion for pigs because much later in life she owned a farm and bred Vietnamese potbellied pigs. She was one of my biggest fans when it came to pig stories, and to this day is extremely fond of pigs, which was disturbing to her Jewish grandmother!

With a short story, John would either buy it or not buy it, absolutely black and white. But with a novel, he would work with you, often over a period of years. I think *Deathworld* was three or four years. I started *Deathworld* in New York, worked on it in Mexico, took it to Europe, to Italy, then came back to New York and I had some more copy, and I gave it to John, but it wasn't the whole book. He was very annoyed. "I thought you were handing me the whole book here; I don't want to read more copy!" So I settled down and in a few weeks wrote enough copy to finalize the book. The hero of *Deathworld* has got psychic powers, which John was into then and it fitted the plot, and became very important to the plot. I very quickly got rid of the normal psi stuff and had just this overall psychic "feeling" that this guy has. The money for *Deathworld* got me out of New York, because I had no money then. John was paying three cents a word; a book is sixty thousand words, that's eighteen hundred dollars. I bought tickets to Denmark on SAS.

When I was eight or nine years old in school in the States, we had an alcoholic science teacher. She'd usually come in and give us a chapter to read and answer questions, and she'd have her "cough medicine" in her bag. One day she decided to show us that when metallic sodium is put into water, it bursts into flames. Sodium comes in a jar under oil, and you take a dry knife and take a bit like a fingernail paring and put it in a basin of water and it goes SHOOF! Very dramatic. She took this thing out and cut a piece about the size of a lozenge! And she dropped it in the water and it went WHHEEEENG!!! and burned her hair and turned her face coal black! The piece of sodium shot up and stuck in the plaster ceiling and smoked and burned like crazy! And we were *impressed,* I'll tell you! "What are you going to do next week, Miss?" That was "science" for me! For years, until I left the school, you could see a bit of black stuck in a hole in the ceiling. . . . And the nonfiction articles in *Astounding* were also an essential part of my education and that of other young readers. I think the first time I heard the word "ecology" was in an article in *Astounding*. I was very interested and started buying a few books about it. John educated his readers, dragged them kicking and screaming toward intelligence—I know a lot of physicists and engineers who got into their jobs because of *Astounding*.

I was in the U.S. Army and I was in Moreno, Texas, and we had an old valve radio, and we'd put it on the truck in the morning and play it, and then we'd have to push the truck back at night because we'd drained the battery in four hours. We were shooting off the guns and then the broadcaster came on and said: "A bomb has been dropped on Hiroshima—a bomb of a new type, reputed to have the power of ten thousand tons of dynamite."

"Oh," I said, "must be an atomic bomb." The newsreader said: "It's called the Atom Bomb." The guys said, "Wha? How'd you know?" I said I read it in *Astounding*. It was all there . . . including in an early issue a spaceship powered by gasoline going pop-pop-pop-pop all the way to Mars! An internal combustion spaceship! John never pretended, he was always right!

John was a physicist; he went to M.I.T. and graduated from Duke University. He was a very hard-headed man, but he was also very open to new ideas. He wrote an editorial called *We Must Study Psi*. There were articles on dowsing. I never knew whether he believed in this nonsense, because he was a born troublemaker and liked to shake people up. When Dianetics first came along he believed in it, I think, like many people. By the time opinion changed he'd moved on to something else. I remember when Dianetics first appeared, it was in an article in the May 1950 issue of *ASF* and there was a very fine review of the book by Jim Blish. About three months later there were some very nasty letters destroying Jim Blish's arguments completely—and they were written by Jim Blish! He'd read the book again and said: "That's absolute nonsense!" John's brother-in-law Joe believed it all, and he picked up an outboard engine and died of a heart attack. Belief can kill you.

People came up with these mad ideas and he would print them. Like the Dean Drive: Dean was an airline pilot who took a power drill and attached these fourteen balls to his drive and put it on a scale and photographed the scale, which said, I don't know, twelve pounds, then turned the drive on and it weighed only eleven and a quarter pounds—three-quarters of a pound less. The correspondence came in—"It violates the law of conservation of energy!"—which of course it does (http://en.wikipedia.org/wiki/Dean_drive). John R. Pierce was an engineer, head of Bell Telephone Laboratories for a long time, and a good science fiction writer. As a physicist he couldn't accept this: he knew conservation of energy was conservation of energy. So what John did, being a good researcher, was he went out and bought a scale with the same name on it, which was a spring scale and not a balance scale, and did the whole bit with the damned Dean Drive and set it working, and found that it didn't decrease the weight of it—the vibration of this rotten apparatus caught the moment of vibration of the spring and affected the reading! If John Pierce hadn't done this . . .

———————

John Campbell wrote a lot of nutty editorials. John's word for them was "eclectic." They were argumentative, profound, and absolute madness sometimes. When I came back to New York—I was living in Denmark then—he said, "I've got a great idea for a book, Harry. A collection of my editorials." I said, "Gee, what an idea for a book." He said, "Yes, and I want you to edit it." I said, "Gee, what a *great* idea for a book, John!"

At first I didn't think it would be successful, but then it occurred to me that there'd be an ad every month in *Analog*—a free ad for the book. So I said yes. I went to work and started reading editorials, right back to number one. As soon as I saw the words "rocketry" or "nuclear power" I left it, because (a) it would be out of date and (b) it would be very boring. And John was often wrong about these things. I went through and it took quite a while. There were a lot of good editorials, and there were a lot of really bad editorials. And I put together a good book.

John read it and he liked it pretty well, but he said, "There's one more I want you to include." It was an editorial about rioting, and it said very simply that any riot, anywhere in the world—Calcutta, Belfast, London, New York—was controlled by the Communists in Moscow. The concept was absolute nonsense. "It is absolutely true," John said. I said, "John, this is nonsense. How can they control all the riots from Russia?" "They have their ways," he said. "They have a computer." And it went on. We had no problem except on this one. I'd see him every couple of months when I'd be in New York, and he'd say, "Harry, you've really got to put it in." And I'd say, "No, I can't really use it." And so finally I had the book approved and ready to be set in type, and he was still arguing about it, so I said to him, "Look, I'm very sorry, John, if you want to put it in, put it in, but take my name off the book. I will not be associated with a book that contains this editorial." And he said, "Okay, you're the editor!" The editor edits the editor! But he made me suffer for it.

I recall one day in his office, G. Harry Stine was there—he was writing juveniles under the name Lee Correy—and some moron in West Virginia had produced research that proved that the negro mentality was less than the white mentality because of a smaller braincase or whatever. And they had a curve—a bell-shaped curve of intelligence, with the whites up here and the blacks down there or something, and I said: "No, no." They said: "But it's proved in West Virginia." And G. Harry was nodding his head. And I said, "You could prove anything in West Virginia!" Then finally in desperation I shouted: "Gentlemen, you can't reduce everything in life to a bell-shaped curve." And they both said: *"Yes, you can!"*

That was the thing with Campbellian theory; everything was analyzable that way.

John was not right wing, he was not a fascist. He was a technocrat. He loved technocracy. If you want to know what technocracy is, read a Bob Heinlein story called "The Roads Must Roll." Basically the idea of technocracy arose in the States in the '30s during the Depression—it was that all problems are solved by bell-shaped curves. Engineers would rule the world and they would take care of us. On a scale of left to right you might call it right, but I call it technocracy.

John didn't really force his writers to accept his point of view. I'd argue with him often. And he'd win! You couldn't win, but you could sometimes fight him to a draw.

One of my books, *In Our Hands the Stars,* had a character on Mars looking out at the view and giving a lecture expressing my point of view—not just about politics but about evil—and I'd typed two or three pages of conversation: I'd let the readers enjoy themselves a bit and now I was giving them the propaganda. It was really very left-wing politics, and John wrote back and pointed this out and said, "Harry, you're making a point here that I disagree with completely. You're being unfair, Harry, because the other guy isn't replying. He shouldn't say, 'Oh, I understand,' he should say . . ." And John had written about a page and a half of counterpropaganda. I looked at it and said: "Well, it's his magazine. And I want to sell it." So I put it in. I had John's words coming out of the other guy's mouth. I did bend the knee that once, but so what? But when the book edition came out I threw it away! It was *my* book! A small victory.

In Our Hands the Stars was about an imaginary machine that allowed a spaceship to accelerate at one gee for half the journey, then turn about and decelerate at one gee. John had written an editorial on this, and I kept thinking about it. I wrote the book about ten years later—I stole The Daleth Effect from this editorial of John's. I wrote about a gravityless drive, and it works fine, but there was no explanation about where it comes from. You just leave that out. It just *is*. Because I wanted to have a gravityless drive. And no one queried it. John had said that with one gee continuous acceleration and one gee deceleration, it would take three days or whatever to get to the moon. I wanted to be more accurate, so I went to a computer expert, a science fiction writer who was living in San Diego. He had a dumb terminal connected to a mainframe, and he did the figures for me. The big Cray came up with the same figures John had worked out on his slide rule!

———————

I'd written *Deathworld* what felt like thirty or forty times and published it in various disguises, and I felt that there were other books in the world besides *Deathworld*. I wanted to get out, and that's why I had the idea for *Bill, the Galactic Hero,* which is a satirical book. When I wrote that, I knew John wouldn't buy it. Months after it was published he asked me, "Why did you write *Bill, the Galactic Hero*?" I said, "I'd be happy to tell you why I wrote it if you'll tell me how you know I wrote it." He said, "I saw it on a newsstand, so I bought it." He didn't read enough manuscripts that he bought paperbacks?! So I gave him some sort of waffling answer: I didn't want to say, I didn't submit it to you, John, because you wouldn't have published the damned thing.

I spent a year writing *Bill,* and getting very depressed. I'd write it and I'd laugh, and then I'd read it next morning and think it wasn't funny. I've learned one thing writing humor: don't cut it—if you laughed in the first place, leave it in. *Bill* was a completely different book. Terry Pratchett said he was inspired by *Bill, the Galactic Hero,* and Douglas Adams said *Hitchhiker's* was inspired by my book: he said it once to me on a radio show, and never repeated it in public! But it was a seminal book. People read it and laughed—there's not much to laugh at in science fiction normally.

John Wood Campbell, Jr., died July 11, 1971. I wrote a brief obituary for *Analog.* I went over to New Jersey for the funeral. I met with Gordy Dickson—he was staying in the Algonquin, where all the writers stayed. He had a room and I couldn't get a room so I slept on the floor. In the morning a car pulled up, Isaac Asimov was driving, and Lester del Rey was in the passenger seat, and somebody else was there. Gordy Dickson and I climbed in. There was a really good turnout; every single writer of note was there at the funeral home. His wife, Peg, had contacted them all. The only person not there was John. There was no *body* there—a good Campbellian funeral! We didn't know where John was, and we were afraid to ask. "Where's John?" I asked. "He's not here," the others said. "I know he's not *here,* but where is he?" He didn't want a funeral at all. He was cremated, I think, his ashes scattered somewhere. Peg wouldn't say a word. Isaac read something from the Old Testament, George O. Smith read something, and I read from one of his editorials—one of the nasty ones. We had some food and made some jokes, and we knew John was up there enjoying the whole thing. Jim Gunn said we should have some kind of memorial for him and that stuck in my mind. Out of that came the *John W. Memorial Anthology,* a final edition of the magazine he edited. And then a few years later, after the Hugo had been bought and sold one more time, we were so annoyed at the award for best novel of the year that we founded the John W. Campbell Memorial Award. We put together a jury of academics who are also fans—we figured their choice could be no worse than the ones made by the fans or the writers. It seemed like a good idea at the time.

Although we were opposites politically, John and I got along extremely well; we spent a lot of time together and became good friends. During one of our conversations he said he wanted me to edit the magazine after his death. "God forbid," I said. I didn't say, when you die the magazine dies with you, but my feeling was that

John *was* the magazine. "You're going to live forever!" I said. Ben Bova edited it after John, and did a fine job, but it wasn't Campbell's *Analog.*

John Campbell was responsible for the Golden Age of science fiction. When Brian Aldiss and I edited our Decades series we chose the best stories, and everyone selected for the 1940s volume was from *Astounding.* It wasn't done on purpose, it was just that the best writing in the field was going on there. The first SF novels published in paperback in the '50s had all been sixty-thousand-word *Astounding* serials. This is all ancient history, which I can sum up in one sentence: John Campbell invented modern science fiction.

MAKE ROOM! MAKE ROOM!

It was in 1970 that a Hollywood lawyer called my agent, saying how much he loved my book *Make Room! Make Room!* and that he wanted to make it into a film.

"That's great!" I said when the good news reached me. But then I talked to the lawyer, who was gloomy about the future. "We're a small company and it's hard to put much money up front." This was all new to me, but my agent seemed to know what he was doing. Alas, he didn't. In fact he made the deal in an alcoholic haze and was dead of the same within a few months. My agent agreed on a low option fee and a modest price to buy the rights—based on a promise of a decent payment later if the film did well.

This was all dreamland. Before the ink was dry on the contract, they had sold all the rights to MGM for a dollar. The office and the lawyer were just a dummy company that had been set up to hide the fact that it was MGM who were buying the film rights all the time. This complicated dummy company and all the fancy footwork were there simply to make sure that I, the author, was completely shafted.

MGM knew what they were doing. *Make Room! Make Room!* had been recognized academically and included on reading lists because it was accessible. It was one of the very first books—fiction or nonfiction—that talked about overpopulation. My interest in the problem of overpopulation dates back a long way, right back to the borough of Queens in New York and the subway exit on Queens Boulevard, where I met a member of the Indian Communist Party. Very few people can say that. (This was after the war—I got out of the army in '46.) When he heard I was a free-lance writer he sighed. "Harry, you will starve with your writing. If you want to make a lot of money, I'll tell you what you can do: go to India and sell them rubber contraceptives."

"I'm a writer, why would I want to do that?"

"Because you'd be helping the world," he said, eyes sparkling with enthusiasm. "India is overpopulated now, and the overpopulation is going to get worse. And, tragedy, India is only the first. Soon the whole of the world will be overpopulated. But you can help. Sell them the contraceptives they so desperately need."

Well, I never did get started in the rubber business. But he had planted the seed in my subconscious. Years later it grew into a book and, along with a great deal of needless thievery, into a film, *Soylent Green*.

As far as I was concerned, the lawyer's call had come out of the blue. It was carefully designed to look that way. But some time later I was having chat with the producer's secretary—the secretary is *always* the one to talk to, they know everything—and discovered that producer Walter Seltzer and Charlton (Chuck) Heston had been trying to get the backing from MGM to make the film for two or three years. They both liked the theme of overpopulation and wanted to get the film made. They didn't tell *me* they'd been trying to flog my book to MGM for three years!

They really got me good. One of the more crooked parts of the contract I signed, in my simplicity, prevented me having any control over the screenplay. I was supposed to sign the contract and fade away into the woodwork. They wanted to be able to change the title and do whatever they wanted with the story. Having bought the rights, MGM said: "Overpopulation? Sorry, we're not interested in that." It wasn't important enough, they said. That was one of the first rejections.

A hack called Stanley Greenberg was hired to write the screen-play. His script transmogrified and denigrated my novel, gutting it like a fish. If you do a screenplay of a book at full length, it would run for twenty hours, so you have to make cuts. Greenberg didn't make cuts. He threw out everything and substituted garbage for it. He reduced it down to a cannibalism tale. In my book, nobody is eating human bodies. In the film, "Soylent Green is people!" Charlton Heston cries out in the last scene. "Yes, my God, cannibalism. That's socially important. The audience will eat that up!" MGM shouted. This tells you something about the powers that be in Hollywood.

My novel *Make Room! Make Room!* is about overpopulation. I worked on it for a total of five years, digging out the material to make an intelligent estimate of what life would be like in the year 2000 AD. At this time, the 1950s, there were no popular nonfiction books on the dangers of overpopulation, overconsumption, pollution, and allied problems. But there was a great deal of talk and speculation in the scientific journals, and that interested me greatly. I researched population growth curves, oil depletion, food growth, etc., and came up with the figures I used in the book. I went to specialists—demographers, pathologists, and agronomists—and read a great number of very thick books. It took a great deal of time to write the novel, which was the longest I had ever done, because as well as getting my facts right I had to write a realistic story set in that near-future world.

Overpopulation had been a recurrent theme for years, but I realized that science fiction had fudged this problem by setting stories in the far future, and they were about as relevant to life today as Doc Smith's Lensman. I picked the year 2000 as being close enough to be a real threat. And I used the character of Solomon Kahn as the link to present-day readers—Kahn is my mother's family name on one side, and I gave him my birthday and military record. I am not Sol Kahn, but I wanted to suggest a parallel. My idea was to set the book in our own lifetimes—twenty or thirty years ahead—and make the worst prediction I could, writing it as a warning of what may happen. Dystopia is something science fiction does very well—shaking the admonitory finger. When it was published it had the spectacular success that science fiction usually had—it sold a few hundred copies in total! It came out too early, before the world at large became aware of these problems, and vanished. But someone decided to turn it into a film. A film that wasn't about overpopulation.

They showed me the screenplay—it was all wrong. I asked them if I could rewrite it. They said no. A clause in my contract said that I couldn't say one word about anything, or there'd be no money. But even though I was forbidden by contract to make any changes to the script, I nevertheless pointed out a number of inaccuracies and mistakes I discovered. I sent little notes suggesting things. Credit goes to the producer for taking instant action.

The film's opening is a prime example. In the dismal script, the action begins in Manhattan, no date given, green fog everywhere: it could be a million years in the future. I said, "You bought this book because, though it takes place twenty or thirty years in the future, it connects with *today*. People alive today will be alive when this film takes place. But the screenwriter has eliminated this. There is no connection with the present at all."

"Harry, you son of a bitch," Walter Seltzer said, "you're costing us a lot of money." It was money well spent—on Chuck Braverman. He'd previously done a short film, *American Time Capsule*: the history of America in two and a half minutes. For *Soylent Green* he did the opening credits as a montage of stills. Music over, no voices. They showed the settling of the Wild West, pioneers chopping down trees, railroads being built, going from wagon wheels to cars, slowly building to the opening scenes in the overpopulated and polluted New York City in the year 1999, very nicely done.

I rang up Walter Seltzer and said I'd like to come down and watch them shooting, and he said, in a moment of unusual largesse, "Any time you like, Harry." Being on the set meant I could make suggestions that helped bring the film closer to my book.

I went down to MGM, driving majestically through the great front gate, taking copies of the original novel with me, propagandizing everyone in sight, from cameramen and technicians to actors. Chuck Connors was a big, solid guy—an ex-baseball player, built like a tank, six foot four or something. I stopped him on set and he said, "Yeah, what do you want?" And I choked out, "I'm the author of the book the film was adapted from, and I'd like to give you a copy of the book." He looked at it and nodded. The director was setting up a scene and Chuck Connors yelled across to him.

"Hey, Dick, why aren't you using this title instead of that crappy *Soylent Green*?" The answer, which Fleischer perhaps did not know, was the decision made in high places that my title might be associated with a long-dead Danny Thomas sitcom called *Make Room for Daddy*. I feel that the title *Soylent Green* is weak. They didn't even know what Soylent was! In the book I mention Soylent burgers. I made up that word as a combination of soybeans and lentils. I'd always imagined they'd only have vegetarian food. In the film they call Soylent "the miracle plankton food," made from microscopic plant life. . . .

On a movie set there is always a photographer wandering round with a big still camera. I was on the set with Joan and the kids, and I asked Chuck Connors if I could have a picture of him with my wife and kids. No problem, Harry, come on up here. He put his arms out, wide enough to get everybody in his arms. Joan and the children are smiling—it was nice to be hugged by Chuck Connors. And I'm on the far left, and he had his hand on my shoulder, and just as the photographer took the shot, Chuck squeezed, his fingers crushing bone—and the picture shows everyone smiling except me, who's doing an agony take. He had a good grip, I'll tell you.

I was shown the set for the "meatlegger" sequence. Meat is in very short supply in the future. The meatlegger is like a bootlegger selling meat of dubious origin; dog is hinted at. I was suitably impressed until I saw that they had plastic bags on the counter. "Where do you get these plastic bags from? They are made from petroleum, and all of the world's petroleum had been used up by this time."

"Then what do we do?" Wail of agony.

"What all the Europeans do—take a bag with you."

The plastic bags were instantly whisked away.

The final sequence in *Soylent Green* was shot at the Hyperion sewage treatment plant, which was right by the sewage outlet. They built this new sewage plant and the state of California had some problem with it, so they just shut it off. The plant had been closed for a number of years. They were shooting all the outdoor scenes there. In addition they had an outdoor lunch set up on tables—it was really great food. The women disagreed. None of them would eat outdoors because of the dust blowing by—they were sure it was dried sewage. All the guys were eating outside. It wasn't macho—they just couldn't have cared less.

Real evidence of the dubiety of the screenplay was driven home to me when I overheard Edward G. Robinson say to the director, "Dick, I read the script and I don't understand my role." With good reason: there was nothing there to understand. Summoning up my courage, I introduced myself and offered to provide answers about his character. He ignored my rudeness, invited me to lunch with him, then listened closely while I explained the character he played as I had visualized him in the book: "You are the only person in this film who has lived in the world that we know now, who has seen a world of plenty. He can survive in this world of pollution, overpopulation, and chronic food shortages. That doesn't mean he has to like it." Robinson said: "That's a very good idea. Why didn't they tell me? It isn't in the script."

This conversation led, a few days later, to an act of cinematic creation that it was my privilege to witness. They were shooting on a closed set, which means no visitors allowed, just the technicians who were shooting the film plus the grips, carpenter, and electricians, who were standing by in case of any emergency. These guys, as usual, were bored to death. They were shooting a key scene that occurs about halfway through the film where they talk about how the world got that way. Sol (Robinson) and Thorn (Heston) are eating some pilfered black-market food. The scene runs for two or three minutes, shot as a unit, with intercuts done afterward. They had to memorize lines for this, which is hard for some actors. The script was devoid of directions or content, the dialogue banal. They did the scene and Robinson muffed a line—"I'm seventy-nine years old, I'm allowed to waste a bit of film." They did it a second time. And then the third time. Then Robinson took this really dreary, badly written scene and before our eyes built a new scene that embodied the essence of the book and the film. Old wooden-faced Heston had to actually act a little bit—pantomiming simple pleasure at the loathsome artificial food—which is all he has ever known. Robinson virtually embodied repulsion and despair. And it's not in the script. They're not saying anything, really. Robinson is *acting* and inventing the role on camera. When Fleischer called out "Cut!" all of the bored professional audience, carpenters, grips and technicians—no visitors—burst into spontaneous applause. This was artistic appreciation at its very best. The impressive results grace the film.

I was impressed by two inescapable facts: the truly professional ability of everyone connected with the making of the film and the truly appalling quality of the script. That a successful film was made despite what might be considered a major obstacle can be credited to the art and set designers; the director, Richard Fleischer; and to the fine actors. As well as to, I submit with suitable humility, the strength of the novel.

The film has its strong visual content, the correct utilization of the large screen, the escape from television's talking heads, and much credit is due to the art director, director, and cameraman. The green pall that hangs in the air makes the viewer aware at all times of this polluted and overcrowded world. It also adds emphasis to the beautiful Braverman graphics—with Beethoven's *Pastoral* playing in the background—during the suicide parlor scene. A perfect example of visual strength overriding content. In the book, Sol is a loner, a survivor, and dies after taking a public stance for the very first time in his life. The one thing that he would *never* do would be to commit suicide. Completely ignoring this fact, the inept screenwriter brings in that old SF cliché, the suicide parlor. Something I would never do. Ironically, it worked, since it was new to cinema audiences. The scene, which includes images of the clean and beautiful world as it once had been, also adds to the film's impact.

This continual visual onslaught conveys the message of the book—modified for the film. The idiotic cannibalism-crackers (not in the book) and the "big" revelation that they are made from corpses will have been twigged by the audience early on. This, and the cornball chase sequences, and the "furniture" girls (not in the book) are not what film is about and are completely irrelevant. The film, like the book, shows what the world will be like if we continue in our insane manner to pollute and overpopulate Spaceship Earth. This is the "message" of film and book. Both of them deliver this message in a manner unique to science fiction: the technique of background-as-foreground. This means simply that the story played out by the characters is not the major story. It is a means to capture the reader or viewer's attention, to reveal a greater truth in the setting where the foreground takes place. The film is a visual success. The background of this terrible world is punched home like an inescapable drumbeat.

The aftershock is very strong. Almost every person that I have talked to had the same delayed reaction: a week or more after viewing the film, memory of the action had dimmed—but the feeling of horror of this world had grown and intensified. The background had become the foreground. This is what good science fiction can do. It has a residual shock content. The technique goes back to dear old Verne and Wells. It dramatizes the situation and explains the unexplainable.

MGM originally had the amusing idea of releasing the film on a Tuesday, because in the film "Tuesday is Soylent Green day." They rescheduled at the last minute when some genius pointed out that the Tuesday they'd picked was Yom Kippur, the Jewish holy day when no one eats!

Soylent Green was released without much hype—they advertised it, but there was no Hollywood Boulevard, no arc lamps. It opened in forty thousand theaters at the same time. I was living in San Diego and went to see it with friends and family. It being California, they had the usual popcorn and Coke, and because it was a hot climate there they had cold slushy. They had orange slushy and lime slushy. But since they were showing *Soylent Green* the manager put up a sign saying SOYLENT GREEN SLUSHY. The audience had plenty of Soylent Green slushy on the way into the theater. And then hearing that "Soylent Green is people" they're coming out barfing at the green machine.

Soylent Green was the only movie MGM made that year that made money. That was the year of a movie called *The Great Waltz*, which sank into oblivion and lost millions. *Soylent Green* was shown in the States and all over the world and enjoyed quite a success during its release, and it has since become a "cult classic" on TV and video. But somehow it was still in the red—according to the powers that be, it has never made any profit. Creative bookkeeping made certain none of the film's profits reached the author. MGM loaned the money to the producers, and it takes its interest first every year. The returns come in and Charlton Heston draws on the gross. MGM take their interest off the net, which is very small at this point. I have points of the profit—and there's no profit.

I should have made money on the rerelease of the novel. What you should do with a paperback as soon as they sign an option is say *Soon to be a major film!* And the week the film is released the book is there waiting with *Now a major film!* MGM worked with the publicity department of Berkley Books, they had a fine illustration, everything was worked out, and the book was finally reissued—six months after the opening of the film!

If I sound bitter, it is because I am bitter.

It was an exciting experience to see a major film produced by a major studio. Also fun and exciting for the kids and Joan, as they got to visit the set and watch filming. It was a humbling experience to meet Edward G. Robinson, a great actor and a great human being. He alone knew he had terminal cancer when he made the film. He must have chosen to make one more film rather than sit quietly at home and await death. He saw the dailies, which he enjoyed, but he didn't live to see the finished film. It is a tribute to the hard-nosed film executives that they considered cutting out the suicide parlor scene before the film was released. But it is such an integral part of the film that it could not be done: his great performance remained untouched. Credit also goes to critics and filmgoers, none of whom complained about bad taste.

Ultimately *Soylent Green* works as a film. It moves, it keeps the interest, it is visually exciting. The message it delivers raises it above simple entertainment. There's really only one thing wrong with it, and that's the script. The screenwriter was a moron who had never even heard of science fiction. I only met him once. The film received the Nebula Award for Best Dramatic Presentation. There was a gorgeous event in Los Angeles—men wearing tuxedos and all of that.

An astronaut who had walked on the moon gave a talk, and I said, "I've got to shake your hand, you were on the moon!" That was a very happy moment in my life when I got to shake the hand of the man who held the flagpole on the moon.

Stanley Greenberg, who knew nothing about science fiction, got up to give his speech in front of the fans and pros in the audience, and said some inarticulate nonsense like, "It's wonderful to be here . . . my pleasure to get this award . . . through art and emotion and sympathy we will conquer the universe. . . ."

I gave him a slow hand clap and said, "Thank you to my inadvertent collaborator, Mr. Greenberg. I just want to say that not one word he said was true. It won't be emotion that will get us to the stars, it will be science, logic, and intelligence." I saw Greenberg scurry out of the back door and I gave him the finger. Everyone else broke up and gave him the finger as well. I had a really nice time because I knew the audience; they were my audience. That was a wonderful bit of revenge! Stanley Greenberg invented the idea "Soylent Green is people"—one of the dumbest ideas in the world. Anyway, the Soylent Green chips are really made of green-painted plywood. I stole a handful of them when I was on the set and gave them to the kids.

Just one final observation. With my hand raised, I promise never to let anyone screw me, or one of my books, again.

ESPERANTO

It was a lovely summer's day in Avoca, County Wicklow, Ireland. Wicklow is called "the garden of Ireland," and with good reason. The rain is far less here than in the west of Ireland, but still more than enough falls to ensure that it is green and blossoming. Not that I saw many of the blossoms. As usual I was working my all-day every-day schedule that I stay with until the first draft of the current book is finished. My study here was at ground level, offering me a small view of the Vale of Avoca through the narrow windows—and even more view of the Volvo parked outside. The phone rang.

"Hello," I muttered, mind still in the book.

"Bonan tagon. Ĉu vi estas sinjoro Harrison?" the voice said in fluent Esperanto.

"Jes, certe," I answered, trying to switch mental gears out of English. The speaker went on to identify himself as the president of the Universal Esperanto Association, the overall organization that oversees all of the national societies. I made appropriate noises. The president went on to explain that he had a request for me and hoped that I would say yes. He asked me if I would like to become an honorary patron of Esperanto. I was taken aback, my mind still in English, still in the book. Dimly, I told him that this was surely a great honor, then asked him how I qualified.

"Patronoj devas paroli Esperanto kaj esti mondfama," he said.

Which translates as, "Patrons must speak Esperanto and be world famous."

"That's me!" I remember thinking as I, not too reluctantly, agreed to accept this honorary position. I was in good company; other patrons included Ralph Harry, Australian ambassador to the United Nations, and Bakin Ba Jin, a member of the ruling committee of China. As well as the former prime minister of Sweden, along with others of this ilk who were ". . . linguists, scientists, and other eminent people who have made important contributions to the Esperanto movement, and who speak the international language."

Well—that is a long way from starting on lesson one of *Learn Esperanto in 17 Easy Lessons* on a hot summer evening in 1944. What sort of Esperanto road had I traveled between these two events? It was certainly a long adventure—with some exciting moments along the way.

My attention was first drawn to Esperanto when I was in the army, during a long, hot summer in Texas, where I saw a notice on the bulletin board.

> *Hey guys! 8 PM in the post church.*
> *Hear about the Simple Second*
> *Language that*
> *you can learn with ease—!*
> ***ESPERANTO!!***
> *Join us and be wowed!!!*

I was intrigued—and not only by the exclamation points. It was certainly better than another night in the steaming barracks. I went, and if not wowed, I certainly was intrigued. I paid six bits for a green-bound booklet titled *Learn Esperanto in 17 Easy Lessons*.

The book's title was true, too. Unlike any of the so-called natural languages, Esperanto is accessible, simple—and fun, which cannot often be said about language studying. That's the plug. If you are interested, enter "Esperanto" into Google and take it from there. Then read on to see what joys Esperanto might bring into your life. . . .

It helped me to survive the army. Learning to read and write

Esperanto kept my mind turning over in the intellectual wasteland of military life. Since the war was still on I certainly couldn't write to Europe; the places I could correspond with were limited to the Americas. There were plenty of *deziras corespondi* (wishes to correspond) notices in the Esperanto magazines. Very soon I had pen pals in Brazil, Argentina, Mexico, and Cuba, but these were handwritten—few of my correspondents had typewriters. Since that one evening in Texas I had yet to hear a spoken word of Esperanto. After the war I returned to New York and, for almost the first time, heard the language spoken aloud. I took a conversational class and very soon was speaking as well as writing Esperanto. I was a great enthusiast, and in the right place at the right time. New York City was the home of the central office of EANA, the Esperanto Association of North America. With great pleasure, I threw myself into the movement, stamping envelopes, sending out mailings, the usual. Joan—to please me, or to please herself; it is hard to draw a line—attended conversation classes and learned to speak the language as well. Eventually I became national treasurer. We made good friends in the Esperanto community and had many fine times. This organizational activity ended when we moved to Mexico—but not my enthusiasm for *la patro lingvo,* the father language.

Once we were living in Europe we found ourselves welcomed by the greater community of Esperantists. Explanation is necessary. There is a cultural and social world out there that extends a warm welcome to anyone who speaks Esperanto. Every country has its own Esperanto association. And there are numerous specialist organizations, like Esperanto-speaking railway workers, Catholics, Quakers, Baha'i, youth clubs, you name it—and there are Esperantists doing it, including myself, who has used the power of publishing.

Among the books I have written is a series about a character called the Stainless Steel Rat. I'll speak no more of it now—other than to make this observation. The publisher was kind enough to allow me a full-page ad in one of the books. It plugged Esperanto and gave a New York address for more information. In the fullness of time the ad was reprinted in the Russian edition of the book. Complete with New York address. Enough to say that thousands of letters in Russian arrived in New York—rather than Moscow. This took many years to sort out. Good fun—though the New York Esperanto office was less than pleased. *Esperanto vivo vi!* Live on, Esperanto!

One of the greatest things about Esperanto is the opportunity to meet ready-made friends speaking the same language in every country of the world. So one of the first things that I did when we settled into Denmark was to contact the local Esperanto society, and I began to appreciate the true value of the language. At the first meeting I attended there were mostly Danes and Swedes, but there was also a German couple on holiday in Denmark, a Yugoslavian doctor working in a local hospital, and three Greenlanders, and Esperanto was our common language. This was wonderful!

Since this was before the days of package tours and cheap travel, they had never met an American Esperantist before. I was invited on the spot to address the Malmö group, a short ferry ride across the Øresund from Copenhagen to Sweden. I had never done this sort of thing before so I made careful preparations. I thought the audience, being internationalists, might be interested in Mexico. I prepared slides from photographs I had taken there and looked forward to the big day. I must admit to a little stage fright since this was a totally new experience for me.

Svend Dragsted, president of the Danish Esperanto Society, introduced me. The sixty or seventy Danish and Swedish Esperantists in the room clapped politely. I spoke a bit about Esperanto in America and could see that I had their attention. I asked for the house lights to be lowered—and the room went black. There was no dimmer switch and no other light source in the hall but there was just enough light from the bulb in the projector to operate it, so I carried on. I showed the usual tourist items first, then ended up with our final drive when we left Mexico. We had driven through the seasonal cloudburst and the shots of the flooded plain and a mired-down truck drew interested murmurs from my unseen audience. Then I showed the pig truck accident.

"You will see that the tires on the truck are completely bald; probably a blowout caused this one-vehicle accident. An ambulance was just leaving, as the driver was sent to the hospital. About half the pigs had been killed while the rest were being rounded up by the police. Since all of this fresh pork would have spoiled quickly in the sun, the local villagers are doing some on-the-spot butchery. This will be a great addition to their normally vegetarian diet. . . ."

This was when I lost my audience. Even in the dark you can tell when people have stopped listening. There were murmurs, and people were obviously moving about. I must have bored these Scandinavians with my travels, gone on too long. I wrapped quickly and asked for the lights to be turned back on. I hadn't lost my audience—I had petrified them! Row after row of staring eyes and gaping mouths faced me. They were shocked. In years to come I understood the provincialism of these people; they had never seen anything like this before. They thanked me kindly enough before they stumbled out into the night. I learned to consider my audience better in future talks.

A few years later we had saved up enough money to make a summer trip to Italy, to Ravenna on the Adriatic. They had a large Esperanto club there. When I wrote in advance they responded with some enthusiasm and promised to help us find a summer rental. This they indeed did. I spoke to the club—noncontroversial, no dead pigs, and the lights stayed on.

The next day the chairman was kind enough to guide us through the various churches, to see their incredible mosaics. It was there

286 / HARRY HARRISON

that we met the president of the local organization, a Capuchin monk named Father Durante. We talked a bit before he was called away. It seemed that a priest had taken ill in a nearby church in the Camacho marshes and he was going to fill in for the man. He invited me to visit him in the church and I gladly accepted. Pastro Duranti was a small man with a squeaky voice—but was a great scholar as well. He was one of the people then working on a new translation of the Bible into Italian. Open on his study desk were texts in Hebrew, Aramaic, and Greek. All of which he read.

As we settled down for a chat there was a knock on the door and one of the local parishioners was admitted by the housekeeper. The monk's voice deepened when he spoke as the voice of the church. The woman wanted to make some funeral arrangements, but first she presented him with a bottle of local wine, a gift to the priest being a local custom. They talked, she left—and he got two glasses and cracked the bottle. It was good wine.

When we chatted he, like all priests, quickly got around to the relevant question—in Esperanto of course—and queried, "Are you a Catholic?"

"No. I'm an Atheist."

"Ĉu, jes!" he said, eyes sparkling with interest, an exclamation like "You don't say!" The lines for intellectual combat were drawn. He bested me in the beginning, since I didn't know what the words for the Holy Trinity and other theological terms were in Esperanto, but I learned fast and soon held my own. Of course theological arguments, in Esperanto, are thirsty work; the wine was there. There were occasional interruptions for church business. The next visitor presented him with a freshly baked pizza Romanoglia, a local oven-baked specialty, flat bread without cheese or tomatoes but coated with fine herbs instead, and delicious. Particularly when washed down with the local wine. We were already on the second bottle when darkness fell. It had been a lovely and stimulating afternoon, the stern intellectual argument softened by numerous bottles of wine. In the end he had to leave to ring vespers; I had to go out by the church wall to relieve my bladder. We embraced and parted, each to his duty.

This wasn't our only trip south. We lived in Denmark for over seven years. After trading the loyal Anglia in for a VW bus—fixed up as a camper—we drove south every summer to Italy, camping on the way in all of the western countries, and many of the then-communist countries. We made many new Esperanto friends that way, with sometimes surprising results. It was in a campsite on the beach in Yugoslavia that we met the eye surgeon from Hungary. We chatted in Esperanto while the kids splashed on the shore. When they had enough he invited us to his tent for a glass of wine. I brought over a bottle of Swiss wine, which was much admired all out of proportion to the quality of the wine. In his experience, shut off behind the Iron Curtain, this was an alien object from another world. Since the wine had proved so popular I dug out another bottle, which proved equally successful. The eye surgeon was relaxed and loquacious about life behind the curtain. It seemed that there was a limit on the amount of foreign currency he could take out of the country. It was the equivalent of $2.35 a day. Right there in the tent on the beach in Yugoslavia a great commercial deal was struck. He was very well off in Hungarian forints. While I was loaded with dollars and other Western currency, having come well prepared for currency exchange. With the simple preparation of closing the toggle on the tent flap we began our happy numismatic exchange. The doc set the rate—something like ten times the legal exchange. He was so cheered by the few U.S. greenbacks that were included in the deal that he said this was still a great cheat if he went to the black market. We finished the Swiss wine and deals were struck that pleased us all. We would be in Yugoslavia for another week, and the gray, limp banknotes really were a viable currency. The wine was gone and, financially happy, we retired.

The rest of our stay behind the rusty Iron Curtain was that much happier now we knew what to do with their decrepit financial system. By hindsight it seemed so obvious. We were loyal warriors in

the Cold War against Communism. We retired well pleased with
our labors.

Esperanto now was really a home from home, a ready-made
circle of friends that extended right around the world. And every
year there is an annual world convention of Esperantists, each time
in a different country. When we discovered that the world convention in 1986 would be held in Beijing, the first time ever in China,
I knew that we had to go; Joan was in complete agreement.

The trip was long and tiring but well worth it. I shall resist the
temptation to write a travel article about China and stick with Esperanto. Suffice it to say the trip and travels around China were
more than worth the visit. And the food! We never ate a Chinese
meal as it is served in the West. And every meal was a gustatory
winner. But back to the convention.

We were staying in a great Canadian hotel. Its existence was a
neat solution to the primitive state of Beijing's lodging in 1988.
The deal was that the Canadians brought in all the plumbing, lights,
elevators—all of the finished products of the West—while the
Chinese supplied steel, concrete—and manpower. We moved into
the just-completed hotel—with cheerful Esperantists on all sides,
all reveling in the *patrolingvo*. There were 2,482 attendees at this
convention—at the time the largest foreign convention held in
China, with attendees from fifty-one different countries.

In the morning I went down to breakfast—after making sure
Joan had her cup of coffee. There was quite a crowd around the
buffet table, which was being constantly topped up. As a tip of the
hat to the multinational crowd there was an oriental and a Western
table. While I do love my curries and tofu, they are not for breakfast. Bacon and eggs were in order and I tucked in.

I don't communicate very well early in the morning and hid behind a muttered *Bonan tagon* (Good morning) or two, but I could
still listen. All around me they were talking Esperanto and I eaves-
dropped automatically. There were two men sitting opposite me,
chatting away.

"I'm from Korea—and you?"

"I'm Chinese—but not a local. This is the first time I have been to Beijing—so far from the mountains where I teach."

"I envy you. I live on the shore."

They chatted on and my attention faded—until the teacher said: "This is all new to me, particularly the food. I don't think I like Western food."

Western food? What was he talking about? I looked up. I wouldn't like it either the way he was eating it—he was eating a piece of cold, dry toast speared on a chopstick!

The convention went from one success to another. It was indeed a feast of communication and a convention to be long remembered. The high point was the banquet at the People's Palace on Tiananmen Square (to become famous later after the man-against-tank standoff). When we went it was filled with a sightseeing crowd eager to see the visiting celebrities. As a patron of Esperanto I was high on the VIP list. On the morning of the banquet an envelope was hand-delivered to our room by a uniformed flunky who did everything but bow. I did everything but bow back. It contained a list of our evening activities, starting at the time of our limo's arrival. After that we were in the hands of conquerors.

As you can imagine, Joan was wondering what dress she was to wear. With no woman present she turned to me for aid, forgetting that I was a weak reed in these matters. Each suggestion of mine was rejected with a sniff of disdain. Eventually I was thrown out of the room altogether. A gaggle of women were passing at the same moment. "Ladies, I need assistance badly. Can you help me? My wife is having trouble choosing what to wear tonight." Since they were dressed to the nines and smelling of all the perfumes of the world, I knew that the ladies in my new audience were not strangers to the problem. I threw the room door open mere minutes since I had closed it and to Joan's amazement herded her new companions in to her aid. I introduced her new assistants and slipped into the hall and closed the door. Fingers crossed I made my cowardly way down to the bar. Upon my return I could expect happy cries of joy or . . . I shuddered and signaled the bar man.

I can only report a happy return; Joan was all smiles and laughter and had enjoyed the brief invasion. A few minutes later there was a knock on the door by our chauffeur, who politely told us that we were ready to leave for the palace of joy. A hulking black limo was waiting outside the hotel. Our fellow Esperantists cheered us on—and took photos of this great occasion. Waving to the crowds, we made our majestic way to the square, where we were slowed by the crowds and other arriving limos. More photos were taken— this time by the Chinese onlookers—and I waved, smiled, and nodded majestically at the crowd; a sharp elbow in the ribs curbed my majestic enthusiasm. We slowed to a ponderous stop, flunkies opened the door, a people's majordomo bowed us onto—yes!—a red carpet. This was the big time. Until they served the food. When I said I never had a bad meal in China my mind was certainly cleansed of this shuddering memory. It began with thousand-year-old eggs and went downhill from there.

Chinese friends later explained that at important banquets only special banquet food is served. Nobody really ate it and honor was satisfied by pushing it around my plate with my gold-tipped chopsticks. And oh yes, ha-ha, my friends explained that the eggs were only a few years old, maybe three or four, and buried in the ground to ripen. . . .

I have come a long way in exploring Esperanto. That demonstration I attended in Texas all those years before has more than earned its worth. I shall be ever grateful to that nameless GI who set my feet on the road to Esperanto. Learning Esperanto was a wise decision that I have never regretted. I can truthfully say *Vivu la patrolingvo kaj eterna mondpaco!* Long live the father language and eternal world peace!

Learning to read and speak Esperanto was fun. One thing about learning this language that I didn't appreciate at the time was that it proved to me that, yes, it was possible to learn a second language, or even a third. To learn to read it and speak it—and *enjoy* it. My linguistic experience in high school left me with no desire or intent to learn any other languages: English was more than enough, thank you.

Forest Hills High School curriculum required at least two years of a language. I opted for Spanish, which turned out to be a disaster—with all thanks to Señorita Murphy. I don't think she cared if we learned Spanish or not. Certainly I have no memory of any attempt to teach us to speak the language. I remember no nouns or adjectives—just lists of grammatical verb forms. (For some reason I still remember the preterite of *ir*—though I don't remember what a preterite is.) After two years of her tutelage I learned barely enough to fail my regent's exam with a massive thirty-one points out of a hundred. To take the exam again I would have to repeat the second year. But salvation was at hand, for I studied that year with Señorita Soller, not the dreaded Murphy. She did her best and I managed to pass the test with a score of exactly sixty-five— which was the lowest passing score at the time. She loved the language, read us some poems by Lorca—and I still remember bits of one of them. But the curse of the Murphy remained; I shuddered away from the thought of learning a language. A good number of years passed before the possibility was raised again by that poster advertising Esperanto!

A number of years slipped by before I thought of the dreaded Spanish again. This was when we had decided to move to Mexico. Were we naïve about this? About packing up the baby, loading the faithful Anglia—and driving to Mexico? Many would say we were. (Many would also think we were bonkers with the whole idea— and told us so.) But we did think about it, to the extent that before we left we studied Spanish privately with an old buddy from my early Esperanto days. Jim Donaldson was now a high school teacher in New Jersey, just across the river. He was always hungry and was more than happy to trade Joan's meals for him and his companion José—we exchanged dinner for them for lessons for us, an arrangement approved by all. Joan prided herself on her cooking and the fact that no one left her table hungry, except for Jim. He was tall and thin and apparently suffering from starvation. No matter what she made he demolished it—then smiled wanly at his empty plate as though wondering where the rest of the meal was. You don't do that to a Jewish mother, particularly one like Joan, who took great—and justified—pride in her table. Of course she won in the end. She forgot haute cuisine and settled for one of our simpler favorites. It was the most inexpensive and filling of meals: stuffed franks. A hot dog sliced down the side and the slices filled with cheese, the whole wrapped in bacon—a delicious and calorific cholesterol nightmare. I could get down one, possibly two of the things. To satisfy her pride she served Jim two, sweetly asked if he wanted another, then brought it with his happy agreement. I think he managed to get down nine of them before he signaled glassy-eyed admission of defeat. She smiled in satisfied triumph as she cleared the table.

The day came when we left for Mexico and, after an adventurous trip, settled into the small market town of Cuautla in the state of Morelos. Our lessons with Jim now proved their worth. The local Indians spoke Nahuatl, the Aztec language, with Spanish as a second language. So we and they learned Spanish together! In the year that we lived there we became quite proficient, learning by ear all the ins and outs of the language that aren't mentioned in the textbooks.

How could we forget the happy pineapple seller in the *mercado* shouting his welcome to the passing girls? The fruit was so cheap—and so ripe and so good. He would slice the top and bottom of the fruit with a wicked machete, then square the sides. Then he would hold it aloft and call out, *"Piña piña para la niña!"* Pineapple, pineapple for the lady!

After Mexico we returned to New York, then decided to move to Italy. Once again we did not think about the language. At this point, my narration is stopped by a hand on the arm and the question of why? Why move to Italy? I can but answer that: it seemed like a good idea at the time. Elsewhere you will find a more satisfactory explanation. Italy was a great fun. We felt at home the moment we stepped off the Naples ferry in Capri. We had the advantage of speaking conversational Spanish—the two languages are very much alike. The grocer in Anacapri, where we settled, cheerfully corrected us.

"No, signore, 'pan' es español. 'Pane' en Italiano."

"Pane . . . ?"

"Bene!"

Now we could eat bread. *Pane,* simple enough. I must take a moment to reassure the linguists and the purists—I hear their teeth grinding together. I know that my grammar is simple and probably wrong, my spelling impossible, my accent very regional. I can only say that I get by with no complaints from the locals, the barmen, grocers, and all the rest of the casual conversationalists. Life is too short for me for linguistic perfection. I happily settle for conversational Esperanto, Spanish, Italian, Danish, Norwegian, German, and French.

We left Italy only because Joan was pregnant and the Italian doctors more than incompetent. Back to New York, where our daughter Moira was born—and the world became a far brighter place. It seemed logical at the time to move to Denmark, and move we did. It was supposed to be a three-month visit . . . seven years later we were still there. A good idea at the time . . . By hindsight we never thought about learning Danish—in the beginning we seem to have learned it by osmosis. We were just settling into Denmark when Joan met Muriel Overgaard. She was English, a Geordie, her husband Kaj was Danish. Four-year-old Todd soon made friends with Thomas; one of their three sons. They were of an age and became close friends. They talked English, though the occasional Danish word would slip in. Thomas was already bilingual; Todd soon joined him. It was easier for Moira, whose first language was Danish. (Her first English word was to our Danish babysitter in Italy. . . .)

All our Danish friends spoke English. The shopkeepers and others did not. One does not pick up Danish by ear; it is not that easy to hear with its five umlauts and glottal stops. However with the help of Danish tutors we soon caught up with the kids—or could at least talk to the mob of them when their friends came round. We skied every winter that we could in Norway and discovered that to our American ears Norwegian and Danish sounded very much the same; add one more language.

We went through France in the summer, on our way to Italy. Joan's high school French worked fine and I tried to catch up. I bought a book titled *Learn French in Seventeen Easy Lessons* and practiced on the poor French next time we took our annual trip south. I got by. German was easier; I simply spoke Yiddish that I had picked up in New York when I shared a studio with a Viennese jeweler. That's enough languages to get by in most any European country. Knowing those, along with Esperanto, we were able to roam Europe and never look back.

RUSSIA

Alexander Korzhenevski, my Russian agent, said to me: "Harry, I don't know how to tell you this, but you are the most popular author in Russia, and also the most stolen!" I didn't know anything about this at the time, and I didn't believe him about my being the most popular. As a result of the Cold War, the Russians never signed up to the international copyright agreement. We talked about this, about how the West stole Pasternak, Lukyanenko, and Solzhenitsyn, and how the Russians stole science fiction. All of my books were stolen—published in unauthorized editions for which I received no payment. Only certain books were officially translated. Other books were seen as anti-Communist. They were illegal. *Deathworld 3* was regarded as anti-Communist, so that and other books were translated by fans, copied and bound by fans, and passed around by fans. That is true fanac, you know! Some copies ended up in libraries. So originally, when they were forbidden by Communist authorities, my books had been published in *samizdat* editions, but now they were being pirated by professional publishers.

The first time I met Alex I remember asking him how he learned to speak English so well and he said it was very important for him to know English because he was an engineer. I asked him what kind of engineer, and he didn't want to talk about it, but finally he told me he was working on weapons, on atomic weapons for tanks: "A very dirty gun." Thanks a lot! But years later I realized that's what you need to take care of publishers—an atomic weapons engineer! Many years later and he is one of only three agents in Moscow who handles science fiction, and they work together, and they're all ex-atomic engineers! They have a Mafia, and that way they can squeeze things out of the various publishers.

After Alex became my agent, he asked me if I wanted to come to Russia, and he said, "We'll pay everything." That's when I first found out that Garry Garrison—the Russians have no aspirate H— didn't have to go through customs: they took our passports and came back with our bags and everything. We had a private car waiting, which took us to the hotel. It was a really posh American hotel where you could have breakfast cooked to order. The doorman in the lobby was about nine foot nine, an armed guard. During the day they stayed out of the way, but at night they walked with us and went up in the lift with us. They didn't say anything.

When they set up the interviews for the media, they had a big black-and-white thing in the lobby with letters on it saying "Garry Garrison at 2 o'clock" and I put on my jacket and tie, and my medals, because it was the fiftieth anniversary of the Great Patriotic War. We had television and radio and the newspapers, all in one giant room, and they interviewed me. Afterward I was a little tired, but I was signing books, and there was the doorman with a book: "Will Garry Garrison sign book for Igor?" So I signed a book for Igor. And that was the first time I realized that it wasn't just a normal turnout, and maybe I *was* popular in Russia!

A lot of people from various magazines came round to interview me. One had three or four million copies sold a week, a boys' magazine. A women's magazine came to interview Joan—they didn't want to see me, they wanted to know how the wife of Garry Garrison lived. The publisher arranged everything: I had a suite in the hotel to do interviews. I had a car and a driver, and I had a very good translator, a woman who was very religious and kept taking me to churches! I kept saying, "I don't want to see another church! I'm an atheist!" I managed to get to some of the places I wanted to see.

Somewhere along the lines there, I don't remember how, we ending up going to a convention in St. Petersburg. My agent Alex got train tickets, and we went on the "vodka express." It was nice, six or eight hours, with sleeping cars and one bar car. We had caviar and vodka all night! And that was the start of the weekend. We had three days in St. Petersburg.

It was the worst hotel we ever saw in our lives. Joan wanted to turn it down; she said, "We can't go to a con here." We got up about seven or eight in the morning, and were drinking vodka by eleven, and the hotel started looking better and better! It was still a dump but most of Russia was very broken down then as a result of the war; everything was either very old or very new, and the very new was not that good.

There was a book fair in St. Petersburg, nothing to do with the con, but all Russians read science fiction, and that's where I found this out. I did a book signing, and there was a long queue. And all my stolen books with the *tirazh* printed in the back. By law in Russia you have to show the number of copies printed. There are no returns in Russia, books are printed and sent out from Moscow, and they go away and never come back, so what you print is what you sell. And the *tirazh* for these books was one hundred thousand, two hundred thousand . . . and one guy had a book with a stated print run of four hundred and fifty thousand copies! That stops you. And no money for Garry Garrison! But they kept bringing me vodka and my agent passed out next to me! We were drinking vodka all night, and everyone passed out. We had a big banquet and everyone passed out. Russian hospitality is not to be underestimated.

The year was 1993 and the location was San Francisco. This was the site of the annual World Science Fiction Convention. One reason I was looking forward to this annual convention was because of the chance to meet up with Alexander Korzhenevski, my "Russian agent." I liked Alex; he seemed a straightforward guy. And he was *bolshoi,* which always helped. This means "big"—but it has other nuances. Big in spirit might be one interpretation. I don't know what literary magic he was working but he had sent contracts for me to sign: always a good sign. As soon as the introductions were over he mentioned in a low voice that he had some money for me—and should we find a quiet place to pass it over?

Quiet? Dusty bank notes pried from the commie coffers? Stalin's loot?

"No way!" I cried. "Let's go to the green room where all my alcoholic peers are tossing it back! Boy, do we have something to show them."

So we went, pushing our way in through the crowd of freeloaders. Then I remember Alex speaking in quiet tones, these words that will ring down through history.

"Do you take hundred-dollar bills?"

Do I take hundred-dollar bills? Is there a pope in Rome?

I discovered that after much discussion the banks had finally opened bank note exchanges and Alex had brought some with him. He passed them over to me, lovely, green hundred-dollar bills, twenty-five of them.

"Quiet, everybody," I shouted to the alcoholic crowd. "I want to introduce my friend and agent from Russia, Alexander Korzhenevski—who has brought me my *first real money from that communist country.*" It no longer was—but it sounded great. "Look at these greenies," I shouted, fanning them out. They fanned nicely, impressive. I noticed that a number of writers wanted a word with Alex. I hope he got a few new clients that evening.

And thus began my relationship with Russia—on a very happy note. It could only go uphill from there. Alex has been my agent for many years now. He no longer has to slip me hundred-dollar bills. I had the best Russian publisher, Eksmo, who produces publishing miracles. Life has been smooth and pleasant on the Russian front. Therefore it was a pleasant surprise when I received again, many years after the first visit with Joan, an invitation from that distant land.

Eksmo invited me to Moscow on a publicity tour. This is the sort of offer that it is impossible to refuse; mainly because I wanted to meet my publisher. Since I was no longer of an age to do much traveling, and could use a little physical assistance on the trip, I brought this up. When I told them this, Eksmo was kind enough to expand the invitation to include my daughter, Moira, and her husband, Mark.

It was a gorgeous Moscow summer day when we arrived at Domodedovo Airport—where an unbelievable reception was waiting for us. Guided by a very official official, we jumped a number of queues and ended up in a cheerful room: flowers and drinks on the table. Our passports and documentation were whisked away and, very soon, our stamped passports reappeared, and all of our baggage. We had been met by a beautiful (and intelligent) young woman who would act as our interpreter. She was a schoolteacher who earned additional income acting as a translator. We also had a chauffeur, Sergey, who was smartly turned out in a suit and who happily whisked us around the hectic traffic in Moscow. This kind of treatment is gratefully appreciated!

From the airport we headed to the Hotel Sovietsky it had pictures of all the old Soviets on the wall. This hotel was luxury on an international level, as good as—or better than—the hotels in New York or Paris. It was quite late and we had the rest of the day off followed by an early start in the morning. After cocktails in the lounge we strolled to the dining room but it had already closed. Because there is a two- or three-hour time difference, we were still at eightish or nineish body-time, but it was eleven o'clock at night, and we had missed a meal. So I ordered up room service: (a) they spoke good English, and (b) they had some very good stuff; I think we ordered salmon, pizza, and sandwiches. And (c) it took them an hour to bring it up, ice cold! And they wouldn't let me sign for it, they stayed there until I paid cash for it. I had to go to the cashier at the front desk with my credit card to get some roubles to pay for room service. And it was about a hundred dollars for three sandwiches! That was the one time we bought in the hotel. Never after that!

We were off early the next morning to one of the bigger book-shops, where we were smuggled in the back way in the freight el-evator. I wondered why—until I saw the large number of readers that filled the store, patiently waiting to meet me, each one clutch-ing a copy of one of my books. I was just beginning to realize the popularity of my books in Russia.

Eventually the staff ordered things in a practically military style. There were guards stationed to see that the customers formed an orderly line. Then they approached me with a book opened and ready for signing. After Alex asked their name I personally signed the book to them. Through the translator they could ask me a ques-tion or something while I signed, and they had to talk very fast! Before they could talk much more another guard saw them out a side door behind the table. This was a mass-production meeting and signing. Writing in the book took me only seconds, since my years as a graphic artist enabled me to write quickly without fa-tigue. Alex estimated that I had signed over a thousand books in the first hour. Then it was down to the hospitality room for nibbles and drinks and gifts for me of some beautiful Russian books that I still treasure. After that it was off to another bookshop with the same reception and then finally to the hotel and the press confer-ence. Now, I have been to a lot of press conferences. Usually there is a small room with maybe a few drinks on the sideboard and a reporter or two with pad and pencil. Some questions and that is it. This is not the way they do it in Russia. Russia is very *bolshoi* to me. The streets are wider, the parks greener. Even the statues, like the fantastic one of Peter the Great, are *bolshoi*. The press conference filled one of the largest meeting rooms in the hotel. There was a table at the front where I sat facing a barrage of lights and the television cameras. Journalists from many magazines and newspapers sat at all of the tables in the room. To me, the very best part was the way everyone clapped when I entered the room. I felt very much at home. Then came the interviews and the questions, and things became very busy indeed. My daughter brought me a glass of wine, which I badly needed!

Television, radio, newspapers, syndicates—they were all there. I spoke until I was hoarse and ready for another glass of wine. It was fatiguing but fun. I felt that I was among friends who read my books and wanted to talk about them—and me. Mark was even interviewed for television, as son-in-law of Garry Garrison! My mother was born in Riga in Latvia and her family moved to St. Petersburg, so in a sense I have Russian roots as well as Irish.

At one point we asked the driver if we could go somewhere to buy some caviar. It cost a hundred and fifty pounds in England. In Russia we found a place where it was twenty or thirty dollars, and we brought a couple of jars back with us and eventually ate it in Moira's sunny garden, washed down with ice-cold vodka. Much to our disgruntlement, Mark, who had previously expressed disgust at the idea of eating fish eggs, found the caviar to be delicious, so we had to share it with him! On the other end of the culinary scale, Moira and Mark ventured out to a small local supermarket to buy chocolate and wine. As Moira browsed the shelves she spotted a huge rat heading down the aisle toward her. She screamed and jumped out of its way, much to the amusement of her fellow shoppers, who were well used to the sight. The rat itself was not bothered at all and continued its journey as normal.

We didn't bring much else back, except the books given to me by the bookshops on Russian art or the Russian navy, very beautifully produced. We were there three or four days. Theoretically the reason we were there is that I had been invited to the Russian national SF convention, which was in the suburbs of Moscow, in the greenbelt. They had an encampment, a professional place for conventions, a sort of Russian Butlins holiday park. It had one main building with meeting rooms and a chow hall, and an auditorium. It was out in the woods, and no one could find the bloody place! Up to that point we had a chauffeur and the BMW, but on the morning of our departure to head for the convention, the chauffeur showed up with his jacket and hat and tie gone, wearing an old dirty lumber jacket, and with his girlfriend on the front seat—we had to wait for her at the tube stop. Our translator was also gone. He drove us out there with our bags. We had a sinking feeling that our world was about to change from the pop star treatment of the last few days. When we finally got out to this place, it was like an old holiday camp or something. The driver went into the reception, found out where we were staying, then drove us over to one of the buildings, carried our bags in, said good-bye, and left us there. There were two suites—I had one myself and Moira and Mark had one; they were quite nice, although Moira would disagree. She covered her pillow with a T-shirt as apparently it smelled of a thousand other heads! But—where in hell were we?!

We had arrived there a day before the convention started. At American conventions, all the fun starts the day before—in Europe too. You have a pre-con and meet all your friends. But in Russia the convention started at noon the next day and not a moment before. There were a few people staggering around from the last convention, but apart from that the place was completely empty. No one spoke a word of English and there were no signs in English.

We unpacked a bag or two, and then walked over to the main building, and into the restaurant. It was about two or three in the afternoon by this time, and we were getting a little hungry. There were three cashiers in little booths, three or four tables occupied, and we sat down at a table, but no one came near us. I went to the cashier's booth—no signs in English, no one spoke English at all, no one had any idea what I was talking about or spoke German or Italian or Spanish, or any other language known to man.

But there was a bar there, so I went to the bar and I exhausted a few of my words of Russian: *vino, pivo,* and ordered a red wine for Moira and two Russian beers, and I paid for it in cash. I know about six words of Russian that I've picked up over the years—beer, wine, vodka, water, and one, two, three, and four in numbers—and most of that was from Yugoslavian and Czech, which have the same words.

We sat and had a drink, and then I went to bother the cashiers again, and eventually got to speak to the supervisor, and while she didn't speak any English either, she was more intelligent, and she figured out why we were in a restaurant: maybe we wanted some food! You were supposed to read the printed sheet with food on it by the cash register, then order and pay for what you wanted, then go into the dining room and hand the receipt to one of the grimly lurking waiting staff. I thought I ordered a meal and paid my cash, and they brought us three of everything: three slices of bread, three orders of soup, and three fried eggs. That was probably the best meal we had there, even if we did fight over the bread! The main meals we had once the convention got started were really bad. We had watery, cold soup and overcooked vegetables with cabbage appearing in many guises, even at breakfast. The meat was served the same way (possibly boiled until dead), irrespective of species. Russian food can be terrible, absolutely awful. The wonderful meals we had in Moscow were but a fading dream. I had a young man, Kyril, coming out to interview me, and as soon as we realized he spoke pretty good English, Moira pounced on him, invited him to join us for dinner, and then let him translate for us so that we actually managed to order a whole meal. He plowed his way through the awful food—nobody leaves food on their plate in Russia, it is still considered a precious commodity.

Moira and Mark were going back home the day before me: I was staying on an extra day after the con to have some fun (I thought). The next day we managed to get a breakfast—there were people coming in for the con, bit by bit, and there was one girl who spoke

English: I stopped her as she came in through the door and asked her if she would help me. And she got a meal for us, three of each again. And about noon the science fiction people started coming in. David Lally turned up, and in response to Moira's concerns about what would happen to me and how I would get back to the airport in Moscow once she and Mark left, offered to let me sleep in his room if I had to. Moira will be forever grateful for his offer. Then my agent showed up, and my publisher, and Moira started working on him. It was all very confused. We sorted the whole thing out—almost. And Moira was very worried about me being left alone there, because the convention ended a day before my flight. Alex and my publisher sorted out my room and got me a car that would drive me to the airport. Moira and Mark left in a broken-down van so decrepit that they kissed the ground when they arrived in one piece at the airport. The agent and publisher finally got it all arranged for me—until they discovered it was the wrong airport! I eventually ended up in a motel at the airport— Alex took me there and we rang Moira to reassure her I was alive and well and at the airport and not languishing in the now-abandoned holiday camp.

But what a difference between poverty and millionaire!

I'd been to Russia once before, in 1987, as a result of World SF. I was invited by Yeremy Parnov and went there with Joan and a few others, including Fred Pohl. It was a one-week conference. We had a little banquet at the Writers' Union, this was the Writers' Union of all Soviet Russia, and Parnov and his apparatchik picked who got published. They were really a power in the land. It was in this very nice, elegant prewar building, with chandeliers and stair-cases, and I went to the toilet to find it was a urinal that was broken in half: your pee went right on the floor. That was it. No one ever fixed the damn thing—it was hanging off the wall, had been for years. You get this strange dichotomy. . . .

We stayed in the Cosmos hotel, which was a real typical Russian-style hotel that held *five thousand* people. When the Russians do it, they do it big. Why they bothered making a hotel for five thousand people I have no idea. They had two dining rooms, one where the food was twice the price of the other, and the same menu, but the food came in five minutes instead of five hours! Somewhere in the middle of the hotel I found a little bar where they served all kinds of Western drinks, Budweiser beer and everything, and you had to pay in dollars. I was with another writer, I forget his name. And they had caviar sandwiches, and we used to go in and have caviar every day, courtesy of foreign currency. In the hotel was an eye clinic, where a lot of Arabs with glaucoma were being operated on. There were big lifts and the doors would open and the elevator would be full of Arabs with patches over their eyes.

We had a very nice translator, who spied for the government, of course. And we did some sightseeing—they took us out to Star City where the cosmonauts were, and I met a cosmonaut. They had a landing capsule there—they landed in Siberia. The American space program did research into food and put it in tubes so they could squeeze it out in space. In the Russian capsule was a box with glass on top, and it was full of tins. The Russians took tinned food with them. Tinned fish, tinned caviar . . . why not? Eight million dollars' research saved right there. They had a cosmonaut there, a little guy, about five foot one—all the cosmonauts were very small, because you save weight that way! My translator was with me, and I said can I ask him a question, and he was a very serious-looking guy, and I asked him if he flew in this capsule, and he said *da,* and this is the food he ate? *Da.* And I said: "Will you ask him, did he remember to take a can opener with him?" She translated, and his face broke into a big smile. . . . He said: *"Da, da. . . . Many* tin openers." Russians are very funny people, and very easy to get along with.

Svetlana, Stalin's daughter, married an American and moved to America, and she always wondered why the Russians and the Americans didn't get along, because they were very much the same kind of people. And we are. Russians have a great sense of humor, and are a lot of fun to be with, they love to eat and drink. We were only enemies because the politicians thought the Cold War was a great idea. When Eisenhower left office—and bear in mind he was a general and president of the United States—his parting shot was: What America needs to watch out for is being taken over by the military-industrial complex. And they took over. They won! That's why we have all these nice little wars all over the world.

The guy who was our translator on that first trip to Russia was very good, a great fan and a great collector: fandom is international. In Russia, everything was late. We were supposed to be going on this coach tour, and we were sitting in the lobby, and Fred Pohl and I were bullshitting each other, and we were talking about who is the ugliest science fiction writer—there's a lot of competition! And we looked up and saw the translator's face: I said, "What's the matter?" He said: "You're talking about my gods!" A true fan.

I was guest of honor at the 2008 Eurocon, which was held in Russia and which was also the Russian national convention, Roscon. My appearance there was reported—or I might say "misreported"—by *Pravda*. I was interviewed and asked a lot of leading questions, and they managed to misquote me just enough to make it quotable: "Within several years of Bush's rule the American democratic power has turned into the state of a fascist or Stalinist type—the president violates the Constitution, such key principles as freedom of speech and freedom of conscience," I am quoted as saying, having been translated into Russian and then back into English for the

Pravda Web site. This led one fan Web site to declare: "Stainless Steel Rat Author Defects to Russia!"

For the record: I did not say that the USA is a fascist state. I said that Bush had consistently violated the Constitution and the Bill of Rights. But America is a constitutional democracy and I have great faith in this document. The inherent checks and balances in the U.S. system would cancel out Bush's violations, I said. I am a great believer in the strength of American democracy. In the long run. Read my Stars and Stripes trilogy if you doubt me.

STAINLESS STEEL RAT

My first sale to John Campbell was "The Stainless Steel Rat," a short story that appeared in the August 1957 issue of *Astounding*. It introduced a character—James Bolivar "Slippery Jim" diGriz— who would stay with me for the next fifty-five years.

I was in New York and making the transition from "Harry the artist" to being a writer. As a comics artist I'd collaborated with Wally, Ernie Bache, and others, and when I started writing men's adventures and confessions I worked with my old friend Hubert Pritchard. I met Katherine MacLean at the Hydra Club, and somehow we ended up collaborating on a story called "Web of the Norns." It just seemed natural—a lot of writers were collaborating back then. We passed chapters back and forth, and were going to expand it into a novel, but we never did. I eventually published it in *Fantasy,* which I was editing at the time.

At that time there was a mouse in my apartment; it used to steal my cereal. I'd catch it and shove it in a paper bag and release it up on the roof, and by the time I got back to my typewriter he was back in the cereal box! I'm pretty sure that the idea came up in a conversation with Katherine that while we have flesh-and-blood mice in our apartments, in the future they will have steel mice, or she may have said mechanical mice. I'm happy to give her credit for that idea, because I was able to put it together with an idea I'd had in mind for an antihero in the future.

I write stories that I would like to read, and I'd always admired Rupert of Hentzau from Anthony Hope's *The Prisoner of Zenda*. It's a wonderful device to have the villain as hero. Raffles was a real criminal in the early stories, then along came morality and he confessed his sins and the series faded away. I wanted to have a real Rupert of Hentzau type, who gets away in the end and gives everybody the finger! That sort of character, a criminal who's good at his job, has much more dimension to it, and you can explore things like the Rat's opposition to violence: I wanted to have a hero who doesn't believe in killing people.

The final piece that fell into place for the original short story was a narrative hook that I wrote. At the Hydra Club I'd sit around and talk with the other writers, and one of the things we discussed was the narrative hook. When you were writing for the pulp magazines, the first page of a manuscript for a story would have the name and address of the person to be paid for the story up in the left-hand corner, and in the right-hand corner the number of words in the story. That's the money sorted. Then you jump to the middle of the page—leaving lots of white space for the editor to write on—and type the title, double space, "by" any name at all, double space, then the first paragraph of the story. And it's all double-spaced! At this point you have six or eight lines on the first page of the manuscript in which to write something that will "hook" the pulp editor's attention and get him to turn the page. So much garbage comes in front of him that if you can catch him with the hook he says, "My God! I turned the page . . . I'll buy it!"

I was practicing writing narrative hooks and wrote a dozen or so, and I wrote one that hooked me. The first page of "The Stainless Steel Rat" is written in the first person:

> *When the office door opened suddenly I knew the game was up. It had been a money-maker—but it was all over. As the cop walked in I sat back in the chair and put on a happy grin. He had the same somber expression and heavy foot that they all have—and the same lack of humor. I almost knew to the word what he was going to say before he uttered a syllable.*

"James Bolivar diGriz, I arrest you on the charge—"
I was waiting for the word "charge," I thought it
made a nice touch that way. As he said it I pressed
the button that set off the charge of black powder in
the ceiling, the crossbeam buckled, and the three-ton
safe dropped through right on the top of the cop's
head. He squashed very nicely, thank you. The cloud
of plaster dust settled and all I could see of him was
one hand, slightly crumpled. It twitched a bit and the
index finger pointed at me accusingly. His voice was
a little muffled by the safe and sounded a bit an-
noyed. In fact he repeated himself a bit.
"On the charge of illegal entry, theft, forgery—"

After writing this I thought, "What's happening here?" And I
kept thinking about it and thinking about it. And I put it together
with the idea of the mouse and the villain-as-hero, and that started
the whole thing going.

That first story was popular and got the extra penny a word because the readers said they liked it. And I thought this was a character that could be developed, that other stories were possible, so I
wrote a second story, "The Misplaced Battleship." In that story I
introduced Angelina, and initially she was just another device to
forward the plot. The Rat was chasing a guy who has stolen the
battleship, which is pretty straightforward, and then I had the idea
for a twist at the end: the villain has an assistant, and it happened
to be a female assistant, and I thought it's a nice reversal if he ar-
rests the wrong person. He gets the guy but she's the *real* villain,
and she escapes.

After *Deathworld* I wanted to do a second novel, and I had it in
the back of my mind that I'd like to do something lighter—I really
wanted to write humor. And I had this property that had been well
received, the readers liked it, and it was slightly humorous. . . .
The two short stories became the opening of the novel, and I car-

ried on from there. In a mainstream story, people are established and the story comes out of their character. In science fiction it's the opposite: you have a plot established, things have to get done, and the characters fit the roles in the machinery of the plot. But you have to do a decent job, you shouldn't have one-dimensional characters—though many writers do. Although I'd invented Angelina as a plot device, she was now my supervillainess and I wanted to give her a real motivation. It's not enough to say that she's evil. I had to justify her actions. I don't believe in that James Bond thing where pretty girls are psychopathic killers; they're not. Murderesses in jail don't look like that. I asked myself how she could be beautiful now and yet insane and ugly inside. What happened? I made it so that she was ugly when young, such that the world hated her, and this provided her motivation. She was intelligent and committed crimes for the money for operations to make her beautiful. So she is very beautiful outside, but inside she's a very ugly girl who hates the whole world. It builds from there.

As a novel, *The Stainless Steel Rat* came out as an original paperback from Pyramid in 1961—and it was completely invisible! Nothing happened with it, and that may well have been the last we heard from Slippery Jim. But fate stepped in, in the form of Toby Roxburgh, a Scotsman with an Oxford accent, living in America. In the early '60s he was an editor at Walker, which was a publishing house that had come up with a very good idea. Back then there were a lot of very good original paperbacks that never appeared in hardcover, and Toby was buying up these rights for five hundred dollars and doing a small edition in hardcover, mostly for library sale. He had the pick of the bunch because no one wanted to do them in hardcover. He asked me if he could have *The Stainless Steel Rat,* and I said sure, but five hundred was not enough for me. I worked out a deal with Walker and Bantam for two thousand dollars—I would write a new book for Bantam to publish in paperback, and Walker would get the hardback rights to both *The Stainless Steel Rat* and this new book. I wrote *The Stainless Steel Rat's*

Revenge for them. I'd never thought of it as a series, it was just a one-off. That means Toby is probably responsible for it becoming a series.

Many years later—name dropping—I'm sitting with Kingsley Amis, drinking, and he mentioned that he'd just read *The Stainless Steel Rat,* and he told me how much he liked it, and he said, "You know, it's the first picaresque science fiction novel." And I nodded and said, "Perhaps, Kingsley, perhaps." And then I rushed home to see what "picaresque" meant. It's a story with a villain or rogue as the hero. Jim is antiestablishment, and he's also antiwar. Except for the one time when he had to save Angelina's life, he's never killed anyone in all the ten books. Not bad for adventure novels. From that character the whole thing grew.

I never tired of the character because there was always a gap between the books. After a very heavy book, when I was feeling depressed, I'd write another Rat book to cheer myself up. Graham Greene used to call books like that his "entertainments"—you do a serious book and then you do an entertainment. I don't count myself in Greene's category, but I'd still do something important, some of which would take three, four, or five years, and fill in with a Rat book or something like that, an adventure book. I'd only ever write a new Rat book when I had a mad idea to motivate it. I remember one time reading in a newspaper about a South American election, and I said to myself, "These South Americans think they know about crooked elections, but wouldn't it be interesting if you had a planet very much like South America and you had an election there and the Rat got involved!" *Click!*—plot for story. That was the whole idea.

The first two are quite serious books except for a few jokes, but as time went on the Rat books grew lighter and lighter and madder and madder. I was writing *The Stainless Steel Rat Wants You* and had his world invaded by various horrible aliens who hate all humans because they're soft and squishy (or hard and crunchy, I forget which) and the Rat needs to disguise himself as one of these creatures so he can infiltrate their lair. He looks at photos of all these aliens, then has the computer put together the ugliest thing ever, combining claws and teeth and eyeballs and scales and whatever. And he gets into his disguise and flies out there. As I'm writing, I know he's gone to rescue his wife or something, and as he approaches the alien planet one of these horrible creatures appears on the view screen and Jim says, "Hello." And this thing says, "Hello, sweetie." And I thought, "Eh? *Hello, sweetie!* Did I write that? Where the hell did that come from?" But then it's obvious—in creating the ugliest thing to us, he's created what the other aliens think is the most attractive alien in the world. At that point the whole plot went ape, and he's wearing pink negligees and they're all trying to seduce him—it became an alien in drag story. *Hello, sweetie*—I typed it first and I read it second.

The Stainless Steel Rat books have always been popular with readers. In the UK their popularity was boosted when three of the books were adapted for the comic *2000 AD.* They wanted to adapt an existing property, and they were all science fiction fans who wanted to do it well. My only criticism is that they were perhaps being too true to the stories by keeping all my dialogue. I kept telling them, "Cut! Cut! Keep the action moving!" But the comics were very popular. Judge Dredd got top votes for the violence, and the Rat came second with the readers' poll because Angelina was sexy! The artist, Carlos Ezquerra, did a great job. Book dealers in Britain used to tell me that they stocked copies of the Rat books because so many kids read *2000 AD* growing up and went on to the paperbacks of the same character.

The books weren't always so well received by the critics. Brian Aldiss did a history of SF years ago called *Billion Year Spree,* and on the whole he was pretty favorable about my work, but I was a little hurt that he inferred that the Stainless Steel Rat books were "hastily written" potboilers that "hardly add to his reputation." Twenty years or so later he did *Trillion Year Spree*—and the Rat books had been popular all that time—and he still says the same thing about them. I guess even Brian's opinion is wrong sometimes! They have been my most popular books, in English and in translation. And Brian does go on to quote a couple of pages from the first novel, so he can't have hated it that much.

The problem is that fast-paced humorous adventure stories are rarely taken seriously. Books that appear to be written quickly are actually harder to write. The story moves at a faster pace, but only because of the work the author has put in. Sentences are shortened and paragraphs have fewer sentences. Punctuation becomes simpler, with commas dropped so that the reader zips through the sentences. Dialogue is punchier. It is disappointing when critics say "he writes hastily." I still have to do my homework and get my facts right.

Humor is often dismissed too, as if it cannot carry serious themes. But satire like *Bill, the Galactic Hero* is more serious than a lot of fiction—it's a serious look at the military and the future of war. *The Stainless Steel Rat Gets Drafted* is a variation on the same theme.

I have a great interest in languages, as well as in science fiction, and the two of them finally met in the Stainless Steel Rat books. When I do a book and I need an alien language for another planet, I use a foreign language. I have dozens of language dictionaries and I just pick one off the shelf. On one planet, for example, everyone speaks Turkish. But the universal language in Slippery Jim's universe is Esperanto. The Stainless Steel Rat speaks Esperanto like a native. I say that in fun, but the idea of a "universal" language designed to remove a barrier to communication is a serious one.

Unusually for an action-adventure hero, the Stainless Steel Rat has aged as the years have passed. The downside of this is that you risk writing yourself into a corner. After six books he was gray-haired and had grown-up sons—he's pretty long in the tooth. Did I want to write about a stainless steel senior (or pensioner)? I did, in a short story, "The Golden Years of the Stainless Steel Rat." But where did that leave the series? How could I continue? If in doubt, steal an idea from another writer, preferably a great one. C. S. Forester went back and wrote about Hornblower in his younger days—I could do the same with the Rat, and did.

There were a couple of good reasons for wanting to write a prequel. Firstly, you have an established character and you can go back and find out how he got to be that way. What happened in his past is intriguing, for both reader and writer. Secondly, it saves you endless research and re-reading! I'd written the books over a period of twenty years or so, which meant I had to go back and remind myself what I'd written—what had happened where and getting everybody's names right.

There was also a third reason. The Rat novels have a big teenage readership—every book I'd sign for a teenage fan would be a Rat book. Why not give them a teenage Rat? Making him a teenager in *A Stainless Steel Rat Is Born* meant that I didn't have to show his family life. We hear about his parents, and they sound pretty square, which will resonate with intelligent kids who read science fiction. Jim's parents were porcuswine breeders on a backward planet and he escapes to a new life of his own. The porcuswine started as a one-liner—Jim's father is a porcuswine farmer. But it grew from there and I had Jim hiding out at McSwiney's and eating nothing but porcuswine burgers. "It's the food of my generation," Jim tells the Bishop at one point.

I brought the porcuswine back for the final Rat book, *The Stainless Steel Rat Returns!* It brings the story full circle, with Jim's relatives—all porcuswine farmers—destroying the tranquility of his retirement. The porcuswine are yet another example of John Campbell's influence—him and his damn pigs again. . . .

WEST OF EDEN

Book ideas usually grow and develop and it is very difficult to pin the genesis down with any degree of accuracy, but with *West of Eden* I remember the whole process. I got the idea from a television documentary that showed what an intelligent dinosaur would look like today. It was a very obvious idea. In fact, on my shelf I had a few nonfiction books about the same thing, so the idea had been around for a long time. But no one had ever done it in fiction.

I thought about it and I thought it was too big an idea to throw away on a single book. The size of the thing—it is now sixty-five million years later and we have intelligent dinosaurs. Now where did they come from? What happened there? Where is mankind?

I was talking to Tom Shippey about it, and I said: "Why don't I get some professional help? Perhaps a professional from every field?" I approached Jack Cohen, an eminent reproductive biologist, to talk to me about all things biological to do with intelligent dinosaurs. There was no trouble getting Jack Cohen to talk—can you imagine! I think one time we even managed to tire Jack out! Jack, being his usual acerbic self, had seen the program about intelligent dinosaurs, and he said: "It's all nonsense! It's all wrong! They got all the biology wrong." He said many of the details, such as the eyeballs, were wrong. It looked like an alien—skinny with big eyeballs.

Jack Cohen is an incredibly bright guy, an incredibly good teacher, and incredibly temperamental. He did research into prostitutes and syphilis and enjoyed working with the Birmingham-area prostitutes. He found out that some of them become immune to things like AIDS and syphilis because of overexposure. Interesting stuff. He knows everything about biology—and if he doesn't, he fakes it so well that you'd never know!

Tom and Jack and I met in Birmingham to have a meal and do some work. Jack had a couple of geckos there. They would sit and not even move their eyes. If you came near them they would follow you with their eyes, but that was it. Jack poked this wooden pencil near one, and the gecko bit it in half. I was very interested in all this, but when I looked at Tom his eyes were bulging. There is an innate fear of lizards in most human beings. I didn't know that. Right away we had the idea that each species fears the other one. That goes in the plot.

The Yilanè (the intelligent reptiles) had only biological science, no heat. Chemistry will work at any temperature, we just use heat to speed up the reaction. About twelve o'clock one night I called Jack and I said: "Jack, do you have to use a centrifuge?" And he said, "Absolutely, I couldn't work without it."

Damn! You can substitute specialized animals for many things, but if you spin an animal it is eventually going to have to stop and spin in the opposite direction. We can't have that. A centrifuge must keep going for a couple of hours to separate out all your chemicals. I said, "Jack, could you do it with a fractioning column?" He said, "Well, you could, but it would take a *long* time." I said, "That's okay, we've got sixty-five million years!"

When I had a query, instead of trying to answer it myself, I'd go to a specialist and they'd do it for me. When you talk to specialist, you find out what is going on in the field. There's research going on that will take a year or two to get published, and it can be four or five years before they get any results. In addition you make them think. They dig out recondite material that can be used in the book.

Early on when we were designing the Yilanè, we were looking at Jack's gecko, and Jack said, "Like most lizards, he has two penises."

I said, "What do you mean *like most lizards*? I never heard that before."

Jack said, "It's a commonly known fact."

"Only to you, what's the second one for?"

"Obvious. If the first one gets tired, they use the second one."

I was accused by the feminists of being anti-women because of the Yilanè. But it came out of creating the opposite of the humans at all times. So the females must be dominant. There are an awful lot of lizards and amphibians that go into a torpid state. There is also one species of frog where the male carries the eggs on the back of his neck. Another carried the eggs in his mouth. So I had a torpid period when the Yilanè males are pregnant. And if they're torpid when they're pregnant, that makes the females dominant, as they must protect them. Biology has assigned the "female role" to men and the "male" to women.

While I was listening to Jack expatiating, I realized that intelligent dinosaurs would be just as alien as creatures from the stars. It was somewhere about here that the big idea clicked.

Why isn't the alien world, everything about it, the direct opposite of mankind? Where the humans would still be in the late stone age, the hunter-gatherer stage.

Jack had done some work for Anne McCaffrey and other writers, and he volunteered to help me as well. That was when I decided no freebees. I thought, no, these academics are friends of mine and they're hard-working guys, I'll pay them real money. That way they can come and go, and I have the work that I've paid for. I can either use it or not as I see fit.

In science fiction there are many mansions. Many people I know teach PhD courses and they are more than willing to help. Ask them about their specialty and they can produce endless material.

I was talking about the idea with John R. Pierce—from Bell Labs—and he remembered a story in John Campbell's *Astounding*, a long time ago, that had a flying plane with bird's wings. However when you go inside you see that there's no engine—and no bird—just a muscle attachment. So I thought, why don't I do a biological-based science? I would have to go all the way. There will be no fire. Everything is done biologically and chemically. I worked with Jack on that. Tom Shippey built the language. Leon Stover sorted out the anthropology. Then, somewhere about halfway through plotting, I needed a real religion—that doesn't exist yet—for the Daughters of Life. I dug through the Science Fiction Research Association directory, and there—among all the professors of English Literature—was one professor who taught philosophy and religion.

Next time I was in America I went to visit him and we had a meal and a chat. He was more than happy to design the religion. It was wonderful. I could never have designed anything even close.

I had a bit of money in the bank at this time so I was able to spend two years working on this new book. I had no plot yet, no story—and about thirty thousand words of notes! I wrote to my agent about this and when he looked at the heap of material he said, "This isn't one book—it's a trilogy." He was right. I ended up with about half a million words across three books. I turned this thirty thousand words of research around and I looked at it, closely, and thought, what do I do with the story here?

I built in the separation of the two species so that they didn't meet until the events of my book brought them together. The Yilanè ran all of Africa and Europe, and the Tanu, the humans, had the New World. That caused me some problems, because we are descended from Old World monkeys. The Tanu had to be descended from New World monkeys. We are tailless, but the New World monkeys all have tails. In the book, one group of humans, the Paramutan, have fur and a tail—each problem leads to its own interesting solutions.

In my book there is a new ice age that is coming on. Leon Stover was upset at this. He said that once you change what happened

65 million years BC, you louse up the whole cycle of the ice ages. I was happy to do this. The ice is coming down, the climate is changing, and it sends the Tanu south to Florida.

In the Old World the Yilanè have elaborate city-states, completely separate from the humans'. One city has been wiped out by the advancing ice; seeking new land the Yilanè send an exploration party to the New World. When they meet the Tanu the feeling of hatred is mutual: they clash. Like Tom Shippey and the gecko, they just loathe each other from the very first moment.

The Tanu and the Yilanè had separate cultures and separate languages. And their innate fear and hatred meant there could be no peace between them. To carry the story I needed a bridge between the two species. I went to history. In America at the turn of the century, there were many books about Native American Indians capturing white children and raising them as Indians. In turn I must have a captured child who grows up among the Yilanè, speaking both languages. The various problems and their eventual solutions developed enough plot for three books. I worked it out so that every detail had its opposite. The story develops from the clash.

The geography of the world is the same as it is now, except that the ice cap is coming down, farther and farther south. I had Bill Sanderson (an incredibly gifted artist) do a map and it turned out that Alpèasak was the Florida Keys. We did the projection of the maps from the Yilanè point of view.

West of Eden is a classic example of how you plot a science fiction book. Although the world is our world, there is still world-building going on there; there are new languages and cultures. The Yilanè are not aliens in the bug-eyed monster sense, they were created as an "alien" race. I was as naïve as the reader. But when you have conflict, you have plot. With plot you have a book or books.

Science fiction people are outsiders, and they know it. I remember going to some convention somewhere, and in the main lobby was a kid reading a science fiction book. Every time I went through the lobby he was still reading the book. He didn't bother going to panels or anything. At home his parents would probably tear his magazines up and throw them out, but here he could sit in *public* and read science fiction! We are just one big family. You can talk to complete strangers but have a common reference point—the science fiction stories you have read. When I was younger we all read the same magazines and could talk about individual stories we liked. And we all have the same rejection by our parents.

I read one story, a serial, in some forgotten magazine. I was so in love with that story that I tore out the three parts and bound them together. I loaned it to a friend of mine—and his mother threw it out!

Then, after the war, one of the small presses printed it as a book. Great! *The Green Man of Graypec* by Festus Pragnell. I've never heard of Festus Pragnell. The story is about Leroy Spoffit, lawn tennis champion of the world. He gets whisked through to another dimension and ends up in a world called Graypec where the green men are fighting a tank war. I bought this book, paid two and a half dollars for it, bound, wow! I started reading it, read about three or four pages, and then the letters all fell off the page in front of my eyes.

It was terrible pulp in every way. Only a teenager—which I was then—would see any value in it.

I have a letter in my correspondence file from Terry Carr saying how terrible "Doc" Smith is. I said, "How old were you when you read it?" He said, "I was twenty-one." I was eight years old, and let me tell you, when you're eight years old it reads pretty well. It's age-dependent, bad writing and stupid plotting, and a lot of juvenility. When I was teaching my science fiction course at San Diego State, a high school kid who got good marks could pick an elective, and a lot of them picked science fiction. Greg Bear was my student at the time, and said he could get me a job teaching teachers science fiction. We decided that "Doc" Smith was science fiction written for boys. And if you open Kimball Kinnison's zipper, he'd be smooth all the way down. He was a prepubescent boy too!

One thing that detective stories share with science fiction is that you have to know the ending before you can write the book. In a detective novel you start at the end and work backward. In science fiction you do the same thing at different points in the story—you do it more often. So in *West of Eden* I needed the hero to speak the Yilanè language, so I had to work backward from there and plot how this came about. Mainstream fiction is oriented around the character—the story comes out of the characters. Science fiction is plot oriented: you get a plot and then you create a character to fit the plot. In science fiction the plot is based on an idea, it is about a novelty and an exploration of that novelty. Someone once said that science fiction was the only form of fiction where the plot was the hero.

I remember one story, written by a very nice Scottish writer who came over to visit me in Denmark. In his story he built a giant robot ship to explore the galaxy. It's all robot operated, and it was a very nicely developed story. They send it out, it goes out to the galactic edge and comes back, which takes a couple of million years or more. When it gets back it lands on Earth and the robots look out and there's nothing there. So it takes off and goes round again! The machine is hero, the plot is hero. You don't do that in other forms of fiction.

In detective fiction and romances and Westerns there are certain standard plots. In science fiction there is no formula plot. The plot comes out of the exploration of the idea. You can use plots from all of fiction.

When I wrote my first piece of science fiction, "Rock Diver," I fell back on the safety of two standard plot ideas: matter penetration and the Western. I had a claim-jumper *under* the rocks. It was not too complex, when you think about it. By setting it underground, you then have all the little problems related to being underground. The gadgetry in the story is integral to the plot. If a story is well written you have complications coming out of the original idea and consequences arising from it.

Hal Clement was not much of a writer, but his stories were successful. He had a story where the planet had very heavy gravity on one side and light gravity on the other, and he worked out all the details. I wrote one story—*Wheelworld*—where I had a planet with no axial tilt. Intuitively I thought it would work, but I couldn't be sure. At a convention I was talking to Poul Anderson, and he didn't think it would work. Harry Stubbs was there, and he thought about it for a while, and he said it was true, and every day is an equinox. When he said that, he solved all my problems. Writers help each other work things out. They come up with ideas that are interesting enough to interest other writers.

Brian said that John Campbell had a little wire that he plugged into every reader's brain, which tickled them and made them think and the writers too. I sent John a one-page letter about the idea for *Deathworld*. He sent me back *thirteen* pages. He didn't tell you what to write, but a lot of the development of the book came out of his suggestions. He never took credit for his ideas. He came up with the Three Laws of Robotics, which Asimov freely admitted.

I wrote a story for the *Asimov's Friends* anthology, a tongue-in-cheek piece called "The Fourth Law of Robotics." Norman Spinrad was around the house one day and he read it, and he said, "You should have called it 'The Mechanical Schwartzers'!" When I submitted it to Isaac, I put that title on a fake cover page—only for Isaac.

ALTERNATE HISTORY

Science fiction embraces change and the fact that we can *change* change. This distinguishes it from all other forms of fiction. This quality is what accounts for the fact that a mainstream novel such as Orwell's *1984* or Shute's *On the Beach* can also be regarded as science fiction. Science fiction is not about rocket ships and robots and aliens—these may be present, but they are not essential. Science fiction is an *attitude* toward change, and explores the impact of change upon people. Throughout the twentieth century the change that has typically been explored is scientific change or technological change, and stories have been set in the present or the future, but SF can explore other forms of change and stories can be set in the past.

During the 1980s and '90s good science fiction was hard to find, crowded off the shelves by fantasy, and fantasy with science fiction trappings. But one form of real SF became increasingly popular—the alternate history. These stories were accounts of our world as it might have been, or will become, following some hypothetical alteration in history. Alternate history comes in three basic forms:

1. The story set in the past where a change occurs that will bring about a different present from the one we know.
2. The story set in the past where a time traveler arrives to change the future.
3. The story set in the present, which has been altered by a change in the past.

I was pleased to discover—after the fact—that I have written novels in all of these categories. The Hammer and the Cross and Stars and Stripes trilogies are examples of the first; *Rebel in Time* and *The Technicolor Time Machine* of the second; and *A Transatlantic Tunnel, Hurrah!* and *West of Eden* of the third. Alternate histories—like all good science fiction—begin with a *what if . . . ?*

What if the Germans had won the Second World War?

What if the atomic bomb had been developed during the Victorian era?

What if the Catholic Church ran the world?

The writing of an alternate history novel requires a great deal of time-consuming research, which, unhappily, many authors are loath to do, and the research is not always appreciated by the reader. I was taken to task by one reader who insisted that a novel of mine, set 140 years in the past, contained many "misspellings"—such as "butty" for "buddy." This despite the fact that the Oxford English Dictionary from 1820 on defines "butty" as a friend or comrade.

The Technicolor Time Machine was structured as a straightforward adventure novel with twists in time, but the humor crept in and it got funny. I tried to be accurate, particularly as it first appeared in *Analog*. Part of the plot was that they were very short of time; they have only a few days to finish shooting the film. They send Charley Chang, the scriptwriter, back into the past and bring him back an hour later, but he was there for three months. He comes back with a beard and scars and everything. The producer says to pay him the highest rate for an hour's work that anyone has ever been paid in California. I'd never been to California, but I knew from the literature that on a clear day you can see Santa Catalina Island—it's about twenty miles off the coast. I put the writer on Santa Catalina Island in the Jurassic and had him staring at the creatures in the sea. I thought I'd better check, and looked it up and Santa Catalina Island is metamorphic rock, so it *was* there in the Jurassic. After it was published in *Analog* I got a letter from the Florida School of Mines or something: Dear Mr. Harrison, Santa Catalina Island was there during the Jurassic period but it was two hundred miles in from the ocean! One person out of the magazine's hundred thousand circulation.

Sam Lundwall published it in Sweden and one academic, a historian from the university, did a review of it for an academic magazine and said it was a very accurate book! He didn't mention the action or the humor, but he liked the Vikings. I had a good time doing the research, and it's about as accurate as you can get. There is very good evidence that the Vikings were in North America. I did a lot of research on the Viking map, which turned out to be a fake later on. But they have traces in L'Anse aux Meadows and Newfoundland of Viking ring forts and they have found runes, stone inscriptions, farther north. They interacted with what they called the *skraelling,* who were probably Eskimos who lived farther south in those days. It's pretty obvious that they did settle along the coast there.

It was very easy to get there from the tip of Greenland; if you sail that latitude you end up in North America. They would do it in summertime when the prevailing winds were great, and they probably did a lot of fishing and brought dried fish back. They brought wood back from North America too, because there was no wood at all in Greenland and they needed the wood for houses and everything. They *were* there, in a place called Vinland, which means "vine land" but nobody knows why because grapes don't grow that far north.

I also used the sagas. The sagas are very straightforward stories: he killed him, and then he killed him, and he was his wife's brother and he came and killed him—they're very straightforward tales of murder and rape! They'd attack from the ocean, kill everybody, and take the cows. We made them heroic sagas afterward, but they were just accounts of people killing each other.

Everything in the book taken from the sagas is true, apart from the Jack Daniel's bottle. There are so many variations of the sagas

that you can pick the one you want. At one point they pacify the
skraelling—the Indians—by feeding them ice cream. In the sagas
there's this unknown word, a milk product—it's obviously ice
cream! When they sailed they could tell the latitude by the angle
of the sun, but the sun isn't always visible at those latitudes. They
had a thing called a *húsasnotra*, which I think is really an Icelandic spar that is polarized so you can see the sun when it's low, even
in fog. But in the book I have it as Viking for "compass repeater."
All this stuff worked out and in the end the lovely twist is that the
only reason the Vikings settled North America was because they
went back in time to make a film about the Vikings settling North
America. It was a lot of fun to do.

In America and Britain the Vikings you see in books are either
sailing dragon boats or wearing horned helmets and wielding axes.
I read the history books in Denmark, and there the Vikings are
treated as what they were—farmers. They had a long wintertime, so
they went out raiding for something to do! They'd go south and raid
England or wherever, snatch a few cows and a few women. They
went from having a farming culture to being landowners. Then they
started these family feuds and they started killing each other. Even
when they came and occupied York they had these family feuds
going on.

My interest in Vikings came from living in Denmark—but I
wrote about Hollywood without ever having been there. I'd been
working with a lot of cheap film companies in England—I'd never
been to Hollywood at that point. I wrote about Hollywood and
went there a few years later and discovered I'd got it right! Cheap
film-making is cheap film-making. Having been surrounded by
Viking culture and then working with these nickel-and-dime companies in England, I had the idea of making a film about Vikings.
How do you film Vikings? You get a time machine.

I started thinking about the time machine itself, and I was so
bored with all the explanatory details about how a time machine
would work, it's all nonsense, so I had this great cracking machine

built by this Yugoslavian professor and they asked him how it worked and he said, "You're too stupid to understand." And that was all the explanation you got! That took care of that, and set the tone for the whole thing.

The book has actually been optioned by Hollywood on and off for years. Like most of my books there is a lot of motion and color and action in there. There was a story editor who was looking at science fiction books and somebody recommended *The Technicolor Time Machine* to her, and she recommended it to Mel Gibson. For a while it looked like it was going to be a Mel Gibson movie.

The Vikings really were very bloody people. Around the merchants' harbor in Copenhagen the wall was originally made of huge tree trunks driven into the ground, and they'd driven each one through a slave's body so that his spirit would go into it and hold the wall up. And they launched the Vikings' ships across slaves' bodies—using them for grease!—for the same reason, so that their souls would go into the keel of the ship. And I told Mel Gibson about this, and he's a Catholic, so I told him they drove the tree trunks through *Catholic* slaves! Maybe they were Catholic slaves, who knows? Mel liked that! I had more Viking stories, but we only had about twenty minutes together.

They actually had the screenplay written, a wonderful screenplay by Marshall Brickman, who wrote Woody Allen films. Allen had agreed to play the Barney Hendrickson character, the second lead: he's a con man film producer, guilt-ridden, stumbling into an unknown future, perfect for Woody Allen. And Mel would be your perfect Viking. He told me that he hates Vikings. It would have been a perfect role for him since he projects self-hatred so well in some of his roles. He'd make a great lead, he's very good. In the first *Lethal Weapon* you look at him and think: The guy's half mad! He's very good at that—humorous and half mad—it's a role made for him! I think Mel Gibson was going to play the actor who breaks his leg *and* the Viking, do it with a fake nose or something. It was a very neat idea: Marshall Brickman is a very good screenwriter, a very sharp guy. He picked out all the humorous bits, kept the names, came up with some more Old Norse words to put in there, did his homework. You wouldn't think of Mel Gibson and Woody Allen together. It would have been great.

They paid a bundle for this great screenplay—far more than they paid me!—and they just put it on the shelf. For business reasons, Mel never made the movie. At the end of the novel there's a throwaway line about them going back to make a movie about Christ. Later Mel Gibson went off to make a movie about Christ—maybe he got the idea from there—the timing was just about right. I may unwittingly be responsible for *The Passion of the Christ.* . . .

The Technicolor Time Machine is a humorous adventure story, and it's also a story about identity. The director, Barney Hendrickson, is really a failed director, and he *knows* he's a second-rater who will never quite make it. That's a very sad position to be in, and I've known writers like that. Barney succeeds by bullshitting and talking people into things. He's always on the edge of failure. The film he makes, *Viking Columbus,* is filled with compromises and it would probably be a crappy film when it came out. At the end Barney is written into the saga. Barney, spelled Bjarni, is a Norwegian name, and Bjarni was one of the guys who went with Erik the Red, who was nicknamed "Ottar" in the book. Barney ultimately became a historical character—as he says himself, he was written into the story.

My father was a lapsed Irish Catholic, my mother was Jewish but from an agnostic family. "Rabbi" means "teacher" and out of my six granduncles, five were rabbis. My grandfather was a watchmaker in St. Petersburg, a working-class Jew. My grandmother was a nihilist—that was a big libertarian movement in Russia, it wasn't just about throwing bombs. He went over to America to work in a clock factory and sent over for the family one at a time. Neither of my parents went to church, they wouldn't talk about it, and so religion played no part in my upbringing. This was a great big lacuna there, which I felt a little bit guilty about because many of my friends were Jewish and Catholic. When I was about thirteen years old I read an English book published by a society that is the Humanist Association now, and I remember the author's name was Chapman Cohen—a good English name and a good Jewish name!—and it was called *Theism or Atheism* and it took every argument for religion, like the watchmaker and original design, and he would explain carefully what the theory was and then he would destroy it! I went through the whole book, and when I finished it I thought, "Oh, thank god, there's no god!" I became an atheist at that point and never looked back.

I've written a number of stories that oppose organized religions as being narrow-minded, bigoted, and medieval in their use of physical and psychological torture. Having lived in Mexico I've seen how Catholicism destroyed a whole culture. I'm very much against that kind of destruction of anything that is "against god."

At the beginning of *The Hammer and the Cross* I have the quote from Gore Vidal about Christianity being the worst disaster that ever befell the West. Tom Shippey translated it into Latin. I wrote to Gore and he approved of the Latin and corrected the wording of the original quotation, which I'd gotten from an interview in a literary magazine somewhere. It was the perfect quote to start the book with.

Religion does no good. Christianity has been called the slave religion: you give up all of your physical life in this world for a promise of "pie in the sky by and by," as the old folk song has it. You are kept enslaved by this stupid idea, and it destroys your *real* life. Not only is there nobody home upstairs, there is no upstairs. I see that as a form of evil—people live stunted lives because of it, especially the poor nuns and priests. It is an unnatural state. It is wasteful of human resources, of human lives.

Why do people feel a need for religion? It's pretty obvious: they want some death insurance! It's all black out there. They don't want to believe that there's no life after death. That's why every religion on the planet has its creation myth and its Christ myth. There were seventeen crucified saviors before Christ; it's a near-Eastern myth that was picked up by this Jewish cult. When the state religion doesn't work for them anymore they go back to the "new age" stuff—they just need someone to supply them with *something*. And there's no shortage of nutcase ideas.

Religion always takes responsibility for the moral system, but there was morality before there was religion. People live with each other and they learn how to get along. There are morality systems like Buddhism that don't believe in a god at all. Religion takes credit when they don't deserve it. We don't need religion, that's the whole point. It doesn't supply anything, but it takes a lot of money from people's pockets. It is very negative. And they end up being very bigoted: religious bigots are the worst in the world. Anti-Semitism comes out of it.

The Hammer and the Cross is an alternate history that explores what the Western world might have been like if it hadn't been dominated by Christianity, and if there was another religion that wasn't as narrow-minded or as bigoted.

It started off with a short story that I wrote with Tom Shippey. Greg Bear asked for an alternate history story, and Tom Shippey said, "I've always wondered what would have happened if King Alfred had made peace with the Vikings." Tom and I are old friends from way back. He had already done a lot of work for me on *West of Eden*—he did all of the linguistics for the different races. And he wrote the Latin joke for me in *The Stainless Steel Rat Gets Drafted*. We kicked the idea around and wrote the short story together. It has a great last line. Alfred has fought the battle and won, and he's trying to decide whether to become a Catholic or not, and he has the symbols of the crucifix and the Viking hammer on a silver chain.

> There was the tiniest sound in the silent room as
> metal touched metal.
> Or was it the loudest sound the world had ever
> heard?

Tom and I talked about the idea behind the story and decided there was a book there. We turned it into an outline for a book, but it grew so big we decided it should be three big novels.

The books were also an opportunity to use some of the material about Vikings that you couldn't use in a book like *The Technicolor Time Machine*. The Vikings were pretty ruthless bastards. That whole "blood eagle" thing that we describe in there and the torture in the snake pit—it was all absolutely true. It wasn't that they were godless, they really enjoyed their religion, it backed them up. The Norse religion didn't promise pie in the sky. They worked on this life here. Their tortures were so great because they wanted to make sure you suffered pain in this life before you died. They had a very gloomy vision of Valhalla, and only the top guys could go there. There's a quote in the book:

> . . . the world seemed like a king's hall on a winter
> evening—warm and brightly lit inside, but outside
> dark and cold, and a world no one could see. And
> into that hall . . . flies a bird, and for a moment it is
> in the light and the warm, and then flies out into
> the dark and cold again.

They saw our lives as being a sparrow flying through the night and the whole world's dark, and there's a little neat hole there and he flies up to the hole and there's warmth and light, and then back on through the endless night. Our existence is that little bit of something between the nothing on both sides. It's a very gloomy religion!

They believed in *this* life, and that the chance was the afterlife was pretty bad, so make the best of it. They were good family people and they took care of each other.

They believed in live and let live, they didn't have rules for everything. But it was superceded by these family feuds. Family feuds aside, they loved life. The religion itself was never that strong, which is why the Christians won against it so easily. The Vikings were pagans and believed in Thor and Odin and the rest, and theirs was a religion of strength. Bishop Absalon converted all the Vikings to Christianity in a very simple way. He would take the head Vikings and try and convince them to convert to Christianity, and if the Vikings didn't convert, then the Bishop's men would hold the Viking down and put a big *lurhorn* on his stomach and fill it full of rats, and put hot coals on the outside of the horn, and the rats would dig through the guy's stomach to escape. The Vikings appreciated that—"That's a good god you've got!"

Poor old Tom, he didn't have to look this stuff up in a book, he has it all in his head! He can quote the Anglo-Saxon and Old Norse. I hadn't realized that I had only read the "cleaned-up" versions. I'd played it down in *The Technicolor Time Machine,* but in *The Hammer and the Cross* it became an important part of the culture. I tried to ameliorate it, because there were *good* influences in the Viking culture: it was a very humanistic religion. But there was also a very negative side to it. It wasn't inculcated in the Viking religion, it was just part of their national heritage. You *win* the fight. The word *skol*—skål—used by Scandinavians as a toast means "skull" in Old Norse. After they killed their enemy, they cut the bottom off his skull and drank mead out of the skull. That proves you won!

The Vikings were *big* people with big appetites. A smaller body radiates much more heat than a bigger body, it's the inverse square—the surface of something like a sphere may double, but the total volume quadruples or quintuples. If you're big, you conserve your heat better. Even today Scandinavians, like the Russians, are big. A six-month-old baby in a pram looks like a three-year-old! The minimum height for the Royal Guards in Denmark is two meters, and some are much taller than that. And they wear Busbys—which make them look nine feet tall!

Tom had all this information in his head—he never opened a book. He has an incredible eidetic memory. All the material there was out of his brain! He knows a lot of strange, strange stuff. There was a meeting of the Vikings, they'd meet once a year, and they had a tree and they hung the bodies from it and they hung a whole horse from it. That was very impressive. Tom was a font of strange and obscure details that you couldn't find in a textbook. Anything to do with linguistics that I ever asked him he could answer like that.

Tom speaks and teaches Anglo-Saxon, four or five other dead languages, as well as German and the Germanic languages. We kicked the plot around and he had all these basic facts, and I would suggest things for the plot, and he would knock it on the head saying, "You can't do that, but how about this . . ." I'm very strong on plotting. He would make little notes on a card: for a whole evening's conversation he'd have about twelve words and he'd be able to transcribe directly from that. I have the exact opposite kind of memory, it's like a sieve. He'd do up an outline and we'd work back and forth on it. It was a good collaboration. He learned a lot about writing from me, and I learned a lot about history from him. A good collaboration should be synergistic, it should be more than either person could do without the other. It was hard work, but it was a lot of fun to do.

I was ill toward the end and Tom ended up writing the final copy on the third book. Usually one of us would write it and the other would correct it. It turned out that Tom wasn't able to put his own name on *Hammer and the Cross* because he was working at that time for a Jesuit school. They would have been a little unhappy about Professor Shippey putting his name on an atheist book! He used the pen name John Holm.

In a big alternate history like *The Hammer and the Cross* you begin with reality, what we know, and then you add the twist and start sliding away from what really happened. Sometimes that key incident, the twist that gets you where you want to be, is obvious. In *The Hammer and the Cross* everything came out of that original short story. In *Stars and Stripes* I was looking for a turning point, and went through my research on the Trent Affair. There almost *was* a war: the English sent fifteen thousand troops to Canada to invade the United States. Lord Palmerston hated the fact that someone had dared stop a British mail packet, and he wrote a really shitty letter insulting Lincoln, but Prince Albert read it and cleaned it up. That's what happened historically. I had Prince Albert die before he'd had chance to clean it up. You look for the turning point, and then all else follows. Sometimes it's obvious, but sometimes it takes time to find. Sometimes it comes with the whole idea of the alternate world, like *The Hammer and the Cross*.

With *Hammer and the Cross* we had the starting point. A lot of our conversations were about what would logically come out of it. We tried to bend it toward the good, but there was an awful lot of dead Vikings before we got them civilized!

What if the Catholic Church hadn't evolved and run Europe? It wasn't an *anti*-religious story, it was just a *what-if* story. We tried to make a realistic story out of it, an alternate version of the past. Unfortunately the trilogy wasn't as successful as we'd hoped. It didn't break through. If it had been attacked by the religious right we might have sold a lot more copies!

In the Stars and Stripes trilogy I tried to have the Americans doing good for a change, starting in Lincoln's time, in a simpler kind of age—perhaps—when America was not the demon of the world the way it is now. They hadn't done any of the terrible things they've done now. All my Tory friends in America said, "Harry, this is a Republican book!" I said, "No, this is a truthful book. I'm not trying to be right wing, it's just that—for a change—I agree with you."

The basic idea for Stars and Stripes came out of the research I did when I wrote *Rebel in Time*. By the end of the American Civil War there were a hundred thousand soldiers in total on the two sides, and they were a *modern* army: if they had been united, they could have beat every other army in the world at the same time. Everyone else was still using Brown Bess muskets and outdated tactics.

Science fiction sales have fallen, and there's no backlist anymore. All of my books used to be in print and on the shelves, and I could rely on them to make some money, but not anymore. To make money now you need a *big* idea, something like *West of Eden* or the Stars and Stripes trilogy. Big ideas, my agent says, make for big advances.

I like writing the "big idea" alternate history because it allows you to exercise your imagination, and it is hard to do, which means that lazy writers don't do it, so there's less competition. Alternate history requires an awful lot of research if you're going to do it well. I like that, it's fun, but it puts off a lot of people. The other benefit of an alternate history novel is that it can "break through" and pick up sales beyond the usual science fiction readership.

Some reviewers and readers believe that alternate histories need a big change to a pivotal historic event, the Nazis win the Second World War, for example. But I don't really believe that. I much prefer there to be a succession of changes, one building on the other. I wanted to make the changes subtle, so that the reader is never quite sure when I've left the real world behind.

I made my pivotal change after the Battle of Shiloh, the first meeting of the two armies in the American Civil War. In two days the North lost twelve thousand men and the South lost ten thousand, and the battle lines didn't change at all. By the end of the war, two hundred thousand soldiers were dead, and another four hundred thousand people died from disease and other causes. Six hundred thousand people, or about 2 percent of the American population, died; it was death on a massive scale. I had to stop the war before it got past the point where the two sides could be reconciled, so I stopped it at Shiloh.

The combined forces of the American armies would have been the most powerful army in the world, but so what? The trick was to find a reason for them to come together. If I stopped the war early enough, it might happen, but how could I do that? Finally I came up with the idea of the English invading. A lot of English reviewers and readers hated the fact that the English were the villains, but in this story they had to be. And if you're going to make them bastards, they have to be bastards. I had them as the heroes in *A Transatlantic Tunnel, Hurrah!* so I have been even-handed, and the real "hero" of Stars and Stripes isn't the Americans, it is the Constitution, democracy.

Science fiction, like the mystery story, requires backplotting. That means you *know* where the story is going to end, and you build to that. That's the *craft*. The *art* is disguising the fact you know the ending, so that the reader is surprised by it. The reader must see new things that they never knew were coming, that way they'll keep reading. But it all has to be within a logical flow, so that *with hindsight* you can see it's logical, but you couldn't actually see it coming. That's very important in alternate history.

With this kind of story it's a matter of changing things gradually, so that it becomes like a snowball going down a hill, slowly picking up speed. It is fun making those changes, but as with all science fiction there is a limit to the number of changes you can make. H. G. Wells said that if a pig came flying over a hedge toward you, you'd be surprised. But if you then saw cows flying and then houses, it would soon become boring.

I accelerated history a little bit in the second book by bringing in the Gatling gun a few years earlier. The observation balloons were there; the telegraph was there; utilizing trains for troop movements was there; there was trench warfare—the American Civil

War really was the first modern war. I'm accelerating just a few things by just a few years. I'm not *inventing* technology, I'm just having it come on stage a few years early, which is not that bad a crime. I have the ironclad ships being used in warfare—in reality most of them were sunk for targets!

The Constitution is what keeps America working; even though Washington is full of crooks, the Constitution will hold up. I'm a Constitutionalist, I believe very much in the Bill of Rights, and I'm writing about the good stuff in it that *could* have come out of American history if American politics hadn't been so full of crooks. The bribe-taking crooks then were even bigger than they are now. In a way I have written a utopian novel—and as for the fact that it's an American utopia, that's totally beside the point. It's about how the history of the world could have been so much better with a few slight changes.

Every once in a while the American Constitution comes through, because it is written out clearly. And it's very hard to amend. All the amendments were pretty decent amendments, except giving up drink—they had to amend the amendment there. But they built it better than they knew. So even though it is religious as hell there, the schools are still nonreligious, the Constitution says you must separate the church and the state. The only time in my life that I agreed with Newt Gingrich was when he said the Constitution was the most important legal document ever created.

I'm *not* anti-American. I have spent a lot of my time in Europe defending America: most Europeans knock America for the wrong reasons. I *am* very much anti the "actions" that America carried out in Vietnam and places like that. I wanted to try and give America a decent role in the world. It's a way of looking at a possible future by rewriting the past. *Stars and Stripes is* a utopian novel.

HARRY HARRISON—
BIBLIOGRAPHY OF FIRST EDITIONS

Compiled by Paul Tomlinson

NOVELS

Deathworld. Analog, January, February, and March 1960; New York: Bantam, September 1960.

The Stainless Steel Rat. New York: Pyramid, November 1961.

Planet of the Damned (as: *Sense of Obligation*). *Analog*, September, October, and November 1961; New York: Bantam, January 1962.

Vendetta for the Saint (Published under the name "Leslie Charteris"). *The Saint Mystery Magazine*, January, February, March, and April 1964; New York: Doubleday (Crime Club), 1964.

Deathworld 2. New York: Bantam, September 1964.

Bill, the Galactic Hero. New York: Doubleday, October 1965.

Plague from Space. Science Fantasy #79 December 1965, #80 January 1966, and #81 February 1966; New York: Doubleday, September 1965.

Make Room! Make Room! SF Impulse #6 August, #7 September, and #8 October 1966; New York: Doubleday, 1966, 216pp., hbk. Jacket: Charles & Cuffari.

The Technicolor Time Machine (as: *The Time-Machined Saga*). *Analog*, March, April, and May 1967; New York: Doubleday, 1967.

Deathworld 3 (as: *The Horse Barbarians*). *Analog*, February, March, and April 1968; New York: Dell, May 1968.

Captive Universe. New York: Putnam, 1969.

Spaceship Medic (as: *Plague Ship*). *Venture Science Fiction*, November 1969; London: Faber & Faber, April 1970.

In Our Hands, the Stars. *Analog*, December 1969, January and February 1970; as: *The Daleth Effect*. New York: Putnam.

The Stainless Steel Rat's Revenge. New York: Walker, 1970.

Stonehenge (by Harry Harrison and Leon Stover). London: Peter Davies, April 1972.

A Transatlantic Tunnel, Hurrah!. *Analog*, April, May, and June 1972; as: *Tunnel Through the Deeps*. New York: Putnam, 1972.

The Stainless Steel Rat Saves the World. *Worlds of If,* September / October 1971, January / February 1972, March / April 1972; New York: Putnam, 1972.

Montezuma's Revenge. New York: Doubleday, 1972.

Star Smashers of the Galaxy Rangers. New York: Putnam, 1973.

Queen Victoria's Revenge. New York: Doubleday (Crime Club), 1974.

The Deathworld Trilogy. New York: Science Fiction Book Club (Doubleday), 1974.

The Men From P.I.G and R.O.B.O.T. London: Faber & Faber, October 1974.

Lifeboat (by Harry Harrison and Gordon R. Dickson). *Analog*, February, March, and April 1975; New York: Harper & Row, 1976.

The California Iceberg. London: Faber & Faber, March 1975.

Skyfall. London: Faber & Faber, September 1976.

The Adventures of the Stainless Steel Rat. New York: Science Fiction Book Club (Doubleday), 1977.

The Stainless Steel Rat Wants You! London: Michael Joseph, September 1978.

Planet Story (written by Harry Harrison and illustrated by Jim Burns). London: Pierrot, August 1979.

The QE II Is Missing. London: Futura, November 1980.

Homeworld. London: Granada, August 1980.

Planet of No Return. New York: Simon & Schuster, September 1981.

Wheelworld. London: Granada, March 1981.

Starworld. New York: Bantam, June 1981.

To the Stars. New York: Science Fiction Book Club (Doubleday), 1981.

Invasion: Earth. New York: Ace, April 1982.

The Jupiter Plague. New York: Tor, July 1982.

The Stainless Steel Rat for President. New York: Doubleday (Book Club), September 1982.

A Rebel in Time. London: Granada, February 1983.

Stonehenge: Where Atlantis Died (by Harry Harrison and Leon Stover). New York: Tor, September 1983.

West of Eden. New York: Bantam, August 1984.

A Stainless Steel Rat Is Born. London: Titan Books, August 1985.

You Can Be the Stainless Steel Rat: An Interactive Game Book. London: Grafton, October 1985.

Winter in Eden. London: Grafton, September 1986.

The Stainless Steel Rat Gets Drafted. London: Bantam, August 20, 1987.

Return to Eden. New York: Bantam, August 1988.

Bill, the Galactic Hero on the Planet of Robot Slaves. New York: Avon, July 1989.

Bill, the Galactic Hero on the Planet of Bottled Brains (by Harry Harrison and Robert Sheckley). New York: Avon, 1990.

The Turing Option (by Harry Harrison and Marvin Minsky). New York: Warner Books, August 25, 1992.

Bill, the Galactic Hero on the Planet of Tasteless Pleasures (by Harry Harrison and David Bischoff). New York: Avon, January 1991.

Bill, the Galactic Hero on the Planet of Zombie Vampires (by Harry Harrison and Jack C. Haldeman II). New York: Avon, April 1991.

Bill, the Galactic Hero on the Planet of Ten Thousand Bars (by Harry Harrison and David Bischoff). New York: Avon, September 1991.

Bill, the Galactic Hero: the Final Incoherent Adventure (by Harry Harrison and David Harris). New York: Avon, September 1991.

The Hammer and the Cross (by Harry Harrison and John Holm). London: Legend Books, June 1993.

The Stainless Steel Rat Sings the Blues. London: Bantam Press, March 31, 1994.

One King's Way (by Harry Harrison and John Holm). London: Legend Books, December 1994.

King and Emperor (by Harry Harrison and John Holm). London: Legend Books, July 18, 1996.

The Stainless Steel Rat Goes to Hell. New York: Tor, November 1996.

Stars and Stripes Forever! London: Hodder & Stoughton, March 1998.

The Stainless Steel Rat Joins the Circus. Moscow: Eksmo / A. Korzhenevski, March 1999. Translated by Gennady Korchagin.

Stars and Stripes in Peril. London: Hodder & Stoughton, April 2000.

Stars and Stripes Triumphant. London: Hodder & Stoughton, 2002.

The Stainless Steel Rat Returns. New York: Tor, 2010.

SHORT STORY COLLECTIONS
(English language editions only)

War with the Robots. New York: Pyramid, September 1962.

Two Tales and Eight Tomorrows. London: Gollancz, May 1965.

Prime Number. New York: Berkley, July 1970.

One Step from Earth. New York: Macmillan, 1970.

The Best of Harry Harrison. New York: Pocket Books, June 1976.

Stainless Steel Visions. New York: Tor Books, February 1993.

Galactic Dreams. New York: Tor Books, April 1994.

50 in 50: Fifty Stories for Fifty Years! New York: Tor, June 2001.

ANTHOLOGIES

Nebula Award Stories 2 (edited by Brian W. Aldiss and Harry Harrison). New York: Doubleday, 1967.

Apeman, Spaceman: Anthropological Science Fiction (edited by Leon E. Stover and Harry Harrison). New York: Doubleday, 1968.

Best SF: 1967 (edited by Harry Harrison and Brian W. Aldiss). New York: Berkley, March 1968.

SF: Author's Choice (as: *Backdrop of Stars*). London: Dobson, March 1968.

Farewell, Fantastic Venus! (edited by Brian W. Aldiss and Harry Harrison). London: MacDonald, October 1968.

Best SF: 1968 (edited by Harry Harrison and Brian W. Aldiss). New York: Putnam, 1969.

Worlds of Wonder: Sixteen Tales of Science Fiction (edited by Harry Harrison). New York: Doubleday, 1969.

Four for the Future: An Anthology on the Themes of Sacrifice and Redemption. London: MacDonald, February 1969.

Blast Off!: SF for Boys. London: Faber & Faber, June 1969.

Best SF: 1969 (edited by Harry Harrison and Brian W. Aldiss). New York: Putnam, 1970.

The Year 2000. New York: Doubleday, 1970.

SF: Author's Choice 2. New York: Berkley, May 1970.

Nova 1. New York: Delacorte Press, 1970.

Best SF: 1970 (edited by Harry Harrison and Brian W. Aldiss). New York: Putnam, 1971.

SF: Author's Choice 3. New York: Putnam, 1971.

The Light Fantastic: Science Fiction Classics from the Mainstream (edited by James Blish and Harry Harrison). New York: Charles Scribner's Sons, October 1971.

Best SF: 1971 (edited by Harry Harrison and Brian W. Aldiss). New York: Putnam, May 1972.

Nova 2. New York: Walker, 1972.

The Astounding-Analog Reader, Volume One (edited by Harry Harrison and Brian W. Aldiss). New York: Doubleday, December 1972.

The Astounding-Analog Reader, Volume Two (edited by Harry Harrison and Brian W. Aldiss). New York: Doubleday, April 1973.

Astounding: The John W. Campbell Memorial Anthology. New York: Random House, 1973.

Best SF: 1972 (edited by Harry Harrison and Brian W. Aldiss). New York: Putnam, July 12, 1973.

Nova 3. New York: Walker, 1973.

A Science Fiction Reader (edited by Harry Harrison and Carol Pugner). New York: Scribner, 1973.

Best SF: 1973 (edited by Harry Harrison and Brian W. Aldiss). New York: Putnam, 1974.

SF: Author's Choice 4. New York: Putnam, 1974.

Best SF: 1974 (edited by Harry Harrison and Brian W. Aldiss). New York: Bobbs-Merrill, 1975.

Nova 4. New York: Walker, January 1975.

Science Fiction Novellas (edited by Harry Harrison and Willis E. McNelly). New York: Charles Scribner's Sons, 1975.

Decade, the 1940s (edited by Brian W. Aldiss and Harry Harrison). London: Macmillan, November 1975.

Decade, the 1950s (edited by Brian W. Aldiss and Harry Harrison). London: Macmillan, April 1976.

Best SF: 1975, the Ninth Annual (edited by Harry Harrison and Brian W. Aldiss), as: *The Year's Best Science Fiction, No.9.* London: Orbit, June 1976.

Decade, the 1960s (edited by Brian W. Aldiss and Harry Harrison). London: Macmillan, January 1977.

There Won't Be War (edited by Harry Harrison and Bruce McAllister). New York: Tor, November 1991.

NONFICTION (BOOKS)

Collected Editorials from Analog (by John W. Campbell; selected by Harry Harrison). New York: Doubleday, 1966.

Ahead of Time: Noted Scientists Prove that Truth Can Be Stranger than Fiction (edited by Harry Harrison and Theodore J. Gordon). New York: Doubleday, 1972.

Science Fiction Horizons, 2 Volumes in 1 (edited by Harry Harrison and Brian W. Aldiss). New York: Arno Press, February 1975.

Hell's Cartographers: Some Personal Histories of Science Fiction Writers (edited by Brian W. Aldiss and Harry Harrison). London: Weidenfeld & Nicolson, May 1975.

Great Balls of Fire!: A History of Sex in Science Fiction Illustration. London: Pierrot Publishing, September 1977.

Mechanismo. London: Pierrot Publishing, September 1978.

Spacecraft in Fact and Fiction (by Harry Harrison and Malcolm Edwards). London: Orbis, September 1979.

SHORT STORIES

"Rock Diver." *Worlds Beyond* #3, February 1951.

"An Artist's Life." *Rocket Stories* #3, September 1953.

"Web of the Worlds" (with Katherine MacLean). *Fantasy Fiction* #4, November 1953.

"Navy Day." *Worlds of If,* January 1954.

"The Velvet Glove." *Fantastic Universe*, November 1956.

"World in the Balance." *Fantastic Universe*, June 1957.

"The Stainless Steel Rat." *Astounding*, August 1957.

"Welcoming Committee." *Fantastic Universe*, October 1957.

"Captain Bedlam." *Science Fiction Adventures*, December 1957.

"Open All Doors" (with Hubert Pritchard). *Fantastic Universe*, February 1958.

"The Repairman." *Galaxy*, February 1958 (British edition).

"The Robot Who Wanted to Know." *Fantastic Universe*, March 1958.

"Simulated Trainer" (as: "Trainee for Mars"). *Fantastic Universe*, June 1958.

"The World Otalmi Made." *Science Fiction Adventures*, June 1958.

"Arm of the Law." *Fantastic Universe*, August 1958.

"The Robots Strike." *Fantastic Universe*, January 1959.

"I See You." *New Worlds* #83, May 1959.

"Hitch Hiker." *The Saint Mystery Magazine*, December 1959.

"The Misplaced Battleship." *Astounding / Analog*, April 1960.

"Case of the Comic Killer." *Tightrope* #2, May 1960.

"The K-Factor." *Analog*, December 1960.

"Survival Planet." *The Magazine of Fantasy and Science Fiction*, August 1961.

"Toy Shop." *Analog*, April 1962.

"Death at 60,000." *The Saint Mystery Magazine*, May 1962 (British edition).

"Terror in Tivoli." *The Saint Mystery Magazine*, June 1962 (British edition).

"War with the Robots." *Science Fiction Adventures* #27, July 1962.

"Death in Mexico." *The Saint Mystery Magazine*, August 1962 (British edition).

"The Pliable Animal." *The Saint Mystery Magazine*, September 1962 (British edition).

"The Streets of Ashkelon." *New Worlds* #122, September 1962.

"Captain Honario Harpplayer, R.N." *The Magazine of Fantasy and Science Fiction*, March 1963.

"The Ethical Engineer." *Analog*, July 1963 and August 1963.

"Fuzz-Head." *The Saint Mystery Magazine*, October 1963 (British edition).

"Down to Earth." *Amazing Stories*, November 1963.

"Ms. Found in a Bottle Washed Up on the Sands of Time" (verse). *The Magazine of Fantasy and Science Fiction*, February 1964.

"Incident in the IND." *The Magazine of Fantasy and Science Fiction*, March 1964.

"Final Encounter." *Galaxy*, April 1964.

"According to His Abilities." *Amazing Stories*, May 1964.

"Unto My Manifold Dooms" (as: "The Many Dooms"). *Galaxy*, June 1964.

"How the Old World Died." *Galaxy*, October 1964.

"Portrait of the Artist." *The Magazine of Fantasy and Science Fiction*, November 1964.

"Rescue Operation." *Analog*, December 1964.

"They're Playing Our Song." Fantastic Universe, December 1964.

"Not Me, Not Amos Cabot!" *Science Fantasy* #68, December 1964 / January 1965.

"A Matter of Timing." *Analog*, January 1965, by "Hank Dempsey."

"Famous First Words." *The Magazine of Fantasy and Science Fiction*, January 1965.

"The Outcast." *Science Fantasy* # 70, March 1965.

"I Always Do What Teddy Says." *Ellery Queen's Mystery Magazine*, June 1965.

"At Last, the True Story of Frankenstein." *Science Fantasy* #76, September 1965.

"The Greatest Car in the World" (as: "Detroit è Sempre Detroit"). In *Il Grando Dio Auto: Racconti di Fantascienza Automobilistica*, edited by Roberta Rambelli. Rome: Automobile Club d'Italia, October 1965. Translated by Adrianno Zannino.

"Rock Pilot." *Fleetway Boys Annual*, 1965.

"Mute Milton." *Amazing Stories*, February 1966.

"The Gods Themselves Throw Incense." *SF Impulse* #1, March 1966.

"CWACC Strikes Again." *Analog*, June 1966.

"Contact Man." *Alien Worlds*, July/August 1966.

"The Voice of the CWACC." *SF Impulse* #10, December 1966.

"A Criminal Act" (as: "Gesto da Criminale"). *Galassia* #71, November 1, 1966. Piacenza: Casa Editrice la Tribuna. Translated by Ugo Malaguti.

"You Men of Violence." *Galaxy*, April 1967.

"The Man From P.I.G." *Analog*, July 1967.

"A Civil Service Servant" (as: "The Fairly Civil Service"). *Galaxy*, December 1967.

"I Have My Vigil." *The Magazine of Fantasy and Science Fiction*, February 1968.

"The Secret of Stonehenge." *The Magazine of Fantasy and Science Fiction*, June 1968.

"Waiting Place." *Galaxy*, June 1968.

"The Powers of Observation." *Analog*, September 1968.

"No War, or Battle's Sound" (as: "Or Battle's Sound"). *Worlds of If,* October 1968.

"If" (as: "Praiseworthy Saur"). *Worlds of If,* February 1969.

"From Fanaticism, or For Reward." *Analog*, March 1969.

"The Ghoul Squad." *Analog*, June 1969.

"The Man from R.O.B.O.T." *Analog*, July 1969.

"Pressure." *Analog*, August 1969.

"By the Falls." *Worlds of If,* January 1970.

"One Step from Earth." *Analog*, March 1970.

"The Life Preservers." *Analog*, April 1970.

"Heavy Duty." *Analog*, May 1970.

"A Tale of the Ending." *Analog,* June 1970.

"Wife to the Lord." *The Magazine of Fantasy and Science Fiction*, June 1970.

"Commando Raid." In *Prime Number*, July 1970.

"The Final Battle." In *Prime Number*, July 1970.

"The Finest Hunter in the World." In *Prime Number*, July 1970.

"The Pad: a Story of the Day After Tomorrow." In *Prime Number*, July 1970.

"American Dead." In *The Year 2000*, edited by Harry Harrison. New York: Doubleday, 1970.

"The Ever-Branching Tree." *Young Scientist*, 1970.

"Brave Newer World." In *Four Futures*, edited by Robert Silverberg. New York: Hawthorne, 1971.

"The Wicked Flee." In *New Dimensions 1*, edited by Robert Silverberg. New York: Doubleday, 1971.

"Roommates." In *The Ruins of Earth: an Anthology of Stories of the Immediate Future*, edited by Thomas M. Disch. New York: Putnam, 1971.

"Strangers." *The Magazine of Fantasy and Science Fiction*, October 1972.

"We Ate the Whole Thing." *Vertex*, April 1973.

"The Defensive Bomber." *Nova 3*, edited by Harry Harrison. New York: Walker, 1973.

"An Honest Day's Work." In *New Writings in SF* #22, edited by Kenneth Bulmer. London: Corgi, 1974.

"The Mothballed Spaceship." In *Astounding: the John W. Campbell Memorial Anthology*, edited by Harry Harrison. New York: Random House, 1973.

"Ad Astra." *Vertex*, August 1974.

"The Whatever-I-Type-Is-True Machine" (with Barry N. Malzberg). *The Magazine of Fantasy and Science Fiction*, November 1974.

"Space Rats of the CCC." In *Final Stage: the Ultimate Science Fiction Anthology*, edited by Edward L. Ferman and Barry N. Malzberg. New York: Charterhouse, 1974.

"Speed of the Cheetah, Roar of the Lion." *The Magazine of Fantasy and Science Fiction*, March 1975.

"Run from the Fire." In *Epoch: the State of the Art of SF Now*, edited by Roger Elwood and Robert Silverberg. New York: Putnam, 1975.

"The Last Train." In *The Second Bedside Book of Strange Stories*, edited by Herbert Van Thal. London: Arthur Barker, 1976.

"Pass the Book, or, An Irish TV Report on the Origin of Modern Science Fiction." *Starburst* # 1, January 1978.

"The Stainless Steel Rat Wants You." *Isaac Asimov's Science Fiction Magazine*, Fall 1978.

"The Greening of the Green." In *Anticipations*, edited by Christopher Priest. London: Faber & Faber, 1978.

"All Wheels, Gears and Cogs." *The Visitors' Book: Short Stories of Their New Homeland by Famous Authors Now Living in Ireland*. Dublin: Poolbeg Press, 1979.

"The Day After the End of the World." In *After the Fall*, edited by Robert Sheckley. New York: Ace Books, 1980.

"A Fragment of Manuscript." In *Microcosmic Tales: 100 Wondrous SF Short, Short Stories*, edited by Isaac Asimov, Martin H. Greenberg. and Joseph D. Olander. New York: Taplinger, 1980.

"The Return of the Stainless Steel Rat." *Ares: The Magazine of Science Fiction and Fantasy Gaming* #10, September 1981.

"A Dog and His Boy" (as: "Un Chien et Son Gors"). *Antares* #19. (2010) Translated by George W. Barlow.

"After the Storm." In *The Planets*, edited by Byron Preiss. New York: Bantam Spectra, December 1985.

"The View from the Top of the Tower." *The Magazine of Fantasy and Science Fiction*, May 1986.

"In the Beginning." *Amazing Stories*, May 1986.

"Ni Venos, Doktoro Zamenhof, Ni Venos!" In *Tales from the Forbidden Planet*, edited by Roz Kaveney. London: Titan Books, October 1987.

"The Curse of the Unborn Living Dead." In *The Drabble Project*, edited by Rob Meades and David B. Wake. England: Beccon Publications, April 1988.

"Luncheon in Budapest" (as: "Lunch i Budapest"). *Jules Verne-Magasinet* #433, February 1989. Translated by Sam J. Lundwall.

"The Fourth Law of Robotics." In *Foundation's Friends: Stories in Honour of Isaac Asimov*, edited by Martin H. Greenberg. New York: Tor, September 1989.

"Samson in the Temple of Science." *The Microverse*, edited by Byron Preiss and William R. Alschuler. New York: Bantam, November 1989.

"A Letter from the Pope" (with Tom Shippey). In *What Might Have Been? Volume II: Alternate Heroes*, edited by Gregory Benford and Martin H. Greenberg. New York: Bantam Spectra, January 1990.

"Tragedy in Tibet." In *Confiction Souvenir Book*, edited by Johan-Martijn Flaton. The Hague: Confiction, August 1990.

"Dawn of the Endless Night." In *The Ultimate Dinosaur*, edited by Byron Preiss and Robert Silverberg. New York: Bantam Spectra, September 1992.

"The Golden Years of the Stainless Steel Rat." In *Stainless Steel Visions*, February 1993.

"Bill, the Galactic Hero's Happy Holiday." In *Galactic Dreams*, April
   1994.
"The Road to the Year 3000." *Nature*, December 16, 1999.

Note: A full bibliography of the Works of Harry Harrison
   can be found at *www.harryharrison.com.*